MW01109366

Cult of Defeat in Mexico's Historical Fiction

Cult of Defeat in Mexico's Historical Fiction

Failure, Trauma, and Loss

Brian L. Price

First published in 2012 by
PALGRAVE MACMILLAN®
in the United States—a division of St. Martin's Press LLC,
175 Fifth Avenue, New York, NY 10010.

Where this book is distributed in the UK, Europe and the rest of the world, this is by Palgrave Macmillan, a division of Macmillan Publishers Limited, registered in England, company number 785998, of Houndmills, Basingstoke, Hampshire RG21 6XS.

Palgrave Macmillan is the global academic imprint of the above companies and has companies and representatives throughout the world.

Palgrave® and Macmillan® are registered trademarks in the United States, the United Kingdom, Europe and other countries.

ISBN: 978–1–137–00847–3

Library of Congress Cataloging-in-Publication Data

Price, Brian L., 1975–
    Cult of defeat in Mexico's historical fiction : failure, trauma, and loss / Brian L. Price.
        p. cm.
    Includes bibliographical references and index.
    ISBN 978–1–137–00847–3 (hardback : alk. paper)
    1. Historical fiction, Mexican—History and criticism. 2. Defeat (Psychology) in literature. 3. Literature and history—Mexico. I. Title.

PQ7207.H5P76 2012
863'.08109972—dc23   2011050705

A catalogue record of the book is available from the British Library.

Design by Newgen Imaging Systems (P) Ltd., Chennai, India.

First edition: June 2012

10 9 8 7 6 5 4 3 2 1

Printed in the United States of America.

Hay que hacer la historia de las derrotas. [The history of defeat needs to be written.]

—Ricardo Piglia, *Respiración artificial*

Yo sé (todos lo saben) que la derrota tiene una dignidad que la ruidosa victoria no merece... [I know (everyone knows) that defeat enjoys a dignity that noisy victory does not deserve...]

—Jorge Luis Borges, "Nota para un cuento fantástico," *La cifra*

Crisis, however, facile the conception, is unescapably a central element in our endeavors toward making sense of our world.

—Frank Kermode, *The Sense of an Ending*

I spoke just now of "having suffered together" and, indeed, suffering in common unifies more than joy does. Where national memories are concerned, griefs are of more value than triumphs, for they impose duties, and require a common effort.

—Ernst Renan, "What Is a Nation?"

I'm writing for the survivors, that they may know what it was they survived. I'm writing, if you will, for posterity, that people may understand what went wrong and resist the historical imperative of judging us too harshly.

—Don Delillo, *Great Jones Street*

Ever tried. Ever failed. No matter. Try again. Fail again. Fail better.

—Samuel Beckett, *Worstward Ho*

Contents

Acknowledgments

I will admit that the potential irony of failing to write a book on failure crossed my mind more than a few times during the process of completing *Cult of Defeat*. Fortunately, I have been associated with and surrounded by good colleagues, honest readers, and supportive friends and family who helped me keep focus, refine my ideas, and push through. I owe a debt of gratitude to Nicolas Shumway, who has been a good friend, outstanding mentor, and enthusiastic supporter of this project for many years. I am also grateful to Héctor Domínguez Rubalcava, Charles Rossman, and César Salgado at the University of Texas at Austin as well as to Sara Poot-Herrera at the University of California, Santa Barbara, who offered valuable insights on early drafts of this manuscript. The quality of this book was immeasurably improved by Ignacio Sánchez Prado and José Luis Venegas, two great friends who read the entire manuscript, made invaluable bibliographic recommendations, and were generous with their time and considerable talents. Thanks are also in order for Rebecca Biron, Margaret Ewalt, Jerid Francom, Kristine Ibsen, Ryan Long, Kathryn Mayers, and Anna Nogar, who each read and commented on various chapter drafts. My appreciation to the anonymous reader at Palgrave Macmillan for thoughtful and constructive criticisms, and to my editor, Farideh Koohi-Kamali, and her assistants for their support in publishing this book.

Over the years the ideas in *Cult of Defeat* were started, shaped, and refined in conversations, conference panels, and cafés with many professors, colleagues, and friends: Leopoldo Bernucci, Jonathon Brown, Irma Cantú, Cristina Carrasco, Russell Cluff, Oswaldo Estrada, Samuel Gordon, Rob Martinsen, Robert McKee Irwin, Seymour Menton, Garrett Oleen, Sarah Pollack, Nicolas Poppe, Sara Potter, Howard Quackenbush, Cristina Rivera Garza, Miguel Rodríguez Lozano, José Ramón Ruisánchez, Ryan Schmitz, Michael Schuessler, John Trimble, Elena Urrutia, and Oswaldo Zavala. I would like to express heartfelt appreciation to my colleagues at Wake Forest University for their support and mentoring: Irma Alarcón, Mary Friedman, Luis González, Anne Hardcastle, Linda Howe, Sol

Miguel-Prendes, Jessica Shade, Peter Siavelis, Emily Wakild, and Byron Wells. Another debt of gratitude is owed to my student assistants: Barbara Arinci, Ian Gray, David Inczauskis, India Prather, and Dillon Sanders. My appreciation to the librarians, curators, and support staff of the Perry-Castañeda Library and the Nettie Lee Benson Latin American Collection at the University of Texas, the Biblioteca Daniel Cosío Villegas at the Colegio de México, and the Z. Smith Reynolds Library at Wake Forest University. A special vote of thanks is owed to Michael Hironymous for guiding me through the treasures of the Rare Books Collection at the Benson. Financial support from the William S. Livingston Graduate Fellowship from the Graduate School and numerous E. D. Farmer Fellowships from the Teresa Lozano Long Institute for Latin American Studies at the University of Texas at Austin, in addition to the Z. Smith Reynolds Foundation Junior Faculty Leave for Research and several Archie Research and Professional Development Travel Grants from Wake Forest University contributed to the completion of this book.

Cult of Defeat would not have been possible without my family. My mother, Cecily Price, has been a boundless source of love, travel advisories, and welcomed editing advice. My father and stepmother, Brian and Suzanne Price, have served the dual function of sounding board and cheerleaders for many years. I am also grateful to my in-laws, Tom and Linda Draper, for their encouragement. And most importantly, I offer my love and thanks to my wife, Janine. We were married shortly before I started graduate school and, since then, she has accompanied me through every phase of this project, listened to every farfetched idea, read every word, weathered every revision, and has done so with intelligence, humor, wit, patience, and grace. I dedicate *Cult of Defeat* to her and to our two children, Cora and Samuel.

All translations from the Spanish language are mine with four exceptions: for quotations from Ricardo Piglia's *Respiración artificial*, Fernando del Paso's *Noticias del imperio*, Ignacio Solares's *La invasión*, and Ángel Rama's *La ciudad letrada*, I have followed *Artificial Respiration* (trans. Daniel Balderston, 1994), *News from the Empire* (trans. Alfonso González and Stella T. Clark, 2009), *Yankee Invasion* (trans. Timothy G. Compton, 2009), and *The Lettered City* (trans. John Charles Chasteen, 1996), respectively.

Introduction: The Stellar Moments of Mexican History and the Rhetoric of Failure

The National History Museum at Chapultepec Castle in Mexico City houses some of the finest murals dedicated to the nation's past, but the most striking is Gabriel Flores' *Los niños héroes* [The Heroic Children] (1967), which covers the expanse of the castle's main cupola. Along the perimeter, phantom horses and riders heralded by tattered stars and stripes trample through the debris of war and smoke from the blazing city walls ascends in the form of an imperial eagle. In the center of the mural, a doe-eyed boy wrapped in the Mexican flag, falls headlong from heaven toward the abyss. Tears stream from his eyes as he witnesses the invading Yankee army wrest sovereignty from his beloved homeland. The story of the *niños héroes* has become an intriguing part of national mythology. On September 13, 1847, American forces under Winfield Scott bombarded and then assaulted Chapultepec Castle, which at the time served as the military college for up-and-coming young officers. Legend has it that the cadets, bereft of arms and training, held off the invading Americans as long as they could and, when hope seemed lost, climbed to the top tower, draped the national standard on their shoulders, and jumped to their deaths rather than be taken prisoners. Monuments commemorating their deed adorn the grounds of Chapultepec today as a testimony of heroism in the face of foreign intervention. The story has become a mainstay of Mexican nationalist mythology despite its questionable historical veracity. While there was a brief battle between US forces and academy cadets, there is no documentation about the exact number of children who jumped, their ages, whether they donned the flag or not, or if the event actually happened. Little mention of the *niños héroes* was made until nearly three decades after battle, and since then the legend has been modified by successive presidential administrations to meet the needs of the present (Parra 277). The story is further complicated by its similarity to Cervantes's historical tragedy *Numancia* about a small band of Spanish Christians who throw themselves from a tower in order to avoid being brutalized by an army of invading Romans in the second century. But the story continues to hold a permanent place in the Mexican imagination despite questionable historical grounds, which leads me to ask: Why is this story so important? Why has the suicide of military cadets come to symbolize an integral part of Mexican nationalism?

Both the mural and the myth interest me for what they say about the manner in which nationalism is both historically constructed and constructed historically. By this I mean that nationalism is both the subject of a developing historical process that involves the transmission of myriad images through artistic representation, as well as a discourse that is firmly rooted in an actualized concept of the past. Intellectuals, historians, politicians, and artists who witnessed the Mexican-American War worked assiduously to understand what happened and make others understand its lessons. As their work filled the voids of public memory, certain stories, ideas, and concepts became the bedrock foundation for all conceptualization of national character articulated after the war. Thus the immediate impressions of those who survived—the sense of outrage, impotence, and violation—in time became the central narrative line. As these notions of defeat were incorporated into the national narrative and disseminated through public education, contemporary crises came to be viewed through the lens of the past. No one questions whether the Mexican-American War actually took place because the evidence of its reality is readily apparent in the treaty that ended hostilities, the written testimonies of those who experienced it, and the border that amputated a significant section of the country. Yet, from what by all accounts was the most astonishing failure of Mexican history, the nation has been able to create a narrative of heroism and resistance that endows tragedy with a sacralized patriotic sentiment.

The central contention of this book, to paraphrase Marx's dramatic opening to *The Communist Manifesto* (1848), is that the specter of failure haunts Mexico's historical imagination. This is particularly true for representations of the independence movement and the nation-building process of the nineteenth century. One of the most recent, not to mention entertaining, descriptions of the period comes from *México: Lo que todo ciudadano quisiera (no) saber de su patria* (2006), Denise Dresser and Jorge Volpi's cheeky parody of the free civics and history textbooks that the federal government distributes to all Mexican schoolchildren. "Una sola cosa puede decirse del siglo XIX: fue un absoluto desastre. Todo lo malo que podía pasarle a un país, pasó," [Only one thing can be said for the nineteenth century: it was an absolute disaster. Everything bad that could happen to one country, happened,] they warn readers. "En realidad, lo mejor que podría hacer el alumno o la alumna es olvidarse de esta malhadada época y pasar de una vez por todas a la Revolución mexicana, la cual no fue menos catastrófica, pero al menos sí un poco más divertida" [Really, the best thing a student could do is forget this unfortunate period and proceed directly to the Mexican Revolution, which was no less catastrophic but much more entertaining] (66). Carlos Monsiváis put it even more succinctly when he mused that "los momentos estelares de la historia mexicana tienden a ser fracasos" [the stellar moments of Mexican history tend to be failures] (14). At first glance these summations may seem exaggerated and undeservedly infused with cynicism. Nevertheless, a cursory examination of nineteenth century Mexican history reveals that they might not be too far afield. The major events that come to mind are the short-lived insurgency under the direction of Miguel Hidalgo that ended three months later with the destruction of significant infrastructure and the capture and execution of all the major conspirators, the loss of Texas 15 years later to Anglo settlers who refused to submit to the Mexican government and rose up in open rebellion, the wholesale despoiling of half the national territory by an invading Yankee army that overran a beleaguered and poorly armed militia of conscripts, decades of ideological contention that undermined the political and defensive well-being of the nation and bankrupted the coffers, and the invasion by French forces that drove the legitimate president into a lengthy sojourn across the country while a Habsburg monarch established an illusory throne in Chapultepec. And this list, for the sake of scope and brevity, leaves off before the complex twentieth-century revolution, the bloody vying for political power by revolutionary generals, the establishment of a single dominant political party, the social upheavals that occurred as a result of governmental repression of student protests, and the mismanagement of major financial and natural disasters.

While Dresser and Volpi's sweeping rejection of the nineteenth century and Monsiváis's aphoristic quip might be regarded as unduly pessimistic dismissals of Mexico's history, they are clear examples of what I will refer to as the rhetoric of failure in Mexico's historical imagination. Lois Parkinson Zamora employs the term "historical imagination" as a critical metaphor that embodies the various literary guises used to construct a sense of continuity between the past and the present. Instead of disavowing the errors of the past, Parkinson demonstrates that Latin American writers "search *for* precursors (in the name of continuity) rather than escape *from* them (in the name of the individual); to connect *to* traditions and histories (in the name of a usable past) rather than disassociate *from* them (in the name of originality)" (5). My contention in *Cult of Defeat* is that authors connect with the tragic moments of their history by employing a series of discursive strategies that highlight, reinterpret, and even poeticize perceived cultural, political, and social shortcomings. Writers resort to failure for many reasons: to revise history, to explain failed utopian ideals, to undermine opposing political ideologies, to promote platforms of social change, to consecrate messianic missions with martyrdom, or to express pessimism about the future. Failure narratives often mediate between lofty aspirations and unsatisfied goals. They seek to ameliorate the psychological trauma resulting from loss. At times loss itself becomes a matter of national pride. Additionally, these narratives are fiercely nationalistic and intimately tied up with the nation's guiding fictions. As authors employ the rhetoric of failure, they reinterpret the nation's foundational moments and at times this serves to challenge official stories in an attempt to invite citizens to rethink their nation, their history, and their commitment to progress. We will see, however, that the realization of that goal is not always accomplished.

My approach to failure differs significantly from the one employed by John Ochoa in his book, *The Uses of Failure in Mexican Literature and Identity* (2005). I am interested in examining the ways that intellectuals actively engage with failure in their historical representations, whereas Ochoa opts for a deconstructive approach to foundational Mexican texts that "contain the *precise moment* of failure, and not necessarily its long aftermath or its reconstruction in hindsight" (7). His primary concerns are the epiphanic moments when failure surprises and even overcomes the author. Ochoa's is a daring proposition that works well in his analyses of Bernal Díaz del Castillo's attempts to correct Francisco López de Gómara's inaccurate account of the conquest of Mexico while simultaneously adhering to the work's structure and narrative line, or Humboldt's fascination with human perception and his paradoxical inability to suppress his own subjectivity in order to adequately express the American experience. And, as will become clear in a number of the historical novels examined in this book, Ochoa's approach provides great insight into the ways in which authors are at times unable to fulfill their own lofty aspirations. But, by contrast, what draws my attention in these historical novels are the ways in which authors conscientiously frame their national history as a long succession of defeats, mistakes, and missteps. I study the rhetoric of failure as being neither accident nor epiphany. Remembering Kenneth Burke's basic definition that rhetoric is the use of words by writers to form attitudes or to induce action in others (41), the rhetoric of failure is the product of a deliberate narrative choice. This is to say, then, that I understand the rhetoric of failure not as a "marker of a certain modality of analysis but as indicative of the way in which historical circumstances have created a predicament that has in turn constituted the context for the Spanish American performance of cultural discourse" (Alonso 5). Moreover, a study of failure discourse is only possible when performed within "the complex web of dominant ideas and events in its immediate historical context" (Mercieca 4). I contend that authors engage in a rhetorical appropriation of failure to reconstruct the stellar moments of Mexican history for the express purpose of responding to present crises.

Mexico is not alone in its fascination with defeat. Failure has formed an integral part of Spanish America's thinking on history, sovereignty, and identity since the fifteenth century and has intimate ties to notions of cultural and political dependency upon foreign powers. When spectacular successes abated during the New World campaigns, conquistadors framed their trials and tribulations as a demonstration of their fidelity and perseverance in their crown's cause (Pastor 116–17). In the nineteenth century, Latin American intellectuals on both sides of the political spectrum framed independence histories as failures in order to justify their redemptive political agendas. Charles A. Hale explains how the crushing defeat of the Mexican army by US forces in 1847 initiated a crisis among intellectuals that provoked "a disposition towards self-examination and a renewed search for remedies to Mexico's ills" (*Mexican Liberalism* 11–12). Nicolas Shumway observes that Argentine intellectuals of the Generation of '37, who witnessed firsthand the failure to unite the nation's disparate provinces and the inability of *porteño* political leaders to provide adequate and inclusive leadership, set out to identify the problems besetting the new nation and, in doing so, went about explaining those failures "with a mercilessness that borders on self-defeating negativism" (112). Nicola Miller notes that Spanish American intellectuals attempting to justify their independence following the imperial experience grounded their sense of nationhood "on the idea that Spanish American experience was best represented as in some fundamental way *lacking*, and that dependency was therefore an inevitability" (177). Forced to forge a national narrative that effectively broke with the Spanish Crown and governmental system in order to justify its claim to sovereignty, Spanish American identity discourse began from a discursive vacuum where the nascent nation was constructed as perennially belated and in need of tutelage and guidance from more mature democracies. For Carlos Alonso, this vacuum allowed Spanish American intellectuals to incompletely and paradoxically inhabit both the modern and the traditional, and eventually led to a weakness in American intellectual thinking. Nevertheless, near the close of the nineteenth century, that weakness no longer constituted a mark of inferiority but afforded Spanish American intellectuals a certain amount of cachet: "If at the banquet of modernity we were always a second-class invitee, history finally rewarded us when sveltness [sic] became the universal fashion.

This interruption has the attractiveness of turning into a virtue what was previously a defect" (154–55).

José Martí's banana wine offers an interesting paradigm for thinking about how the prestige of inferiority structures Spanish American identity discourse. In his classic essay, "Nuestra América" (1891), Martí argued for the development of authentically American political systems that responded to the cultural and historical idiosyncrasies of the American experience without necessarily depending upon European models for inspiration. Spanish American political systems, like Spanish American alcohol, should be made from native elements with native processes. Instead of importing European wines, his countrymen ought to make their own wine with whatever they have on hand, including the banana if need be. And if the wine is sour, so be it, exalts Martí, because bitter or not, banana wine is authentically American. What stands out here is the rhetorical twist in Martí's expression that transforms inherent inferiority into an authentic expression of Spanish American identity. Martí already accepts the probability that domestic products are innately inferior to foreign ones and that this inferiority is part and parcel of the American experience. But, through the rhetorical construction of this failure, Martí is able to recover a positive Spanish American solidarity. This a priori expectation of failure has become deeply embedded within the fibers of twentieth-century discussions of national character throughout the continent, as studies on national identity construction in Cuba, Puerto Rico, Argentina, and Mexico have shown.

This emphasis on failure may run counter to the bold, triumphal concept of nation that appears in many texts on nationalism, because one of the challenges confronting an analysis of the rhetoric of failure is the seemingly inherent aversion to recognizing defeat. Greil Marcus writes that

> There are events that are real but that dissolve when one tries to attach them to the monuments—wars, elections, public works projects, universities, laws, prisons—out of which we make our history. There are people who act and speak but whose gestures and words do not translate out of their moments—and this exclusion, the sweep of the broom of this dustbin, is a movement that in a way is far more violent than any toppling of statues. It is an embarrassment, listening to these stories and these cries, these utopian cheers and laments, because the utopian is measured always by its failure, and failure, in our historiography, is shame. (17–18)

The case of national discourse in the United States offers a useful illustration when compared to Mexico. Carlos Fuentes remembers that, as the son of a Mexican diplomat growing up in Washington DC, he was encouraged to read Mexican history in his home. The names, places, and events that he learned constituted "a history of crushing defeats," which stood in stark contrast to the historical narrative that was taught in his DC public school that "celebrated victories, one victory after another" (*Myself with Others* 4). The disjunction between these two stories became nowhere more evident to him than when he realized that sometimes "the names of United States victories were the same as the names of Mexico's defeats and humiliations"(5). This is not to say, however, that the United States has not suffered loss and humiliation. Instead, the mythologies that underpin this country's sense of being tend to exclude, explain, or erase failure in favor of an epic story of victory. This is why, for example, the Second World War continues to hold an alluringly seductive frame for thinking about what it means to be an "American" while the wars in Korea and Vietnam have been largely suppressed. Where the former was considered the apogee of American culture and military strength—we should not forget that those living during that time are frequently referred to as "the greatest generation"—the later conflicts left indelible marks in national conscience because they were, at best, incomplete exercises of flawed foreign policy or, at worst, painful and costly debacles. The film industry instinctively picked up on this distinction as can be illustrated by comparing the heroic tales told in the HBO miniseries *Band of Brothers* or Steven Spielberg's *Saving Private Ryan* with the heartbreaking stories of defeat such as Francis Ford Coppola's *Apocalypse Now*, Oliver Stone's *Platoon*, and Stanley Kubrick's *Full Metal Jacket*. Linnie Blake comes to similar conclusions in *The Wounds of Nations* (2008) when she argues that the discursive gap for dealing with failure in the United States and Britain is overcome through a film language that metaphorically expresses the trauma of war through depictions of dragons, zombies, and horrific hillbillies. In short, the national myth that exaggerates the United States' sense of exceptionality has limited its ability to develop the narrative strategies that other countries possess to deal with failure in a straightforward manner.

The United States' inability to locate a suitable place for failure within the scope of its national narrative does not mean that other countries have failed to do so. In fact, a number of recent studies have shown how tropes of victimization, defeat, and traumatic loss have paradoxically come to form the central core of what Benedict Anderson called the "imagined community", or the imaginary construct that binds heterogeneous groups into a collective community by establishing bonds of deep, horizontal camaraderie. However, as Claudio Lomnitz points out in *Deep Mexico, Silent Mexico* (2001), the appeal to imaginary constructs alone cannot generate the kinds of personal sacrifice in the name of the nation that Anderson considers to be the hallmark of nationalism. Sacrifice demands a more visceral motivation. Dominick LaCapra has identified a tendency in modern culture to covert traumatic experiences into sublime moments of nationalist organization. Horrific events, such as the dropping of atomic bombs or genocide, become occasions for negative sublimity or displaced sacralization and "give rise to what may be termed founding traumas— traumas that paradoxically become the valorized or intensely cathected basis of identity for an individual or a group rather than events that pose the problematic question of identity" (23). In a similar vein, Ian Burama writes that history, and especially the most painful and gruesome elements of it, enable societies to construct a common identity that differentiates them from other groups. Fraternity is developed through a shared sense of outrage and injury. Defeat and failure become so important for identity construction because it is easier to imagined personal insult and injury than it is to see one's personal sacrifice contribute to the well-being of the group. What is needed to activate the imagined community is a brush with annihilation. And in this regard, negative emotions, especially the sense of injury that follows upon the heels of failures to thwart attacks against national sovereignty, exercise a greater hold on individual citizens than do the lofty sentiments of self-determination and freedom. Indeed, as Jing Tsu eloquently argues in her study of Chinese nationalism, a sense of inferiority is a paradoxically central component of nationalism because the redemptive mission of nationalism is preconditioned by crisis: "The fundamental paradox of nationalism is its testimony not to greatness but to the need for greatness. Oddly, its persuasion and legitimacy derive from the lack of precisely these elements on the basis of which its ideology can be reified. The identity of the nation must be perceived as having failed in some way in order for nationalism to come to its rescue" (24). The rhetoric of failure, then, requires the deployment of powerful, negative images for the purposes of inspiring inciting reflective and communal action.

Because the redemptive mission of nationalism is predicated upon the threat of political and social dissolution, the rhetoric of failure emerges more forcefully in moments of crisis. If we could plot the high and low points of a nation's history on a graph, it would look like a rolling wave, with troughs and peaks occurring at fairly regular intervals. Troughs would be characterized by economic problems, social disarray, civil war, foreign invasions, authoritarian control, and reductions of democratic rights, while peaks would represent moments of growth, prosperity, success, democracy, confidence in government, and general well-being. The rhetoric of failure surfaces in the troughs and look backward, past the peaks, to other troughs in search of answers for present dilemmas. The rationale is that something must have occurred in the past that led the nation to its current state of malaise. Since the peak is a time of prosperity, when everything is going well, the problem must logically lie before, in prior troughs. Because these highs and lows are cyclical, so are narratives of failure. When nations experience highs, narratives of failure tend to disappear. As they descend into troughs, intellectuals begin to ask questions and to look for answers. An example from nineteenth-century Mexican historiography might help to exemplify this ebb and flow. Lucas Alamán, the leading conservative through the first half of the nineteenth century, published his multivolume *Historia de Méjico* in 1852, one year prior to his death. The year is significant because the country had been mired in political turmoil for more than three decades. The situation had reached its lowest point and the government struggled with its inability to maintain social order. Backed by recalcitrant *santanistas*, Alamán determined that the strong hand of a dictator was needed to restore order. He offered the post to Antonio López de Santa Anna, gave him unlimited powers, and bestowed upon him the title of "His Most Serene Highness." In *Historia de Méjico*, Alamán argued that the turmoil besetting Mexico in the 1850s was the direct result of the 1810 independence movement led by Father Miguel Hidalgo y Costilla. He railed against Hidalgo for establishing a precedent of political violence, mixed with a healthy dose of racial hatred and covered in a blasphemous veil of false religiosity. Because Hidalgo offered such a bad precedent, he continued, regional caudillos followed suit and military pronouncements such as the one made by Hidalgo became the standard operating procedure for political transition. Alamán also decried Hidalgo's anti-Hispanic attitudes as xenophobic, narrow-minded, and destructive. Unfortunately, he failed to recognize—or chose to ignore—that the general he supported as the nation's dictator in 1853 had rebelled against more governments than nearly any other in Mexican history. Still, Alamán's argument exemplifies a common trend in the rhetoric of failure. At a low point in history, he delved into the past to find a scapegoat for the present's maladies.

The emotional appeal of failure in the construction of national identity finds its most important expression in the ability to invest the present with the transcendental value of martyrdom. That was precisely the concern for José Vasconcelos, the early-twentieth-century Mexican intellectual who headed up the postrevolutionary push for public education, ran for president in 1928, and ultimately withdrew from public life to write Mexico's history after losing in what he considered to be fraudulent elections. The most important of Vasconcelos's histories for our purposes was *Breve historia de México* (1956), which took inspiration from Alamán's *Historia de Méjico*. They coincide, for example, in their mutual admiration for Hernán Cortés and disapproval of Miguel Hidalgo. The most striking contribution that *Breve historia de México* makes to this discussion of failure and the historical imagination comes midway through the chapter on the independence war, where he notes that José María Morelos, who had taken charge of the insurgent army following the execution of Hidalgo, was a substandard military leader whose only contribution to the legacy of the nation was being a substandard martyr. Concerned that his nation had become enamored with fallen heroes, he chided Mexico for having populated its national pantheon with martyrs, "como si la milicia tuviera por objeto preparar a sus hijos para que sean víctimas, lo que es oficio de santidad, no de milicia" [as if the military's main objective were to prepare its children to be victims, which is the job of religion and not the military] (279). Vasconcelos termed this fascination with failure "un culto a la derrota" [a cult of defeat] and wondered how much "la circunstancia de que nos hemos dedicado a adorar fracasados influye en el temperamento nacional pesimista y en la insistencia con que hablamos de 'morir por la patria', cuando lo que necesitan las patrias es que nadie muera, sino que todos vivan en plenitud y libertad" [our tendency to worship failures influences our pessimistic national temperament and our insistence of speaking of "dying for the nation," when what nations really need is not for people to die but rather to live in prosperity and liberty] (279). For Vasconcelos, what lays at the heart of the Morelos's legacy and other stories of defeated Mexican heroes is not simply a story about self-sacrifice. It is instead a process whereby failure is assigned a transcendental value, becomes a central component of the national narrative, and leads to a flawed model of citizenry.

Vasconcelos was not alone in his preoccupation over the potential dangers of the rhetoric of failure. They also appear in the philosophical quest for a definition of national character that was the primary work of the Hiperión group, which included important twentieth-century thinkers like Antonio Caso, Emilio Uranga, Samuel Ramos, Jorge Portilla, Leopoldo Zea, and Luis Villoro. As Anne Dormeus points out, these "writers regarded philosophy as central to the understanding of the Mexican. By offering self-awareness, they believed it could lead Mexicans to abandon their imitation of imported doctrines and overcome their self-denigration—a by-product of cultural dependency" (158). In *Naciones intelectuales* (2009), Ignacio Sánchez Prado demonstrates that despite the Hiperión group's best efforts to establish an existential and historicist model of philosophical argumentation that distanced discussions of national identity from mythological essentialisms, methodological weaknesses in the work of Uranga and Portilla opened the door to them by codifying certain archetypal figures like *el pelado* or behaviors like *el relajo* (198–206). It was not until the later works of Zea and Villoro that the essentialist bend in Mexican identity discourse was overturned in favor of analyses that focused on endemic social problems derived from economic and epistemological relationships of power. The philosophical and methodological advances made by Zea and Villoro were almost immediately overturned, however, by the mythologizing function of Octavio Paz's iconic essay, *El laberinto de la soledad* (1950). Sánchez Prado has effectively argued that the literariness of the book granted Paz greater access to the public sphere than did the rigidly philosophical writing of his predecessors. Sánchez Prado observes that, around 1950, "el pensamiento verdaderamente crítico se encuentra confinado en las instituciones académicas, mientras que en la esfera pública se consagran los mitos que los mexicanos comienzan a creer como propios" [truly critical thought is confined to academic institutions while in the public sphere intellectuals consecrate myths that Mexicans come to adopt as their own] (237). Though the mythical social misfit known as the *pachuco* had disappeared decades earlier, the national myths that were propagated by Paz's writing essentialized the notion that "'el mexicano' es un hipócrita que se esconde tras la máscara y el disimulo, un estoico al que la muerte le es indiferente, mientras que la mujer es 'enigmática'" ["the Mexican" is a hypocrite that hides behind masks and deception, a stoic who is indifferent to death while women are "enigmatic"] (239). This pointed summary of the main points of *El laberinto* is purposefully reductive because the central tenets of the essay are familiar for many readers and, for that reason, I will not offer a lengthy exegesis. Rather, I pause briefly to reemphasize that it was not the strength of the book's ideas but rather the literary merits of Paz's writing that captivated the public's attention. The high literary quality of phrases like "El mexicano venera al Cristo sangrante y humillado, golpeado por los soldados, condenado por los jueces, porque ve en él la imagen transfigurada de su propio destino" [Mexicans venerate the bloody Christ, humiliated and beaten by the soldiers, condemned by the judges, because they see in him the transfigured image of their own destiny] (*El laberinto* 107) make Paz's overly essentialist reading of Mexican character more palatable despite its negative implications for a discussion of national character.

This reading of *El laberinto de la soledad* goes against the grain of critics who hope to find in Paz the exaltation of the poetic national spirit. Ochoa, for example, takes a much more generous look at his work, arguing that a careful reading of the essay reveals that Paz "never states, either explicitly or implicitly, that Mexicans *are* failures or even that they regard themselves as failures" (10). Instead, Paz's analysis of Mexican character "teeters between paralyzing pessimism and euphoric action" and this "shocking realization can then spark a refashioning of identity" both at the individual and the national level (10–11). This fits Ochoa's general interest in the epiphanic revelation that failure as a heuristic device can offer. That is to say that, by the sudden realization of weakness or shortcoming, authors and readers are propelled into a new form of knowledge that produces positive effects for identity construction. The drawback to Ochoa's reading of *El laberinto de la soledad*, however, is that in his push to find a redemptive use for failure, he overlooks the potential damage that Paz's style of essentialist mythologizing can do. While I agree that Paz is not overtly attempting to prescribe the adoption of criminal or irresponsible behaviors, by essentializing them, his essay falls headlong into poeticized solitude and inactivity. In this regard Sánchez Prado is entirely correct in his assessment of the overarching ideological function of the text: it returns to the essentialist discourse that the Hiperión group had attempted to overturn. And, because of the accessibility of its language and its widespread dissemination, it consecrated a number of myths related to failure in such a manner that Mexicans began to accept them as inherent elements of national being.

In bringing up these objections to *El laberinto de la soledad*, I am not impugning the literary value of the essay. Rather, I have used it in an attempt to elucidate a series of ideas about the way the rhetoric failure relates to nationalism and, somewhat more specifically, to the benefits and potential dangers that it offers. Though *El laberinto de la soledad* is arguably the most recognized essay on national identity both inside and outside of Mexico, it was not universally embraced by Mexican intellectuals. Many perceived and responded to problems inherent in Paz's mythologies. In 1975, Claude Fell asked Paz how readers had received his book at publication and the poet admitted that initial reactions were quite negative. "Mucha gente se indignó; se pensó que era un libro en contra de México. Un poeta me dijo algo bastante divertido: que yo había escrito una elegante mentada de madre contra los mexicanos" [Many people got upset; they thought it was a book written against Mexico. One poet told me something really entertaining: that I had written an elegant insult to Mexico] (Paz, *El ogro filantrópico* 18). One who shared this indignation was Rosario Castellanos, the talented novelist, short-story writer, poet, playwright, and essayist. From 1963 until her untimely death in 1974, Castellanos wrote a weekly column for the *Excélsior* newspaper that allowed her to pioneer the women's movement in Mexico and to offer the first feminist critiques of "the clichés, prejudices, norms, and myths that define and constrain Mexican society" (O'Connell 209). When a reader asked her to comment on *El laberinto de la soledad*, Castellanos responded with a scathing parody of Paz's approach in "La tristeza del mexicano" [Mexican Sadness]. She begins by parodically explaining how Paz identifies a cultural trait, explains it in terms of historical referents, and demonstrates how this trait constitutes a fundamental piece of national identity. She then offers a hypothetical explanation for the melancholic Mexican spirit. Following the model established in *El laberinto de la soledad*, Castellanos links the Mexican's inherent sadness to historically verifiable letdowns: Malinche's betrayal, the conquest's brutality, Santa Anna's loss of half the national territory, Juárez's untimely death, Díaz's thirty-four-year dictatorship, and the bloody debacle that was the Mexican Revolution (176). She then uses this historical overview to hyperbolically ask how, in light of so much historical disappointment, can Mexican men be expected to work hard, assume family and social obligations, handle money appropriately, and drink responsibly. Castellanos concludes her parody, suggesting that not only does this sadness justify patriarchal irresponsibility, but that it also ennobles Mexicans: "Pero la tristeza ¿no lo sabía usted?, proporciona un aire de distinción a quien la porta que lo vuelve elegante…[Estamos] muy por encima de todas las pequeñas miserias cotidianas porque lo que ocurre ¡es que somos superiores!" [But sadness, didn't you know, lends an air of elegant distinction to those who possess it…We are above the small daily miseries because it just so happens that we are superior!] (177). Stepping back from the ironic mode of writing that characterized the first portion of this essay, Castellanos adopts a somber tone and identifies in the mythologizing function of Paz's work "no tanto la necesidad de alcanzar el conocimiento puro sino otro afán más turbio y más inmediato: el de justificarnos. Y lo logramos con tal éxito que cuando describimos nuestros defectos…creería que estamos hablando de nuestras cualidades" [not so much the need to attain pure knowledge but another, darker and more immediate concern: the need to justify ourselves. And we achieve it with so much success that when we describe our defects…one would think that we are talking about our virtues] (175). Castellanos's objection to Paz demonstrates the primary pitfall of the rhetoric of failure: the potential propagation of negative images and representations that emphasize the inescapability of failure.

Recent reports on Mexico's drug wars, economic depression, political corruption, and increasing social instability have again raised the specter of Mexico being or becoming a failed state and seem to confirm Walter Benjamin's axiom that the state of emergency in which we live is not the exception but the rule (257). Acknowledging that Mexico has weathered numerous traumatic events throughout its history, it must be recognized that the crisis narrative that pervades the historical imagination is nevertheless a rhetorical construction. To be clear: failure to achieve a given goal can be empirically demonstrated and therefore considered a fact. Crisis, on the other hand, is one of a number of discursive strategies that assign "some kind of order and design to the past, the present and the future" (Auerbach 94). Frank Kermode, sensing danger in the crisis mentality of modern society, warned that "myth, uncritically accepted, tends like prophecy to shape a future to confirm it" (94). Edmund Morgan later reformulated this truism when he observed that, because "fictions are necessary, because we cannot live without them, we often take pains to prevent their collapse by moving the facts to fit the fiction, by making our world conform more closely to what we want it to be" (14). Thus, the rhetoric of failure is predicated upon the notion that Mexico got off to a bad start and has never fully recovered its footing. The effect of this transformation is a kind of stasis that locks the historical imagination into a fixed position wherein society hinges on the brink of destruction, continually focused on present ills and future decadence, which Kermode describes as the transition from an imminent state of crisis to an immanent psychological state. Regardless of whether these perceptions reflect a political reality, they form part of a long-standing tradition of viewing contemporary problems as the natural consequence of past mistakes. Nowhere does this fascination with failure become more evident than in fictional reconstructions of Mexico's past, particularly of the nineteenth century independence and nation-building period.

If failure forms the backbone of so many historical representations in Mexico, to say nothing of Latin America as a whole, then why should we reduce the scope of this study to the historical novel? Why not, for example, examine Fernando de Fuentes' early trilogy of revolutionary films, the role that false modesty played in the early years of Mexican feminism, the historical murals of Diego Rivera and Juan O'Gorman, the socially committed chronicles of Carlos Monsiváis or Elena Poniatowska, or even the writings of nineteenth-century historians like Carlos María de Bustamante, Lucas Alamán, José María Luis Mora, and Justo Sierra? Indeed, a powerful argument against literary studies as a whole has been offered by cultural studies critics who assert that because being cultured in the modern Latin American sense corresponds to literacy, and because literary texts do not enjoy the widespread diffusion that characterizes the American or European markets, literary studies constitute an antiquated and, dare I say, failed method for observing and analyzing culture (García Canclini 42). Historically speaking, one of the most striking aspects of Latin American literature is the abysmally small size of first-run printings for fiction and poetry. Editions of one thousand to three thousand copies are not uncommon and, assuming that every copy from one of these editions were purchased and read by 70 different people in Mexico City, with more than twenty-one million inhabitants, it would still only reach about 1 percent of the total population. And that, too, without taking into consideration outlying cities where access to new publications is reduced by the absence of major retail bookstores like Gandhi and El Sótano. The disparity between those who enjoy material access to literature and disposable time to consume it and those who do not leads Roderic Ai Camp to argue that

Mexican intellectuals exercise only a limited influence over the values of society at large "because large numbers of the population do not come into contact with intellectual products" (*Intellectuals* 58). But all is not lost.

While these concerns are certainly valid, in recent years history in its many forms and guises has become a good for mass public consumption. Just as the progressive philosophical work of the Hiperión group lost ground to Paz's mythologies, history has entered the public sphere in the form of television shows, film, video games, reenactments, and historical fiction in an unprecedented manner. This historiocopia, or the "overflowing plenty and abundance" of historical products, leads Jerome de Groot to argue that the study "of these different forms and discourses is important in order to gain some small understanding of the multitude and variety of ways in which contemporary society engages with and consumes the past" (13). Publication trends over the last ten years demonstrate a growing demand for historical novels in Mexico. Powerhouses such as Alfaguara, Planeta Mexicana, Joaquín Mortiz, and Grijalbo Mondadori have keyed in on this uptick and have flooded the market with new and oftentimes untried authors in order to meet that demand. In Mexico alone more than thirty historical novels have been published in the last five years, and this number does not account for the legion of popular histories, biographies, and children's books that hit the stands. Likewise, bookstores through the Spanish-speaking world have dedicated ever more space to historical fiction and publishers have inaugurated a number of special series and literary prizes for novels that recreate significant moments of the past. The increased demand for historical fiction can be attributed to two principal causes. First, as Georg Lukács pointed out in *The Historical Novel* (1962), and Seymour Menton later confirmed in *Latin America's New Historical Novel* (1993), the "appeal to national independence and national character is necessarily connected with a reawakening of national history" (Lukács 25), to which we can add that the renewed appeal of history that accompanies anniversaries likewise engenders a reawakening of interest in the historical novel. Second, the national narrative that developed from the ideological platforms of the Mexican Revolution has ceased to provide a cogent explanation for contemporary problems. This is a matter that I will take up again throughout the chapters to follow and will therefore not elaborate here. But what I want to suggest is that the failure of revolutionary rhetoric has forced Mexicans to reevaluate history. Historical fiction about the nineteenth century has become a new and accessible repository for stories, heroes, and myths in Mexico.

This surge in the production of historical novels offers an excellent opportunity for Mexican authors to reinterpret their history, especially the nineteenth century, and to question the grounds upon which contemporary society stands. The historical novel "no cancela la historia sino que redefine el espacio declarado como 'histórico' por la tradición, la convención y el poder, postulando y configurando en su lugar las *historias híbridas* que tratan de imaginar otros tiempos, otras posibilidades, otras historias y discursos" [does not cancel history but redefines the space called "historical" by tradition, convention, and official sources by postulating and configuring in its place *hybrid histories* that try to imagine other times, other possibilities, other histories and discourses] (Perkowska 42). To that end, I argue that these historical reconstructions acquire deeper meaning when understood as part of broader contemporary debates about globalization, neoliberalism, and the continued existence of the nation. The novels studied in *Cult of Defeat* all correspond to significant moments of crisis when authors find themselves pressed to explain the missteps of the present in terms of past's mistakes. The period between 1960 and 2010 include some of the nation's worst economic fiascos, devastating natural disasters, and important political transformations. It encompasses the economic crisis of the late 1970s and early 1980s, the implementation of neoliberal economic reforms which eventually culminated in the North American Free Trade Agreement (NAFTA), as well as the resulting macroeconomic imbalances and political instability that eventually paved the way for the 1994 political and economic turmoil. This period also witnessed the end of the 71-year rule of the Partido Revolucionario Institucional (PRI) and the resurgence of Mexican conservatism under the auspices of the Partido Acción Nacional (PAN). The novels analyzed throughout this book appear at a time when Mexican authors are actively rethinking their society and criticizing the neoliberal reforms espoused by conservative administrations. Throughout this book, then, I will draw explicit parallels between the texts and the political and historical context in which they are written to demonstrate that the historical novel, more than a reinterpretation or redecoration of the past, is a conscientious criticism of the present.

To make these connections, the chapters that follow will deemphasize what have become the standard methods for analyzing the historical novel in favor of a historicist approach that focuses on how the novel responds to the contemporary problems. In general, recent theorization of the genre in Latin America has fallen back on what are now relatively antiquated formulations of metafictional narratology grounded in Hayden White's groundbreaking work on narratological studies of historiography in *Metahistory* (1973). Subsequent studies on the historical novel like Linda Hutcheon's explanation of historiographic metafiction in *A Poetics of Postmodernism* (1988) and Seymour Menton's reliance upon Bakhtinian dialogism in *Latin America's New Historical Novel* relied almost exclusively on White's central thesis that history depends upon narrative tropes and techniques as much as fiction. The impact of Hutcheon's and Menton's works in criticism on Latin American historical fiction was enormous. Santiago Juan-Navarro later adapted Hutcheon's concept to a Latin American context and added layers of complexity in *Archival Reflections* (1999) while Juan José Barrientos reiterated many of Menton's proposals in his study *Ficción-historia* (2001). These studies, however, only infrequently look beyond narratological concerns to think about the way the historical novel engages in an ongoing dialogue about the present state of politics, culture, and society. That is to say, their attention to the internal mechanisms of fiction sidelines important discussions about the relevance of the historical novel in a social context. By contrast, a number of recent studies have emphasized the importance of connecting novelistic representations of the past to present context. This happens, for example, when Magdalena Perkowska explains the renewed interest in the historical novel near the end of the 1980s as a product of the crisis of history that accompanied Latin America's decisions to implement economic policies and embrace globalization (28–31). Diego Osuna Osuna has recently argued that the ability to "revivir el pasado a través de la literatura contemporánea permite encontrar en ella, por parte del lector, elementos que en diversos grados se conectan con la realidad 'extraficcional'" [revive the past through contemporary literature allows readers to find in fiction elements that in many ways connect to the "extrafictional" reality] and that the result of this reliving is the realization that "el pasado, viéndolo bien, no es tan pasado como uno puede creer porque materializa al construir un relato paralelo de la historia contemporánea" [the past, carefully considered, is not as past as one might believe because it materializes when one constructs a parallel to contemporary history] (156–57). In essence, then, what I am proposing in *Cult of Defeat* is a shift away from deconstructive postmodern analysis of the internal mechanisms of fiction toward a study of what makes fiction a vital and active participant in the present.

As a starting point for this shift, I begin with Eelco Runia, the Dutch historian who has most recently been concerned with the "subliminal, mysterious, but uncommonly powerful living-on...of the past" in the present ("Spots" 305). Asserting that the narratological paradigm of historiographic theory offered by White in the 1970s has locked theoretical thinking about the past into a framework that demands the narrative continuity of works of fiction, Runia suggests that discontinuity—or the act of being "surprised by ourselves" because a given action falls outside the logical narration—is equally, if not more, important for understanding ways in which the past seemingly takes control of the present through unconscious repetition ("Presence" 6). This emphasis on discontinuity, he argues, requires an epistemological shift away from the notion of history as what is entirely irretrievable, to one that recognizes history as an ongoing process. Metonymy, more so than metaphor, is the ideal method for transferring historical knowledge because, as a trope of dissimulation that feigns a seemingly straightforward interpretation, it allows the message of history to fill the collective unconscious in a peripheral manner that sidesteps the logical processes of understanding and dissociation. Simultaneously, it functions as a "presence in absence" both "in the sense that it presents something that isn't there, but also in the sense that in the absence (or at least in its radical inconspicuousness) that *is* there, the thing that isn't there is still present" (1). Runia's clearest examples of his theory are articulated in his analysis of monuments to fallen soldiers or victims of terrorism because, while they are capable of representing the past through equivalencies and accumulation, presence "is *not* the result of metaphorically stuffing up absences with everything you can lay your hands on. It can at best be *kindled* by metonymically *presenting* absences" ("Spots" 309). The application of Runia's theorization is relatively straightforward for the rhetoric of failure in that, by invoking the presence of past errors, historical novelists are able to reflect on political, social, and cultural shortcomings in an indirect manner. By focusing on how historical fiction makes the past relevant to the present, we can sidestep the archivist tendencies of criticism that demonstrate more interest in unearthing the truth about a given historical paper trail and return to what I believe is at the heart of historical fiction: understanding why authors dedicate years of their work to researching and writing about a past event, and why these fictions surface at specific moments in history. By resurrecting key moments of historical defeat and linking them to current crises, the authors studied in this book open discursive spaces for vigorous debate about current issues and, in this manner, Mexico's historical novel becomes an ideal medium for understanding the rhetoric of failure.

The best illustration for the way that the historical novel makes the past relevant might be found in Alain Badiou's *Handbook of Inaesthetics* (2005) where he proposes that truth can be determined by studying configurations of works—or subject points—that exist within an infinite array of other possible works. While individual works of art themselves are not synonymous with a given truth, their relationships to each other are. It is this series of relationships that I want to focus on. If, instead of thinking about subject points as works of art, we imagine an infinite array of isolated points that we collectively call the past, the interrelations between these points are determined by the manner in which history is constructed. The process of constructing relationships according to the whims and projects of the historian in question was the central concern for White's *Metahistory*, which offered the first significant examination of the narratological processes that create a sense of causality from seemingly free-floating subject points and bind them together into cohesive narratives. What determines relevance is not the relationship that fiction establishes between subject points in the array, which is the function of historiography, but rather the lines of connectivity between the subject points of the past matrix to a secondary array of subject points known as the present of the novel's publication. In other words, the historical novel pulls subject points out of the array and arranges them as images in relation to a current set of social, cultural, and political circumstances. The relevance of the novel's subject matter is determined by the way it actualizes the past for the needs of the present. When we consider constellations of novels as subject points relating to a given historical period, we can then analyze how the historical novel functions within a given social context. Referring specifically to the novels included in *Cult of Defeat*, each project develops within the context of a significant transitional moment: the financial crisis of the early 1980s, the waning years of Western imperialism in the late 1980s, the decline of the PRI and the ascendancy of Mexican conservatism in the 1990s, the wars in the Middle East of the 2000s, and the bicentennial celebrations of 2010. Taken as a whole, these novels attest to the radical transformations that have significantly altered the nation since the early decades of the twentieth century.

In the pages that follow, I will address these questions of relevance through a series of analyses that focus upon the corrective, recuperative, instructive, and redemptive rhetorical uses of failure in recent historical fiction. The first chapter undertakes a consideration of the corrective aspect of the rhetoric of failure by examining the development of Jorge Ibargüengoitia's version of Mexico's independence story, from its reverential theatrical beginnings in the 1960s to its parodic novelistic end in the early 1980s. I argue that the transition in tone corresponds to increasing levels of artistic freedom for the author, as well as to the declining legitimacy of the ruling PRI party. The second chapter proposes reading Fernando del Paso's *Noticias del imperio* as a recuperative fiction interested in recognizing the historical legacy of the Second Empire in order to metaphorically bury it. This does not mean that the novel apologizes for monarchism; quite the contrary, it is an indictment of conservatism in general. But Del Paso considers the failure to incorporate all aspects of history into the national narrative as a major reason why Mexico has been unable to move beyond it. The third chapter illustrates the instructive aspect of failure by engaging the ethical position of historical and fictional authors in reimagining the past. I contend that Enrique Serna's *El seductor de la patria* provides a manual for reading and interpreting historical and political narratives where readers encounter competing authoritative voices and must sort through biases and concealed intentions in order to sift out their version of historical truth. The fourth chapter offers the clearest contrast between the redemptive and paralyzing aspects of failure by analyzing the impact of trauma on identity construction in the case of three novels that reimagine the Mexican-American War. Each novel's appropriation of the war can be read as a diatribe against the US-led invasions in the Middle East, but what is more significant is the way in which each author either allows the traumatic past to overwhelm his writing or accepts the past and finds a way to turn failure into a form of social, political, and personal salvation. The book concludes with a brief reflection on the bicentennial celebrations of independence in Mexico. A coda of this nature is necessary because the recent editorial boom of historical novels is the product of two extraliterary causes: first, the celebratory fervor of the bicentennial which has inspired readers to seek out additional information about national history in a less academic and more entertaining format; and second, the multiple crises—drug violence, civil unrest, questionable political legitimacy, and economic depression—facing the country at present invite a thorough reconsideration of the guiding fictions upon which the imagined community of nation is based.

Chapter 1

A Mexican Comedy of Errors in Jorge Ibargüengoitia's Self-Correcting Independence History

The word "curmudgeon" is typically associated with cantankerous, surly old men. We think of grumpy septuagenarians with heavy jowls who misanthropically watch a parade of idiocy pass before their rockers. Oftentimes misunderstood as cynics, naysayers, and doomsday pessimists, more often than not curmudgeons are social commentators who bring a unique and oftentimes surly perspective to bear on the contrived manner in which people and institutions govern themselves and others. They are the sarcastic voice of reason in a world where madness prevails. In the Anglo-American tradition, we think of Mark Twain, W. C. Fields, H. L. Menken, Andy Rooney, and Lewis Black, while in Mexico figures like Salvador Novo, Juan José Arreola, Carlos Monsiváis, and Enrique Serna come to mind. But the most talented one of his generation was Jorge Ibargüengoitia, whose curmudgeonly style is best exemplified by a warning he offers at the beginning of his final play, *El atentado* (1962), that any similarity between his work and the historical record is not accidental but a matter of national shame. The implication of this somewhat impertinent forward and all the historical fiction that he wrote afterward is that history is made up of words, actions, and events that do not fit within the neatly cohesive narratives that form the basis of national identity, and that these disjunctive fissures in the texture of national narratives are an "embarrassment...because the utopian is measured always by its failure, and failure, in our historiography, is shame" (Greil 18). Nowhere are these embarrassing little historical details made more readily apparent than in *Los pasos de*

López, the last novel Ibargüengoitia published before his untimely death in 1983, which is a scathingly ironic portrayal of the 1810 struggle for independence. *Los pasos de López,* like most interpretations of the insurgency, hinges on the reputation of Miguel Hidalgo, the father of Mexican independence. Hidalgo presented narrative problems for nineteenth-century intellectuals who knew him personally and had witnessed firsthand the destruction and chaos that his insurgent army inflicted in their march toward the capital; he was perceived by conservatives and liberals alike as being violent, irresponsible, and reckless. The priest's image was later retrofitted by twentieth-century party historians who sought to establish a seamless, teleological narrative reaching from independence to the revolution and beyond. Instead of portraying Hidalgo as the venerable parish priest whose love of country and hatred for authoritarian rule led him to fully conceive a new and independent nation, Ibargüengoitia paints a portrait of a gambling, wine-bibbing libertine who carelessly hurled the nation headlong into armed chaos without much forethought. However, Ibargüengoitia's criticisms should not be understood solely as an attack on Hidalgo's deified persona, but rather, as a broad-spectrum demystification of the mythologies that sustain official nationalism for, as Emilio Carballido writes, *Los pasos de López* "no está hecha contra las ineptitudes de algunos insurgentes, sino contra el hecho de la Independencia" [was not written against the ineptitude of a couple of insurgents, but against the entire independence movement] (264). Indeed, the entire insurgency comes under Ibargüengoitia's iconoclastic gaze and he transforms the epic heroism of Hidalgo and the conspirators of Querétaro into a serious spoof of their foibles and vices.

Los pasos de López has been one of Ibargüengoitia's most popular books, and while readers revel in the follies of the founding fathers, they often overlook the author's own missteps—especially the ones that led to the novel's publication. *Los pasos de López* was, in fact, not Ibargüengoitia's first work about Mexican independence. As early as 1959, he had written *La conspiración vendida,* a rather solemn drama about Hidalgo and the Creole conspiracy that received little public attention and has been retrospectively interpreted by critics as a first draft of the novel. No evidence appears to support that hypothesis. To the contrary, I will suggest that *La conspiración vendida* was the product of a momentary necessity, that Ibargüengoitia in hindsight felt embarrassed by this contribution to pious official history, and that he spent years attempting to make amends. This is to say, then, that there is a process of equivocation, experimentation, growth, and development in Ibargüengoitia's writing about independence that has, to this point, gone unexamined. Reading his works in this manner will allow us to see that *Los pasos de López,* was not simply a novel about national independence but also about personal independence. In this first chapter, then, I want to examine what led Ibargüengoitia to write *La conspiración vendida*, why this play has been swept under the carpet of literary history, and how Ibargüengoitia attempted to make amends for it through his journalism and his final novel. I will conclude by studying how Ibargüengoitia brings this correction around full circle by incorporating theatrical motifs into the structure and theme of *Los pasos de López*. Ever the curmudgeon, Ibargüengoitia exposes the shortcomings of the conspiracy as a whole and interprets independence as one massive theatrical flop, characterized by a faulty script, incompetent directors, bungling amateur actors, and an uncomprehending audience.

This transition in Ibargüengoitia's portrayal of the independence period evinces a growing sense of self-reflection that invites us to pause for a moment and think about metafictional modes of writing. Many scholars working on metafiction have focused on its inward gaze: Robert Alter argued that self-conscious novels systematically flaunt their own artificiality (xi), Inger Christensen suggested that they allow authors to reflect upon fundamental questions of fictional creation (13), and Robert Spires proposed that metafiction is a literary modality that cuts across genre, thematic intent, or historical context to violate sacrosanct conventions by unmasking their arbitrariness and "thereby any illusion that what is being narrated is real rather than mere fiction" (16). But it is an image from José Ortega y Gasset's *La deshumanización del arte* (1928) that strikes me as the best illustration of literary self-reflection to date. Addressing the fallacy of transparency in art, Ortega y Gasset asked readers to imagine

que estamos mirando un jardín a través del vidrio de una ventana. Nuestros ojos se acomodarán de suerte que el rayo de la visión penetre el vidrio, sin detenerse en él, y vaya a prenderse en las flores y frondas. Como la meta de la visión es el jardín y hasta él va lanzando el rayo visual, no veremos el vidrio, pasará nuestra mirada a su través, sin percibirlo. Cuanto más puro sea el cristal menos lo veremos. Pero luego, haciendo un esfuerzo, podemos desentendernos del jardín y, retrayendo el rayo ocular, detenerlo en el vidrio. Entonces el jardín desaparece a nuestros ojos y de él sólo vemos unas masas de color confusas que parecen pegadas al cristal. (17)

[that we are looking at a garden through a window. Our eyes adjust so that our line of sight passes through the glass and rests upon the flowers and plants. Because the object of our gaze is the garden and our line of sight is directed toward it, we do not see the glass; our gaze moves through it without perceiving it. But then, with some effort, we are able to forget about the garden, withdraw our gaze, and focus on the glass. Then the garden disappears from our view and all that is left is a mass of confused colors stuck to the glass.]

Traditional reading focuses our attention on the garden and, while we recognize that the glass is a barrier that impedes direct contact with the outside, we willingly or subconsciously choose to ignore it because what lies beyond interests us. Narrative and textual conventions are likewise a window between readers and stories that simultaneously enable and limit our perception. Metafictional modes of writing call our attention to the artificiality of the window, or the narrative framework that enables us to perceive the text, through a series of textual games—including, but not limited to, the use of narrative self-consciousness, multiple frames of reference, *mise en abyme*, parodic intertextuality, overt references to external literary and nonliterary sources, and direct dialogue with the reader—that allow us to see our own reflection and the writer's in the fictional construct itself. Indeed, it is this emphasis on literary self-awareness that becomes the crux of Linda Hutcheon's treatment of the postmodern historical novel when, in *A Poetics of Postmodernism* (1998), she coined the term "historiographic metafiction" for those novels that refute the commonsense methods of distinguishing between fact and fiction. They refuse to accept the "view that only history has a truth claim, both by questioning the ground of that claim and by asserting that both history and fiction are discourses, human constructs, signifying systems, and both derive their major claim to truth from that identity" (93). Metafiction is a prime vehicle for many authors to question the validity of not only literary conventions, but also the cultural processes that govern discourse at the local, national, and global levels. In Hutcheon's view, historiographic metafictions upset the status quo by presenting new paradigms of historical documentation and cultural perception because the "'real' referent of their language once existed; but it is only accessible to us today in textualized form: documents, eye witness accounts, archives" (93). Thus, we might argue that by means of self-conscious narrators, intercalated theatrical pieces, explicit reflections upon storytelling, and subversive corrections of official history, Ibargüengoitia's metafictional style questions traditional literary ontology by highlighting the arbitrary conventions of commonsense reading, conspicuously calling attention to itself, and evaluating the process of creation. Indeed, both of his most recognized novels, *Los relámpagos de agosto* (1964) and *Los pasos de López* (1982), are highly metafictional works that highlight the ways in which Mexico's historical imagination developed around tropes that cast important moments of national history as a series of failures. However, for the purposes of this chapter, I want to sidestep a straightforward reading of the mechanics of Ibargüengoitia's metafictional writing in order to emphasize the self-reflective development of his historical imagination over two decades.

Ibargüengoitia's writings about independence become more self-reflective over time, perhaps because, as John Brushwood suggests, Mexican intellectuals suffered a crisis of consciousness following the massacre of university students at Tlatelolco Plaza on October 2, 1968. According to his estimate, half of all novels written in Mexico in the 1960s, 1970s, and 1980s were metafictional in nature (*La novela mexicana* 17–56). For Brushwood, Tlatelolco marked an end to the optimism that accompanied the ruling PRI party's willingness to suppress dissident opinions through coercive and violent means. Strikes among railroad workers in 1959, teachers in 1960, and medical professionals in 1965 exacerbated tensions between the polity and public (*Narrative Innovation* 62). But the state-sponsored assault on peaceably protesting students at Tlatelolco pushed Mexican society into an ontological limbo where stability was a fleeting dream and truth, illusory. In addition to the repressive actions of the national government, economic concerns also weighed on the minds of the nation's intelligentsia. Since the 1940s, Mexico has been one of the few Latin American countries to enjoy substantial and continuous growth in the manufacturing, petroleum exports, and technology. Thanks in large part to steadily increasing oil prices, the peso was stronger than it had ever been, and Mexico seemed stable. Throughout the 1960s, the economy remained pinned to petroleum, which led to problems when the 1970s oil crisis cut into profits. To maintain its growth rate, Mexico took out massive loans and transitioned from net exportation of raw materials to net importation. Trouble began in February 1982 when the Banco de México allowed the peso to float on the international market and, in the ensuing devaluation, the peso lost nearly half of its value. Miguel de la Madrid was elected president in a landslide victory over a lackluster field of opposition candidates in July 1982. No one, of course, was surprised: De la Madrid had been personally chosen by the outgoing president, José López Portillo, following the model established by presidents since the end of the Mexican Revolution of 1910. A Harvard-educated businessman with a firm belief in the power of the open market, De la Madrid inherited a wealth of economic and social problems from his successors. Four months after De la Madrid took office, Mexico defaulted on its loans, the national economy crashed, and with it, much of the hope that had been built in the preceding decades.

When we speak of political and social change in Mexico before, during, and after 1968, we must take into account decades of disillusionment with revolutionary promises that never came to fruition; Ibargüengoitia makes this point repeatedly in both his journalism and historical fiction. The literature produced during this period suffered from the same instability and began to probe its own creation. In this regard, the postmodern emphasis on society's flagging confidence in the grand narratives of nationhood makes its most important contribution to the discussion of historical novels. In *The Postmodern Condition* (1984), Lyotard suggested that the "decline of narrative can be seen as an effect of the blossoming of techniques and technologies since the Second World War, which has shifted emphasis from the ends of action to the means" (37). Because Mexico maintained neutrality throughout the war, it was spared the type of epistemological trauma that Lyotard describes for most of the Western world during the 1940s and 1950s, but the upsurge in self-reflective writing at a time when the weaknesses of Mexico's guiding narrative of progress came to light is no coincidence. If metafiction seeks to expose the process by which fictional narratives are created, and if the process by which social and cultural narratives are constructed is similar, then metafictional writing ultimately invites the reader to question both the literary conventions that establish a power struggle between author and reader and the subservient relationship of citizen to the archive, defined by Foucault as the system of organization and censorship that ultimately determines what information is expressed and what is suppressed (130–31).

The Insurgency and Its Interpreters

In order to discuss the changes that occur in Ibargüengoitia's portrayals of the insurgency during this period of social transformation, a few words should be said about how the archive related to the independence movement has developed. In *Through Other Continents* (2006), Wai-Chee Dimock describes the concept of *deep time* as a methodological approach to reading broadly across time and space in order to expand our understanding of the history of national literature. I want to tweak Dimock's method such that, instead of imagining the productive exchange that goes on among cultures and millenniums, we can begin to trace the evolution of the story told about Mexican independence, and more specifically about the image of Father Miguel Hidalgo, over the last two centuries. In this manner, I want to emphasize the transformative effect that time, context, and experience have on the independence story because Ibargüengoitia's challenge to official historiography does not occur ex nihilo.

Political upheavals in Spain resulting from Charles IV's 1808 decision to allow Napoleon Bonaparte to march an army of conquest across Spanish territory en route to Portugal paved the way for American Creoles to declare their independence from Spain. For centuries they had been denied access to seats of power by the colonial regime in both church and governmental hierarchies, and with the empire in disarray, the Creoles saw their opening and moved. The first Spanish American rebellions came from the south: Colombia, Argentina, and Chile. In Mexico, a small revolt in Valladolid (present-day Morelia) was brutally quashed in 1809. By 1810, another plan was hatching in Querétaro under the direction of Captain Ignacio Allende and Father Miguel Hidalgo y Costilla. With the help of the local colonial administrator, Miguel Domínguez, and his wife, Josefa Ortiz de Domínguez, Allende rallied support for independence from military and ecclesiastical ranks, and met under the guise of a literary *tertulia* to hammer out their plans. Plans were set to take up arms in December, but a series of betrayals forced the conspirators' hand. In the early hours of September 16, Hidalgo entered his small parish in Dolores and proclaimed independence in what has come to be known as *el grito de Dolores*. With the revolution in full swing, Hidalgo set in motion a number of sweeping social changes aimed at improving the living conditions for the indigenous population: he abolished slavery throughout the nation and repealed oppressive taxes that had been levied against the indigenous by the colonial regime. From September 1810 to January 1811, Hidalgo's revolutionary army rolled across the central plains taking what provisions they could find from local populations, sacking both European and American haciendas, and massacring any Spaniard who offered the slightest resistance. Simpson, along with many Mexican historians and writers, considers this violence Hidalgo's enduring contribution to national politics. His final evaluation of the priest, as can be expected, condemns Hidalgo "for the rancor and envy which he shared with most Creoles against the Spaniards" and finds it "difficult to avoid the conclusion that his leadership of the insurrection was calamitous, not only in its immediate consequences, but in the legacy of bloody violence which he left behind" (191–92). The violence espoused by the revolutionary army may be most succinctly represented by the massacre at the Alhóndiga de Granaditas in Guanajuato. Guanajuato was, at the time, one of the wealthiest cities in the viceroyalty of New Spain. Spanish royalists, aware of the approaching insurgents, sent their families to neighboring towns and remained to defend the city. Hidalgo sent word to the Spaniards, calling for their surrender. He also made a special arrangement for the local colonial intendant, Juan Antonio Riaño y Bárcena, to leave on peaceful terms. The Spaniards refused the offer and fired shots at the insurgent mob. After a brief skirmish near the outer walls of the city, the royalists pulled back into the fortress-like granary storage known as the Alhóndiga. Hidalgo's forces set fire to the outer doors in an attempt to gain access to the inner courtyard. Realizing their cause was lost, the Spaniards raised the white flag, but to no avail. The insurgent army rushed the fortification and dispatched all the occupants.

From Guanajuato, Hidalgo's forces marched uncontested to the gates of Mexico City and then, unexpectedly, made an about-face and returned. Within months the army disbanded and Spanish officers rounded up and executed the insurgent leaders .

Armed hostilities lasted a brief four months, but the battle for interpretive power raged among intellectuals for the better part of the nineteenth century. One of the most important histories of the insurgency was written by the conservative statesman Lucas Alamán, a man whose energy and productivity is nearly unmatched in Mexican historiography. He founded the Mexican conservative party, advised numerous presidential administrations, worked for the promotion of economic development in the mid-nineteenth century, and penned voluminous tomes on history and politics. Charles A. Hale observes that history was Alamán's primary weapon against liberalism and the cornerstone of conservative political philosophy in Mexico and that his principle goal in writing history was "to combat popular disrespect for Mexico's Spanish heritage and the idea that independence constituted a necessary break from it" ("Lucas Alamán" 128–29). Alamán was raised by aristocratic Creole parents in the prosperous mining town of Guanajuato. At 17 he witnessed the massacre at the Alhóndiga firsthand and was deeply affected by the death of Juan Antonio Riaño y Bárcena, a close family friend and the colonial intendant. This event, colored by an education steeped in the writings of Edmund Burke, led Alamán to look disdainfully on revolutions, especially when the accompanying violence is carried out under the banner of religion. Alamán decried Hidalgo's revolution as the unholy union of violence and religion and noted that, that while the original proclamation included elements referring to government and the king, the popular reduction of Hidalgo's rallying cry focused solely on affirming the Virgin and condemning the Spaniards. His distaste for the 1810 insurgency is epitomized by his consternation that congress selected as Mexico's Independence Day one that had unleashed so much primal fury and bloodshed. Alamán viewed the revolution as the beginning of Mexico's woes because its violence established the precedent for future violence in political transitions. It is worth noting that Alamán published his history in the 1850s, at a time when internal strife and pronouncements had reached a fevered pitch. Presidential transitions were not carried out by the voice of the people, but by the strength of arms. Alamán traced this recourse to violence directly to Hidalgo's actions. Furthermore, Alamán asserted that Hidalgo stirred indigenous masses up against benevolent colonizers. Alamán later proposed September 27 as a more suitable Independence Day because it memorialized Iturbide's relatively peaceful arrival in Mexico City in 1821 and the guarantees he extended to Spaniards.

While Alamán and his conservative faction fumed about the corrupt cleric and his dark-skinned hoards pillaging the nation, liberal historians attempted to turn popular conceptions of the insurgency toward a favorable interpretation. José María Luis Mora, a contemporary of Alamán, and the nation's most prominent liberal, recognized the necessity of a revolution to throw off the Spanish yoke, but reserved little romantic nostalgia for Hidalgo. Mora opened his history of the insurgency arguing that the revolution had been as necessary for independence as it has been pernicious and destructive for the nation. Lamenting Mexico's state following independence as the product of Hidalgo's destructive enthusiasm, Mora describes Hidalgo as a man bereft of sound judgment, moral orientation, talent for organization, or the wherewithal to carry out his plans. Instead, he portrays the priest as being fickle, arbitrary, and irresponsible and offers the following description of the priest: "ligero hasta lo sumo, abandonó enteramente a lo que diesen de sí las circunstancias, sin extender su vista ni sus designios más allá de lo que tenía que hacer el día siguiente; jamás se tomó el trabajo, y acaso ni aun lo reputó necesario, de calcular el resultado de sus operaciones, ni estableció regla ninguna fija que las sistemase" [lightminded in the extreme, he gave himself entirely over to circumstance without ever extending his thought or his plans beyond the next day's activities; he never took the trouble, nor considered it necessary, to calculate the results of his actions, nor did he establish any system of rules] (8). Mora denigrated Hidalgo, praised Allende, and denounced the insurgency's bloodlust. But he ultimately recognized that, as inadequate as the insurgency's leadership may have been, the revolution's final realization was a great achievement.

Subsequent liberal versions of the insurgency, including the contemporary state story, are rooted in Justo Sierra's *Evolución política del pueblo mexicano* and tend to portray Hidalgo as a Renaissance man: an excellent theologian, an industrious entrepreneur, a generous benefactor, and a fatherly leader. The son of a prominent Yucatán lawyer, Sierra was a poet, essayist, educator, and statesman, who promoted an aggressive educational reform and revolutionized Mexico's political institutions. Upon the death of Ignacio Manuel Altamirano, he took the lead as the nation's most influential intellectual force and was the primary mouthpiece for the Porfirio Díaz's administration positivist philosophy. Between 1900 and 1902, Sierra published *Evolución política del pueblo mexicano*, a work whose title clearly denotes its positivist bent and explained the Díaz regime as the logical consequence of a long series of political evolutions. The first step of these evolutions was, of course, Hidalgo's revolution. Interestingly enough, Sierra does not attempt to cover up Hidalgo's faults; rather he shifts the blame to less concrete factors against which Hidalgo was forced to react. Sierra characterized the revolution as a turbulent storm, an uncontrollable mass of passion and fury, and this late-romantic imagery would continue to inform descriptions of Mexican social upheavals through the Mexican Revolution (1910–1917) and its later literary representations. The massacres, pillaging, and violence that swept through the Bajío were not Hidalgo's fault, according to Sierra. Hidalgo attempted to rein in the undisciplined recruits who struck out in retaliation for centuries of oppression at the hands of their Spanish masters, but was ultimately unable to do so through no fault of his own. Sierra does point out Hidalgo's lack of a proper postwar planning, but alleges that time constraints impeded the elaboration of a suitable plan. Additionally, he argues that Hidalgo never thought Fernando VII would be released from prison and therefore declared independence in his name; for Hidalgo, Fernando was a lame duck whose only purpose was to legitimate their call to independence. Instead, Hidalgo emerges from the rubble of history as the father of the Mexican nation. Sierra credits him with the first real conceptualization of Mexico as an independent national entity, even though the documents left behind by Hidalgo do not reflect this burgeoning nationalism. If anything, Hidalgo envisioned—as did his South American counterparts—a liberated America, but did not go so far as to portray an independent Mexico. It might be more appropriate to grant this honor to Agustín de Iturbide. Returning to Sierra's representation of Hidalgo, however, we can attribute this nationalist flourish to Sierra's overall interpretive historical project. Sierra's argumentation is undermined by logical inconsistencies and a patent antipopulist sentiment. The Hidalgo who controls all aspects of the insurgency by virtue of his charisma is unable to maintain order among the militant rabble. By attributing the violence to the mob, Sierra diverts attention from sullying the heroic picture he fashions for Hidalgo. In essence, the people become the villains, and Hidalgo is portrayed as the faithful captain trying to steer a clear course through a violent bloody storm. Ironically, the man who enshrines Hidalgo as Mexico's father feels compelled to denigrate the most fundamental element of the priest's work. Sierra alters the perception of Hidalgo's project by transforming a pro-indigenous movement into a pro-Creole revolution. We will see that this notion is propagated in Ibargüengoitia's novel as well.

The pendulum swung back to the right with the advent of José Vasconcelos' history of Mexico. Vasconcelos argued that all of Mexico's maladies stem from British and American intervention in its domestic affairs, including Hidalgo who was nothing more than a tool of the British government, and a short-lived one at that. Because Vasconcelos enjoyed the luxury of writing about independence from a distance, he employs a continental perspective that Alamán could not. When discussing Hidalgo and Morelos in comparison to the South American liberators, Vasconcelos dismissed the two priests, alleging that if mention is ever made of them, it is only out of "cortesía continental, a la zaga de los grandes libertadores continentales" [continental courtesy, and then only as a footnote to the great continental liberators] (243). This, however, does not keep him from getting his own shots in against the two. Vasconcelos actually spends very little time discussing Hidalgo because, in his estimation, the priest was a local phenomenon whose influence did not extend beyond his region. While post-1910 revolutionary historians have painted him as a great motivator, few people were significantly enticed by his calls. Latin American independence, Vasconcelos argued, was generally the product of a civilized process while, Mexico's, on the other hand, was fashioned by the hand of barbarism. Vasconcelos conveniently overlooks the ideological strife that characterized the majority of Spanish American independence movement for, if it is true that their processes were democratic in character, it was equally true that bitter personal rivalries, partisan inflexibility, and military coups were common tools in these processes. Since Vasconcelos, the postrevolutionary state put its weight behind promoting a sanitized image of Miguel Hidalgo that has essentially allowed the state to float the priest's image regardless of its evolving ideological leanings. The original postrevolutionary system favored modern economic policies such as agrarian reform, land redistribution, and labor unions and used Hidalgo's image to bolster its increasing interest in social policy. Hidalgo became the figurehead of a government backed by the ever nondescript and sacrosanct *pueblo* [people]. Miguel Alemán's election in 1946 marked a transition toward reactionary conservatism. Even though relations with labor were cut and ties with foreign capital were forged, Hidalgo's image survived the change in course.

This transformation continues. Enrique Krauze, popular historian and editor-in-chief of the literary magazine *Letras Libres*, has penned a trilogy of historical biographies that, in many ways, shapes contemporary Mexico's concept of its past. Chafing against the dominance of the liberal perspective in nineteenth-century historiography, Krauze reconfigures the national pantheon, placing conservative figures next to their liberal contemporaries. His version of Hidalgo's biography, for example, leans more toward Alamán and Vasconcelos than toward Mora and Sierra. His closing statement summarizes this bias: "por más entrañable que sea como sustento de dignidad en el pueblo mexicano, el mito—el grito—de fundación ha sido también un llamado justificatorio a la crueldad, un llamado a la intolerancia, de irracionalidad en la historia mexicana: la terrible convicción, puesta en práctica una y otra vez, de que la violencia, sólo la violencia, redime" [no matter how appealing it may be for the dignity of Mexican

people, the foundational myth—the grito—has also serve as a justification
for cruelty, a call for intolerance and for irrationality in Mexican history:
the terrible conviction, put into practive time and time again, that violence
and only violence can redeem] (67). Krauze's interpretation is not the last,
either. Hidalgo continues to occupy a central place in the Mexican historical imagination. Evidence of this can be found in Pablo Soler Frost's most
recent novel, *1767* (2004), a novel whose title alludes to the year Charles
V expelled the Jesuit order from all Spanish territories. After recounting
the atrocities suffered by the order, the novel closes by attributing the 1810
insurgency to Hidalgo's sense of indignation at the expulsion of his Jesuit
mentor during his childhood. For Soler Frost, independence was an act of
individual vengeance.

This brief overview of the historical interpretations of Hidalgo and the
insurgency he led reveals that Mexican intellectuals have typically agreed,
for the most part, that the nation got off to a lackluster start. Violence,
intellectual vacuity, self-interest, and a patent lack of concern for the future
characterize not only their evaluations of the priest, but also of his fight.
Even Sierra, who labels Hidalgo the father of the new nation, was hard-
pressed to explain satisfactorily the man's excesses. Yet, despite the abundance of critical comments made against Hidalgo, the modern state has
subsequently transformed the flawed insurgent leader into a legendary
hero. Where does Jorge Ibargüengoitia fit into this discussion? Does he
side with conservative detractors or lift his voice with liberal enthusiasts?
The answers to these questions are varied and require some sifting through
his literary history in order to draw conclusions about his views on the
insurgency. Only then can we more fully appreciate the impact of *Los pasos
de López*.

Sesquicentennial Subsidies and
La conspiración vendida

Ibargüengoitia's readers owe a debt of gratitude to a broken-down truck.
He had originally studied engineering but dropped out during his third
year and went to work on the family farm in Guanajuato where he ran the
day-to-day operations. In 1951, the diesel motor of his pickup truck broke
down and he had to travel to Guanajuato to pick up parts. While there,
he stopped in to see his mother and found the flamboyant Salvador Novo
standing in his kitchen, promoting a performance of Emilio Carballido's
Rosalba y los llaveros in the Teatro Juárez that evening. He agreed to attend
and was so impressed by what he saw that when the motor protested again

the following morning, he gave up farm life. Weeks later Ibargüengoitia enrolled in a Dramatic Theory and Composition class at the Universidad Nacional Autónoma de México (UNAM) taught by Rodolfo Usigli, the author of the historical *Corona* trilogy and the leading Mexican play-wright of the day, where he quickly distinguished himself as Usigli's prize pupil. Despite this distinction, Ibargüengoitia never enjoyed the master's full approval. Usigli was critical of his colloquial dialogues, emphasis on blasé domestic affairs, and lack of sobriety; Ibargüengoitia in turn was turned off by the master's monumental posturing, heavy-handed epic style, and self-serving criticisms. Despite their rocky relationship, how-ever, Ibargüengoitia was exposed to many of Usigli's critical notions about history, which the playwright criticized for its shallowness, inaccuracy, and obsolescence. These serendipitous encounters with Novo and Usigli shaped the future of his writing by introducing him to Mexico's theater scene where his literary career began and by giving him a venue to vent his frustrations with society, politics, and history. For ten years Ibargüengoitia weathered the tides of theatrical life. He enjoyed the creative process of writing plays like *Susana y los jovenes* (1954), *La lucha con el ángel* (1955), *Clotilde en su casa* (1955), *Ante varias esfinges* (1959), and *El viaje superficial* (1960), which allowed him to refine his natural gift for snappy dialogue and to develop a keen sense of characterization. However, continual dis-agreements with Usigli and his unwillingness or inability to get along the theater crowd alienated him from the stage. Though his plays were rela-tively well received, they were generally not well remunerated.

Ibargüengoitia wrote *La conspiración vendida* in 1959, when Mexico was in the throes of sesquicentennial celebrations. At thirty-two, he was broke and so he turned to Novo, who had recently been reinstated as the director of the Departamento de Teatro de Bellas Artes, for a ten thousand peso advance on future royalties. Novo told him that President Adolfo López Mateo had opened a competition for theatrical works celebrating the fif-tieth anniversary of the Mexican Revolution and the one-hundred-fiftieth anniversary of independence, and Novo commissioned him on the spot for a play on either of the two subjects. Ibargüengoitia set off with half of the money and returned two weeks later with the finished piece only to find that the president had cancelled the competition and Novo was unable to pay the second half. The story does not end there: Ibargüengoitia relates with some satisfaction that later, under the pseudonym Federico Barón Gropius, he entered *La conspiración vendida* in a competition sponsored by the Mexico City government and was awarded twenty-five thousand pesos. A short time later, he found Celestino Gorostiza, one of the committee jurors, in the foyer of a local theater and revealed himself as the author. "Casi se desmayó. Evidentemente habían premiado la obra creyendo que había sido escrita por otra persona con más méritos o mayores influencias. Ni modo" [He nearly passed out. Evidently they had awarded the play believing that it had been written by someone with more merit or more influence. Oh well] (Leñero, *Los pasos de Jorge* 70).

The genesis of *La conspiración vendida* speaks to the close relationship between the lettered city and the state apparatus that subsidizes art. For Pierre Bourdieu, the only way to move beyond celebratory author-based readings of genius and reductively materialist readings of art and literature is to account for the whole field of production from which the work emerges. This, he argues, demands a comprehensive understanding of both how artists create new works and how "the whole set of agents whose combined efforts produce consumers capable of knowing and recognizing the work of art as such" functions (318–19). Unless we understand how state sponsorship relates to the writing of historical fiction, *La conspiración vendida* is an inexplicable anomaly. The timing then is critical: Ibargüengoitia accepted this commission during the sesquicentennial, a period that, as Deborah Cohn observes, saw a massive proliferation of conferences and ceremonies, as well as commissioned historiographic, literary, and artistic projects that attempted to "explore Mexico's past in an effort to understand its present" (172–73). We might argue, as Seymour Menton observed in his landmark study *Latin America's New Historical Novel*, that major national anniversaries promote historical fiction and that authors, inspired by an organic swelling of the zeitgeist, begin to question the historical narratives handed down from official sources. However, Menton overlooks the central role of state patronage, especially that of the Spanish government, in commissioning works that cast the conquest in a positive light, perhaps due to the scope and selection of his corpus. He carves a niche for "new historical novels" that is narrowly constructed as highly artistic fiction that incorporates a number of elements from Bakhtinian poetics. Any texts that lie outside this paradigm are not included, and commissioned works usually lack innovative pyrotechnics. By contrast, Michel-Rolf Troillot notes that official commemorations of historical events sanitize them and "contribute to the continuous myth-making process that gives history its more definite shapes: they help create, modify, or sanction the public meanings attached to historical events deemed worthy of mass celebration. As rituals that package history for public consumption, commemorations play the numbers game to create a past that seems both more real and more elementary" (116). In truth, official patronage on the eve of the sesquicentennial celebration fits the model described by Ángel Rama, who noted that the Porfirian regime was able to win over or, at least, neutralize the opposition press through subsidies and scholarships (88). Combined with the relatively small readership, state patronage ensured a modicum of control over intellectuals who were otherwise unable to make ends meet.

Ibargüengoitia accepted his commission at a time when the state was actively promoting a positive revision of national myth, and he participated in transmitting the official, pedagogical narrative. Reflecting on the play 19 years later, Ibargüengoitia admitted that subsidized theater—even his own subsidized work—was the refuge of indigent writers who relied on the state for support. Works written for commission tend to be contrived, awkward, cumbersome, unwieldy, and uninteresting, and the dynamics of *La conspiración vendida* illustrate exactly this point. It is an elaborate, three-act historical drama with nearly thirty characters and ten distinct locations, including a field outside of Guanajuato, a street in Querétaro, and a number of private residences. The scope reflects Novo's advice to spare no expense in providing a full-scale spectacle for the sesquicentennial celebrations; nevertheless, or consequently, the play was never produced because, though artists fight tooth and nail to write or produce subsidized plays, there is no public to watch them, and once the subsidy expires, no interest in producing them. It is of little surprise, then, that *La conspiración vendida* has been relegated to the dustbin of literary history. The few existing parenthetical references to *La conspiración vendida* force an ironic or humorous reading that is absent from the play. Vicente Leñero notes that the play is somewhat sterile but fails to consider the text, focusing instead on the sentimental education of the playwright. Theda Herz briefly mentions it in an excellent analysis of Ibargüengoitia's representations of theatrics and power in Mexican government, but focuses on *El atentado* ("Carnivalizing the Mexican Ethos" 45). Juan Campesino's *La historia como ironía: Ibargüengoitia como historiador* (2005) offers the most substantive evaluation of the play to date, and yet his analysis falls into well-worn discussion of humor. Even though Ibargüengoitia might have considered the play to be a serious or even solemn work, Campesino argues, the historical event itself was so rife with errors and buffoonery that he did not have to include artificially humorous elements. Rather, he followed the historical record to the letter and the resulting text builds upon ironic juxtapositions that highlight the disparity between the conspirators' lofty aspirations and their flawed results (71). While in general I find Campesino's readings of Ibargüengoitia's work quite insightful, I cannot help but feel that he incorrectly lumps *La conspiración vendida* together with Ibargüengoitia's other historical works, which take an overtly derisive stance toward Mexican history. Campesino forces an ironic reading on a text that, for all intents and purposes, is propagandistic and entirely serious about its portrayal of the insurgency.

And this is precisely why *La conspiración vendida* has been overlooked in most analyses of Ibargüengoitia's historical writing: it does not fit the humorous modality that readers have come to expect from the author of *El atentado, Los relámpagos de agosto, La ley de Herodes,* and *Los pasos de López.* Its most distinguishing feature is exactly what makes it seem least like something Ibargüengoitia would have written. There are no jokes in *La conspiración vendida.* It is a sober piece, bereft of any ironic winks to the audience, veiled jabs at hypocrisy, and critical introspection. It docilely follows the official historical narrative in order to secure Novo's commission. Simply put, Ibargüengoitia understood that violating or carnivalizing historical canons is inadvisable while on the state's tab. Instead of tackling the more complex aspects of Hidalgo's persona or the wartime efforts of the insurgent army, Ibargüengoitia focuses on the mishaps leading up to the declaration of independence. Due to ambition, greed, or weakness, the main characters betray the insurgents' plans to colonial administrators. The play clearly delineates the villains: the junta's scribe, who turns informant in return for a midlevel management position at the local tobacco factory; the royalist drum major of the Guanajuato battalion, who accepts money from Hidalgo in the second act but later recants; and the captain who turns over the conspiracy leaders to save himself. Their unwillingness to sacrifice personal security for national sovereignty earns history's reprobation, but they are not alone: members of the conspiracy, like the dying priest who confesses his role to a royalist curate on his deathbed or the *corregidor* who cannot effectively steer the mayor away from the secret cache of weapons, also contribute. Their crimes are less egregious because they stem from weakness, but they are relegated to incidental roles in national history.

Where Ibargüengoitia lays the sins of almost every character out for all to witness, he maintains reverent distance from Hidalgo, who only appears in three scenes and speaks about twenty lines. He is cast in the official mold: monumental, stoic, and self-sacrificing. The fact that he says relatively little led Leñero to suggest that *La conspiración vendida* was not propagandistic in the least (*Los pasos de Jorge* 70). I disagree. The dearth of lines notwithstanding, the priest maintains his iconic value as the father and savior of the nation throughout the play. He is an unmoving monument, pulled from the pantheon of national heroes to grace the stage for a few moments. When he does speak, he presents a messianic formulation of an independent future utopia created by purging evil and oppression, martyr-like resignation to the role assigned him by history, and a rallying cry. The other characters revere him with bowed heads. Near the end of the play, when the plans have been discovered, and colonial forces move to arrest the conspirators, Allende grimly states, "No nos queda entonces más que Dolores y el padre Hidalgo" [All that we have left is Dolores and Father Hidalgo] (297). Throughout the play, Ibargüengoitia protects the national narrative by truncating significant elements that might damage the reputation of Hidalgo or the government that stands on his reputation. At the end, Hidalgo climbs into the pulpit at the parish in Dolores and delivers his famous *grito*: "Señores, ha llegado el momento. Armarse todos. Vamos a pelear por la independencia. ¡Que viva México!" [Sirs, the moment has arrived. To arms. We are going to fight for independence. Long live Mexico!] (299). The stage directions indicate that enthusiastic cheers are heard offstage, church bells ring, and the curtain falls. Ibargüengoitia eliminates Hidalgo's call for the end of bad government and his support of Fernando VII, the ousted Spanish monarch in whose name every Spanish American territory declared independence. Because such a cry might question PRI legitimacy, or because calling on a Spanish ruler might diminish the American spirit of the father of independence, these embarrassing parts are erased from the historical record. Similarly, because the play ends with the *grito de Dolores*, the audience does not witness the chaotic and destructive march of the insurgent armies through the Mexican Bajío and does not reflect on the ugly aspects of the revolution. Ibargüengoitia symbolically purges the sackings, rapes, and murders from the historical record and leaves us a sanitized, politically correct version. Why? Because any attack on Hidalgo's deified image at an important moment intended to revitalize the national epic would be interpreted as an attack on the nation he founded. And that would have cost him the competition and the commission. Ibargüengoitia kowtowed.

Excélsior and the Freedom of the Press

We can suppose that this momentary weakness bothered him, because he spent the rest of his life working to correct this abuse of history. A year after completing *La conspiración vendida*, Ibargüengoitia wrote one more play and then ended his relationship with theater. This final piece was also a historical drama but completely different in tone. *El atentado* is a farce about the assassination of Álvaro Obregón and, although it won the Casa de las Américas prize in 1963, Mexican officials prohibited its performance. It was censured because it treated an important figure of the postrevolutionary political consolidation with too little reverence, marking Ibargüengoitia as an iconoclast and persona non grata. He received no official recognition for either of his historical dramas: the commission was awarded to the first only because his name was not explicitly attached to it, and the spontaneous one was censured. Ibargüengoitia would later write that his misfortune with *El atentado* allowed him to forsake the theater for

good and dedicate himself to prose fiction. During the period that separates *La conspiración vendida* from *Los pasos de López,* then, Ibargüengoitia
rejected the play's historical model, reformulated his relationship to the
Mexican government, and developed a clear theory about historical writing. He openly attacked the state apparatus that sponsored historical celebrations, a system to which he failed to gain access. Instead of toeing the
pedagogical line, he now aimed his criticisms at historical narratives that
reduced complex stories to bare-bone myths. He argued for a historical
narrative that did not shun human frailty but found within it the material
for elaborating a more true-to-life history. In his journalism, he prepared
his revision by crafting a number of scenes that would appear in *Los pasos
de López.*

Following the celebratory fervor of the 1960 sesquicentennial, newspapers became the locus for articulating a counterdiscourse that questioned
the continued relevance of the Mexican Revolution as a defining narrative
for political organization. Carlos Martínez Assad notes that this discourse
bracketed the pedagogical narrative linking the revolution to a continual
political evolution by underscoring a plurality of revolutionary movements
that did not fit within the official story (232). Once freed from the exigen-
cies of state-sponsored commission, Ibargüengoitia used his column in the
Excélsior's cultural pages to level devastating diatribes against the government and the historical narrative that imagined an unbroken continuum
from the 1810 independence movement through the 1910 revolution to
the present that legitimized its claims to power. Ignacio Corona observes
that these articles allowed Ibargüengoitia to develop a new subjectivity
for his work, one that wrote in the first person and placed his own flaws,
and thereby those of the nation, on display for all to see. That newfound
subjectivity allowed him to establish a critical dialogue with readers who,
picking up on his sarcastic wit and ironic portrayal of Mexican life, could
read his parodic articles at two simultaneous levels: one that mimicked
the official discourse and another that undermined it (320). Notably, he
traded the reverent tone he used to secure his commission for the icono-
clasm that we associate with his later texts. Among reflections on Mexican
society, art, film, and literature, we find his most explicitly theatrical conceptualizations of history and politics.

The *Excélsior* articles take aim at the pretensions of the Mexican government by exposing the theatricality of its public face. He equates reading the news to seeing "una obra de teatro de un nuevo estilo, a veces,
como ver algo escrito y actuado por gente sin talento dramático" [a new
style of theatrical production, sometimes like watching something written
and performed by people with no dramatic talent] (*Instrucciones* 159). He
describes the scene performed for the nation as "un nuevo estilo teatral

(teatro pri), en que la obra está escrita chueca y los actores hablan de perfil, dirigiéndose a un costado del escenario, con el objeto de producir en el espectador la ilusión de que está entre bambalinas, y por consiguiente en la intimidad y que entiende y ve el tcjemaneje del asunto" [a new theater style (PRI theater), in which the play is poorly written and the actors all speak facing sideways, looking to one side of the stage, for the purpose of making the spectator think that he is behind the scenes and, therefore, intimately involved, that he understands, and that he sees the intrigues of the play] (159). He portrays politicians as inept comedians who miss their marks and flub their lines and criticizes the state for its malicious use of pageantry to perpetuate itself in power (Sheridan 225). For Ibargüengoitia, official uses of history, monuments, portraits, speeches, and subsidized historical fiction serve no function other than justifying the present.

The transition from drama to narrative implied a change in Ibargüengoitia's narrative persona, best described as a *pobre diablo*, or luckless schmuck who is constantly involved in campy, vaudevillian mishaps. As Gustavo García keenly notes, the dramatic tension in Ibargüengoitia's work resides primarily in the misery and folly of his characters for who "no hay heroísmos ni epopeyas, sino actos fallidos, marrullerías, acciones desproporcionadas, que conducen siempre al fracaso, al final infeliz y paradójico" [there are neither heroic deeds or epic poems, but rather flawed acts, crafty schemes, and disproportionate actions that always lead to failure, to an unhappy and paradoxical ending] ("Maten al negro"). For Ibargüengoitia, the *pobre diablo* is the Mexican everyman, much in the same way that Mario Moreno's Cantinflas persona or Germán Valdés's Tin-Tan were vehicles for expressing essential commonalities for the Mexican national character. We find the *pobre diablo* in almost every one of his works, a point that Herz makes when she notes that that Ibargüengoitia engages in self-mockery in order to promote his irreverent attitude toward official culture by making himself the butt of his own jokes. By mocking himself, "he establishes his credentials as an insider and diminishes the likelihood that his gibes will be dismissed as mere snideness. The clownish persona's inclusion within the discourse of solemnity ironically confirms the pervasiveness of the folly within Mexico" ("Carnivalizing the Mexican Ethos"). In *Los relámpagos de agosto*, he is Gualaupe Arroyo, the likeable revolutionary general whose continual errors in judgment lead to his military and political defeat. In the short stories collected in *La ley de Herodes*, the *pobre diablo* appears to be Ibargüengoitia himself, who shares one personal failure after another: his inability to seduce a long-lost love, his victimization in a fraudulent property transaction, and his willingness to prostrate himself before an American imperialist doctor who checks for rectal ulcers as part of a mandatory physical exam for a scholarship application. This self-deprecating humor shows up in *Los pasos de López*: the narrator and other players in the seriocomic historical drama are plagued with interminable luckless mishaps. Far from the epic struggle for freedom, independence becomes a madcap adventure frought with comical failures. The construction of a self-ironizing voice became central as Ibargüengoitia refined his ideas about historical narratives in a series of biweekly columns for the *Excélsior* newspaper.

As *pobre diablo*, Ibargüengoitia frequently relied on displaying a feigned sense of frustration at being excluded from bureaucratic processes as a means of critiquing governmental abuses of history. In "El lado bueno de los próceres," he complains about never being invited to participate in "uno de esos comités que se encargan de inventar los festejos con que se va a conmemorar algún aniversario cívico: el del natalicio de algún prócer o el de la muerte de algún héroe" [one of those committees charged with inventing celebrations to commemorate some civic anniversary: the birth of some founding father or the death of some hero] (22). He imagines that a high-ranking official would organize the committee members, give them their assignment, inform them how much money they could spend, and demand a project proposal in two weeks. The national narratives that support the regime are mandated by fiat and composed by committee members whose principal concern is getting on the good side of the politician in charge. Their first priority is to come up with "una frase célebre, que ponga de manifiesto la entereza de su ánimo ante la derrota total" [a famous phrase that makes manifest the integrity of his spirit in the face of utter defeat] (23). These phrases should demonstrate that the hero was not responsible for the defeat, that the blame lies with the cavalry, the administration, or the messengers: "Por ejemplo, inventarle algo que supuestamente el conmemorado dijo al enemigo al deponer las armas: 'Si la caballería no anduviera en las Lomas, estarían ustedes corriendo como conejos'" [For example, we could invent something that hero supposedly said to the enemy as he surrendered his weapons: "If the cavalry had not been in Las Lomas, you would be running like rabbits"] (23). In fact, a long list of such phrases has entered Mexico's popular history. Insurgent general José María Morelos, on trial before the colonial inquisition, heroically stated "Morir es nada cuando por la patria se muere," [death is nothing when one dies for the nation] cited in the title of Pedro Angel Palou's novel, *Morelos: Morir es nada*. Faced with the impending secession of Texas in 1836, Antonio López de Santa Anna harangued: "La línea divisoria entre México y Estados Unidos se fijará junto a la boca de mis cañones" [The border between Mexico and the United States will be established by the line of my cannons]. The phrase that Ibargüengoitia specifically parodies in this article comes from General Pedro María Anaya who, upon surrendering to American forces at Churubusco, declared, "Si tuviéramos parque, no estarían ustedes aquí" [If we had ammunition, you would not be here]. Ibargüengoitia suggests that the historic phrase is everything because that is what will be inscribed in gold letters on every monument erected to the hero, regardless of how the hero acted in his private life. What really matters is the historic phrase because "demasiados rasgos provocarían confusión" [too many characteristics would cause confusion] (23).

The same reductive process is applied to the hero's physical appearance. Heroes should have one or two distinguishing attributes: "Hay que tener en cuenta que la calva del cura Hidalgo, la levita de Juárez y el pañuelo de Morelos son más importantes que su estructura ósea" [We should remember that Father Hidalgo's bald head, Juárez's frock coat, and Morelos's headscarf are more important than their bones] (23). These minimalist symbols exist today in the silhouetted icons for Mexico City metro stops. Catchphrases, iconography, and easily digestible stories are then incorporated into free textbooks published by the government for dissemination to Mexican schoolchildren. This process of watering down complex stories leaves a boring collection of anecdotes. If Mexican history appears boring, Ibargüengoitia argues, it is not due to an absence of interesting historical events. To cite but three examples: Antonio López de Santa Anna occupied the presidential seat eleven times and buried his own leg with full military honors, Ignacio Comonfort staged a coup against his own government, and Benito Juárez loaded the national archive into a train of coaches and moved it around the country for three years during the French intervention. Ibargüengoitia argues that the unimaginative and programmatic way that national history is portrayed deprives schoolchildren of the opportunity to enjoy and take pride in their country's past.

For Ibargüengoitia, the antidote to this uninspired storytelling is imaginative fiction. In his article "El grito, irreconocible," he describes his impressions on overhearing a mother explain to her seven-year-old son that "Morelos es el del pañuelo amarrado en la cabeza, Zaragoza, el de los anteojos, Colón es este, que se parece a tu tía Carmela, Iturbide, el de las patillas y el cuello hasta las orejas. El cura Hidalgo es este viejito calvo" [Morelos is the one with the scarf tied to his head, Zaragoza wears glasses, Columbus is the one who looks like your aunt Carmela, Iturbide has the sideburns and the collar that goes all the way up to his ears. Father Hidalgo is the bald old man] (39). The litany of distinguishing characteristics is transmitted from parent to child without any mention of significant deeds, relative importance, or historical contribution. The mother propagates the boring style of history that she herself learned. Ibargüengoitia confides that his first history lesson was also taught by his mother, outside the Alhóndiga de Granaditas in his hometown of Guanajuato. In 1810, the

Spanish fortified themselves at this fortress-like granary until indigenous recruits broke through the front gate and massacred everyone inside. For Lucas Alamán, founder of the conservative party, this event epitomized the savagery and barbarism of the insurgent cause. Later, the heads of executed insurgent leaders were displayed there as a warning against future insurrections. Ibargüengoitia's mother shared this story with him and then, pointing to the hooks that still adorn the upper wall, said, "De esos ganchos que ves ahí, colgaron las cabezas de los insurgentes" [Those hooks you see up there is where the heads of the insurgents hung] (39). The impression this story left was such that "me quedé convencido de haber visto, no sólo los ganchos, sino también las cabezas" [I was convinced that I had not only seen the hooks but also the heads] (39). For Ibargüengoitia, history should encourage the imagination and invite citizens to think more deeply about the connections between past and present, not simply reiterate a litany of meaningless factoids.

The *Excélsior* articles provided Ibargüengoitia not only a forum in which to vent his frustrations about history, but also a sandbox for imaginative experimentation. These corrective, imagined episodes appear after diatribes against boring traditional history. Many of them—for example, a fictional dialogue between Hidalgo and El Pípila, the insurgent who hoisted a stone slab onto his back and set fire to the gates of the Alhóndiga—never made it into *Los pasos de López*. To the best of my knowledge, only one did. It describes how Hidalgo obtained plans for constructing the insurgency's cannons. After reiterating that all of the interesting elements of Hidalgo's biography get lost in soporific textbook portraits, Ibargüengoitia invited readers to imagine the priest's attempts to build a cannon for his army. As a good student of Rousseau and the French liberals, the natural place for Hidalgo to go for information was the nearest encyclopedia that happened to be in the home of his friend, the colonial intendant, Riaño, in Guanajuato. In *Los pasos de López*, the priest constructs a homemade cannon that is terribly misshapen. The narrator, Matías Chandón explains to his readers that for the average cannon the circumference of the muzzle is smaller than that of the breech. Periñón's cannon, by contrast, inverts those ratios. Like the future revolution, it is poorly planned and awkwardly executed. They propose to solve the problem by turning to the encyclopedia. Narrator and priest visit the intendant's home and, under the pretense of looking up information on planting plums (*ciruelas*), they find in the volume under C an entry for "CAÑONES: su fabricación" (91). The similarity between these episodes demonstrates that Ibargüengoitia was thinking about ways to remodel the historical record and using his journalism to theorize, to experiment, and to refine the story that would become his last novel.

Los pasos de López and the Theatrics of Nation

Ibargüengoitia was not the only critical voice working for *Excélsior*. Editor Julio Scherer García had invited regular contributions from most of the country's leading intellectuals and the newspaper's tone was decidedly opposed to the PRI and, more specifically, to the administration of Luis Echeverría. In July 1976, a group of journalists sympathetic to and encouraged by Echeverría launched a coup against Scherer in a move that has subsequently come to be known as the *Excelsiorazo*. It marked the definitive end of the newspaper's hardnosed criticisms and effectively turned the paper, which under Scherer's leadership had become one of the leading world dailies, into a propaganda machine for the PRI government. Ibargüengoitia left the newspaper following the *Excelsiorazo* and went on to write for *Vuelta*, the literary magazine run by Octavio Paz and one of the many splinter publications produced by the coup. Just prior to leaving the paper, however, he published *Estas ruinas que ves* (1975), the first novel in a four-part series about the Mexican Bajío, the lowland area northwest of Mexico City. The novel tells the story of a middle-aged professor who returns to his hometown of Cuévano, falls in love with a former student, and learns to navigate the petty social circles of a provincial university town. The stage on which this romantic comedy plays out is significant because the Bajío is generally regarded as the birthplace of the Mexican nation. As the narrator pulls into Cuévano, he offers a long list of the local intellectuals, including a historian, Benjamín Padilla, who considered that "la Independencia de México se debe a un juego de salón que acabó en desastre nacional" [Mexican independence was the product of parlor game that ended in a national disaster] (13).

Padilla's evaluation prefigures the final iterations of Ibargüengoitia's thoughts on Mexican independence and hints at why *Los pasos de López* continues to be the most significant literary portrayal on the subject to date. First, it foregrounds the incomplete nature of an independence movement that did not directly produce liberty. Within a matter of months, all the conspirators were captured, tried, and executed, and another 11 years of guerrilla warfare ensued before independence was consummated. Second, it resurrects the sense that independence was seriously flawed from the outset, a constant in Mexico's nineteenth-century historiography; Hidalgo's revolution was not transformed into a truly heroic series of events until after the 1910 Revolution. In 1852, Alamán claimed that all of Mexico's midcentury political and economic woes stemmed from the decision to make September 16, 1810, a national holiday. At the heart of his criticism is a vitriolic diatribe against Hidalgo, whom he considered chaotic, unpatriotic, untrustworthy, and bloodthirsty. His liberal counterpart, Jose María Luis Mora, held a similar opinion of Hidalgo but maintained that the insurgency was as vital to the constitution of a new nation as it was prejudicial. Even Justo Sierra, who designated Hidalgo the father of the new nation nearly half a century later, found it difficult to justify the excesses of the war or to explain its abrupt end. Third, by foregrounding the shortcomings of independence, Ibargüengoitia contradicts the epic genesis story espoused by official postrevolutionary historians. In *Estas ruinas que ves*, the narrator laments that Padilla's version of history had been sidelined precisely because it does not coincide with the story approved by the secretary of education. Finally, the bitter humor that pervades the quote and almost all of Ibargüengoitia's historical fiction levels the sober pretensions of official history and the government institutions that use the independence movement and the revolution as their raison d'être.

Nearly every critic who has written on Ibargüengoitia's work has focused on the demystification of the national epic through derisively humorous writing. The predominance of this paradigm may be attributed to Ibargüengoitia being the most talented humorist of his generation. His stories are riotous, and his novels admit an ironic, playful view of history and literary creation. But Ibargüengoitia was reluctant to identify himself as humorist, specifically because he understood that it could potentially diminish the impact of his work. "Hacer reír no me preocupa en lo más mínimo," [I am not interested in making people laugh] he told Margarita García Flores. "Yo no me burlo, no me río. Me parecería ridículo hacer un personaje con el único objeto de burlarse de él. En cualquier momento, me interesa presentarlo, presentar un aparato que en la novela tenga relación con la realidad, según yo la veo" [I don't joke around and I don't laugh. It would be ridiculous to create a character just to make fun of him. At any given time, I am interested in presenting the character as an apparatus in the novel that relates to reality as I see it] (García Flores 408). He does not make fun of history for the sake of a laugh, but rather offers a fresh, ironic perspective that cuts through fabricated stories to arrive at essences predominantly characterized by failure. Literary critic Evodio Escalante puts it well when he observes that, for Ibargüengoitia, "la escritura es como el ácido; no pretende edificar, sino corromper, volver polvo cuanto toca" [writing is like acid; it does not edify but destroys, turns to dust everything it touches] (499). In sum, the jokes or sarcasm should not be all that remain of Ibargüengoitia's work, but his refusal to accept sacralized textbook history created for the purpose of statecraft. Official historians, not to mention *La conspiración vendida*, breeze over the ugly aspects of the insurgency—rape, murder, pillage, and chaos. Ibargüengoitia's later parody corrects this story by asking readers to consider other dimensions of the nation's birth myth.

Rebecca Biron's insightful analysis of parody in *Los relámpagos de agosto* argues that humor demystifies national figures while constructing a common sense of identity. She suggests that Ibargüengoitia's novel "[performs] national identity not as that which serves a people's psychological need for cohesion in order to function as a political entity, but rather as the people's shared desire for laughter, self-criticism and the pleasure of perpetual cynicism" (626). Readers achieve this sense of community through shared complicity with jokes that meld dark, self-effacing laughter, parody, history, and national identity. In *Los pasos de López*, by laughing at the pretentiously heroic epic foisted on the public by government institutions seeking to legitimate their claims to power, Mexican readers symbolically carnivalize the historical narrative and the institutions that base their legitimacy upon it. Biron's Bakhtinian reading of Ibargüengoitia's historical irreverence is also deeply rooted in Jorge Portilla's *Fenomenología del relajo* (1966), one of the most important documents produced by the post-World War II group of Mexican philosophers known as Hiperión, which included Emilio Uranga, Ricardo Guerra, Salvador Reyes Nevares, Joaquín Sánchez Macgregor, Fausto Vega, Luis Villoro, and Leopoldo Zea. Portilla's contributions were cut short by his untimely death in 1963, but *Fenomenología del relajo*'s philosophical approach to Mexico's devil-may-care irreverence remains intriguing. *Relajo* is a spontaneous communal reaction against authority that nullifies the appropriation or incorporation of a given value. While Biron imagines a community constructed on the basis of shared revelry, Portilla suggests that the show of irreverence toward authority and traditional values acts as the primary cohesive element. Borrowing from both notions we can argue that the humorous elements of Ibargüengoitia's writing do create a sense of community precisely because they are defiantly directed at authorized histories. Ángeles Rodríguez Cadena points out that *Los pasos de López* metafictionally displaces the centrality of official histories by recognizing their existence through parody while simultaneously proposing other, equally valid interpretations of the past (711–15). Thus *Los pasos de López* does create a sense of community, not simply because it is funny, but because it interrupts the transmission, reception, and assimilation of traditional interpretations of Mexico's founding generation, and because it offers an alternative version of independence.

By the time *Los pasos de López* was published in 1982, Ibargüengoitia had achieved a level of personal and professional independence that would allow him to tackle the question of nation's foundational narrative in a critical manner. Moreover, he did so by conscientiously returning to his theatrical beginnings. Luis de Tavira asserts that Ibargüengoitia the playwright and Ibargüengoitia the novelist are the same creator and that he "reescribía sus obras como novelas" [rewrote his plays as novels] (470–71). I think Tavira overstates this kinship. Both deal with the 1810 insurgency, but unlike *La conspiración vendida*, which maintains strict fidelity to the historical sources, names, events, and places—indeed, Campesino identifies the play as Ibargüengoitia's most historical play (70)—*Los pasos de López* recasts history in a fictional space unfettered by archival constraints. It allows him to write what Joshua Lund calls a fiction of "foundational disarticulation"; that is, rather than contributing to the construction of national identity, it reveals the inconsistencies that underlie hegemonic projects of Mexican nationalism (95). *Los pasos de López* tells the story of Mexican independence from the perspective of Matías Chandón, a young Creole officer who moves to Cuévano to take command of the local artillery division. Writing roughly around 1843, he relates how he became involved in the insurgency and shares his personal insights into its events, characters, and, most notably, flaws. Elisabeth Guerrero writes that Ibargüengoitia "thinly disguises the names of the now-famous people and historic places where the events of independence unfolded" and that these name changes reduce the symbolic and semantic value we associate with historically recognizable figures and sites (*Confronting History* 37). If Mexican history is the product of fixed identities that have been arbitrarily assigned and valuated, then she is correct in asserting that this gesture liberates important figures from the symbolic weight of historical association. In this manner, the action of the novel plays out in the recognizable Bajío of central Mexico, but important cities are renamed: Querétaro becomes Cañada, Guanajuato becomes Cuévano, Dolores becomes Ajetreo, and Valladolid becomes Huetámaro. By the same process of transformation, each historical figure is given a new name: Miguel Domínguez / Diego Aquino, Josefa Ortiz de Domínguez / Carmelita de Aquino, Ignacio Allende / Captain Ontananza, Juan Aldaco / Captain Aldama, Father Iturriaga / Father Concha, Bishop Manuel Abad y Queipo / Bishop Begonia, Juan Antonio Riaño / Pablo Berreteaga, General Félix María Calleja / General Cuartana. Howard Quackenbush suggests that, as this playful renaming goes on throughout the novel, "Ibargüengoitia está riéndose irreverentemente mientras disfraza a sus personajes y cambia identidades, bromeando con su público, sin tratar de engañar a nadie" [Ibargüengoitia irreverently laughs as he disguises his characters and changes identities, joking with his readers, without trying to fool anybody] (20). The most significant change, of course, is associated with Miguel Hidalgo, dubbed Domingo Periñón in the novel with a thinly veiled reference to the celebrated champagne and an ironic nod to the priest's failed attempts at winemaking.

Guerrero's emphasis on the transformative nature of Ibargüengoitia's novel is particularly pertinent given the theorization found in the

Excélsior articles. *Los pasos de López* and, more broadly, any historical novel that undertakes a serious revision of the past by creatively transforming it becomes corrective. As Juan Campesino has recently written, Ibargüengoitia does not pretend to faithfully reconstruct the nation's great events, but rather revises and desecrates the key aspects of a series of historical possibilities which constitute "un marco de referencia posible dentro (y sólo dentro) de los universos de ficción que sus obras representan: no se trata de recontar la historia, sino de reinterpretarla" [a possible frame of reference within (and only within) the fictional universe that his works represent: the matter is not to retell history, but to reinterpret it] (16). This historical revisionism comes to the forefront of the novel when, relating his midnight ride to inform Hidalgo that the conspiracy had been discovered, Chandón writes: "El episodio que sigue es tan conocido que no vale la pena contarlo. Voy a referirme a él brevemente nomás para no perder el hilo del relato y precisar algunos puntos que la leyenda ha borroneado" [The episode that follows is so well known that it's not worth telling. I will only briefly refer to it so we don't get lost and to clear up a couple of points that the legends has erased] (117). The narrator's decision to restore elements of the real history that have been hidden by myth coincides with Ibargüengoitia's reinterpretation. Instead of tearing across the plains on a dashing stallion with shocking news of the arrest warrants issued for the conspiracy leaders, Chandón trots along at the pace set by his mare. He relates that there was no fraternal embrace between revolutionaries upon his arrival, no magnanimous freeing of prisoners, and no famous declaration of independence: "Ni él gritó '¡vamos a matar españoles!' ni matamos a ninguno aquella noche" [He did not yell 'Let's go kill Spaniards!' and we didn't kill any that night]. Possibly the most devastating revelation comes when he discloses that instead of launching into fevered preparations for war that night, "Periñón abrió una barrica del vino que él mismo hacía y nos dio a probar. Estaba agrio. Después dispuso guardias y nos fuimos a dormir" [Periñón opened a barrel of wine that he made himself and gave us some to try. It was sour. Later he set guards in place and we went to sleep]) (117–19).

   In an article dedicated to *Los relámpagos de agosto*, Juan Bruce-Novoa and David Valentín note that Ibargüengoitia "demystifies the revolutionary rhetoric of the literature, and in the process, undermines the ruling party, PRI, which still utilizes it to legitimate itself" (15). By demonstrating the superficiality of these rhetorical justifications, Ibargüengoitia:

> converts respected images into arbitrary signs, and finally turns a nation's hallowed history into hollowed, burlesque satire, conscious of itself as facade. With some techniques reminiscent of Brecht, Ibargüengoitia

distances his audience from its symbiotic relationship with those images—
we might even say self-images—and forces evaluation. His ultimate aim
is to violate that sacrosanct imagery that still appears to predominate in
Mexico. Ironically, his violent cynicism serves to underscore the Mexicans'
particular penchant for black humor, but in the process he creates one of
Mexico's most interesting combinations of experimental theatre and traditional Mexican themes. (20)

The allusion to the theatrical is significant because, in writing *Los pasos
de López*, Ibargüengoitia self-consciously returned to his theatrical roots
by incorporating dramatic texts, motifs, and structures as if to underline,
as he had in the *Excélsior* articles, the theatrical nature of historical narratives. *La precaución inútil* is the most important of these plays, both for
what it reveals about the conspirators and its premonition. When Matías
Chandón is welcomed into the conspiracy, Periñón brings him to the Casa
del Reloj, a wealthy residence most notable for an antique clock. The members of the conspiracy are rehearsing the play and Chandón ironically notes
that they do so in an unnatural and artificial tone.

La precaución inútil is a dense title that requires some unpacking. First,
it refers to a common motif in Golden Age literature: an older man seques-
ters a young woman presumably to marry her and obtain her wealth.
His attempts to keep her guarded—his precautions—are rendered useless by a crafty young suitor who breaks through them and rescues the
maiden, as in Cervantes's "El celoso extremeño" (Sedwick 7–10). Second,
the title directly references the subtitle of Pierre de Beaumarchais's 1775
drama, *The Barber of Seville*. In 1782, Giovanni Paisiello wrote a comic
opera based on the play, which was not well received. Decades later, commissioned to create his own *Barber of Seville*, Rossini was concerned that
it would incur the wrath of Paisiello and his followers, so he baptized it
three times: *Almaviva*, the protagonist Lindoro's real name; *The Useless
Precaution*, from Beaumarchais's original work; and finally *The Barber of
Seville*. Since it debuted in 1816, and the conspirators do not appear to be
singing their lines, we can assume that they are reading an adaptation of
Beaumarchais's play. At one level, we might offer an allegorical explanation. From the Creole perspective, the Spanish colonial administrators'
attempts to curtail independence are a useless safeguard that will eventually yield to American desires for liberty. By working together in secrecy,
the oppressed classes, both high and low, will free themselves from Spanish
avarice. However, the play functions more literally within the context of
the novel. The title alludes to the insurgents' flawed preparations. No matter what they do, things turn out badly for them. All their precautions to

maintain secrecy are undone by those they attempt to bring in and those already in the know.

The play is performed by the principal conspirators in Cañada. Of the conspirators, only Diego Aquino, the Crown's representative in Cañada, is out of sight and, for all intents and purposes, out of mind. The characters assume roles that ostensibly reveal something about their personalities. Carmelita, Diego's wife, takes the role of the coquettish Rosina on stage and flirts with Chandón and Ontananza in the wings; Ontananza, who portrays the leading man, aspires to be the secretive lover; Concha, an aging priest who suffers fainting spells and eventually betrays the conspiracy, plays the lascivious old man who locks away the young maiden; and Periñón, both as the primary conspirator and the picaresque servant, moves the action forward and eventually receives all the punishment—excommunication, capture, execution, and years of criticism about his conduct from all sides of the ideological spectrum. The revolution's failure is represented, quite literally, as a comedy of errors, but these parallels are subtly undermined by ironic twists: Carmelita never consummates her flirtations, Ontananza's desire is as frustrated as Chandón's, Concha is not a womanizer but an ancient priest who faints without warning, and Periñón is enshrined in the pantheon of national heroes.

Not surprisingly, the performance planned for Carmelita's birthday ends in disaster. Father Concha, the play's villain, succumbs to one of his habitual fainting spells and misses an important line where he confesses his guilt. As a result, "don Baldomero no confesó su culpa, [y] no hubo manera de que los jueces pusieran en libertad a López, que era el presunto responsable de todos los delitos que se habían cometido en los tres actos de la comedia" [Don Baldomero did not confess his guilt, and there was no way for the judges to free López, who was presumably responsible for all the crimes that had been committed throughout the play's three acts] (79). Chaos ensues. "El desenlace fue grotesco: el elenco cantó: 'Toda precaución es inútil' y el telón cayó con Periñón encadenado y Juanito en libertad, cuando debió haber sido al revés" [The denouement was grotesque: the cast sang "All precautions are futile" and the curtain fell with Periñón in chains and the Juanito free when it should have been the other way around] (79). The failed performance of *La precaución inútil* foreshadows the debacle that follows. In both instances, the cast is carried along as events contrary to the script's original intent develop, exposing the gap between official scripts and everyday life in Mexico or between the performative and pedagogical aspects of national identity in post-Tlatelolco Mexico. Indeed, Bhabha's concept of the performative is enacted by Ibargüengoitia's use of theatricality to undermine the pedagogy of national historiography and national identity. Father Concha's inability to speak ruins the play, while his inability to keep quiet jeopardizes the conspiracy. Periñón, the hero, will not be exonerated but captured and punished instead. When the cast closes the play, singing "All precautions are futile," a dark sense of irony falls over the impending revolution. Its finale will also fall short of the junta's plans. The safeguards they set in place are useless. Their plan to bribe the royalist drum major for control of an important city is a dismal failure. They are incapable of maintaining the group's integrity: Concha, the scribe Manrique, and Captain Adarviles all betray them.

Other small theatrical pieces punctuate the novel. Chapter 15 includes a scripted exchange where Captain Adarviles turns Diego and Carmen over to the mayor and the local inquisitor. The scene is similar in many ways to the penultimate scene of *La conspiración vendida*, but the parodic elements have been sharpened. Matías Chandón, an artillery commander from the military outpost at Perote, travels to Cañada to apply for a position as the artillery commander for the new provincial battalion (11). En route, he meets Domingo Periñón, the priest from Ajetreo, and lodges with the local administrator, Diego Aquino, who will evaluate his performance. He is invited to meet some of the notable citizens, who, unbeknownst to Chandón, comprise the main body of the city's conspirators, and the meeting becomes an interrogation, with Chandón improvising answers to pointed questions, seeking approval and confidence. When Diego asks him about a court-martial for an insubordinate Creole, he quickly picks up on the way questions are supposed to be answered in Cañada. The case dealt with an officer who spoke out against the Crown, saying that Mexico could govern itself just as effectively as Spain. Asked what defense he would offer, Chandón replies, "Dije que estaba borracho cuando había dicho la frase ofensiva" [I said that he was drunk when he made the offensive comment] (25). They all agree that this defense is not good but for different reasons. Chandón laments that the officer was found guilty; the conspirators want something more favorable to their cause. Diego comes to the rescue and reminds the group that "lo que importa no es el resultado, sino que el teniente haya salido en defensa de un oficial independentista" [the outcome is not what matters but that the lieutenant had defended an independence official] (25). The narrator admits to readers that, until that moment, he had never thought of the officer or his ideas as independence-oriented but thanks to this clue, "logré capotear la siguiente pregunta" [I managed to handle the next question] (25). When asked if he defended the officer because he agreed with his ideals or because he was drunk, Chandón, who now understands the how the game is played, responds that he defended the officer because he both agreed with him and because he was drunk.

The next question deals with the promotion of a Spaniard over an equally qualified Creole. Chandón confesses to readers that the question is more complicated than that:

> El español era Topete, a quien en el cantón conocíamos como "Eligio," para no tener que decirle Eligio de Puta. Para evitar que Eligio fuera mi superior inmediato ya había recurrido a todos los medios y el último había sido alegar que había otro con mayor derecho a ascender, Meléndez, un pobre diablo. No me había pasado por la cabeza considerar que uno fuera español y el otro mexicano, pero, claro, esto no lo dije aquella noche, porque ya *iba aprendiendo*. (26, emphasis added)
>
> [The Spaniard's name was Topete, but all of us in the canton called him "Eligio,"which was short for *Eligio de Puta* [son of a bitch]. To keep Eligio from becoming my immediate superior officer I had tried every available measure I could and the last one had been to allege that there was someone else with more right to the promotion, Meléndez, a poor schmuck. It had not even crossed my mind that one was Spanish and the other a Creole but, of course, I did not say anything that night, because *I was learning*.]

He then offers a response full of feigned indignation, peppered with with "lo que entonces decían todos los días todos los oficiales criollos que había en todos los cuarteles" [what all of the Creole officers in every barrack were saying], that is sure to score points (26). He affirms having protested on the principle of equality, "pero en realidad a un oficial nacido en el país le cuesta mucho trabajo ascender: cada vez que una oportunidad se presenta aparece un español recién llegado...o bien se le da preferencia a un gachupín radicado" [but because in reality it is very difficult for an officer born in this country to get promoted: every time an opportunity opens up, a newly arrived Spaniard applies...or else they give preference to some *gachupín* who already lives here] (26). These examples demonstrate that Chandón is able to improvise when circumstances call for it. In this regard, he resembles picaresque characters like Lazarillo de Tormes. He survives because he is astute. Later, we will see that the same cannot be said for his fellow conspirators.

After passing the unofficial examination, Chandón advances to a contrived examination of military skills where three applicants must perform a series of tests to determine who is the most qualified. Chandón is up against Pablo Berreteaga, son of a local colonial intendant, and Pepe Caramelo, a not-so-bright Spaniard whose only purpose for being there is to lend an air of legitimacy to Berreteaga's probable victory. The tests go poorly for Chandón and well for his Spanish opponent. In hand-to-hand combat, Berreteaga bests him with a blow to the kidney. As luck would have it, Chandón draws a skittish horse for the riding test and fails to complete the course. For the map-reading test, he picks a more suitable mount but gets lost. Despite this poor performance, Diego and the Creole conspirators involved in the evaluation seem intent on having Chandón. Diego slips him the answers to the written test, preps him for the oral interview, and turns a blind eye when he orders indigenous artillerymen to fill Berreteaga's cannon with adobe, which drastically alters the distance and trajectory of the projectile. The military test is, of course, a farce to lend credibility to the candidate they had already chosen. When all is said and done, Chandón is awarded the post because he is identified as a fellow Creole officer who will fight for independence... When Diego later asks him if he knows why he received the commission, Chandón naively responds that the members of the jury thought that he was the best candidate. Diego corrects him: "Ganaste el puesto de comandante de la batería y jefe de artificieros por una sola razón: eres de los nuestros. [...] Aunque hubieras cometido el doble de errores en el examen, hubieras ganado la prueba, porque así lo habíamos decidido" [You earned the position as artillery commander for one reason: you are one of us. [...] Even if you had committed twice as many mistakes on the exam, you would have won because we decided that you would] (49).

The Creole governmental officials, Diego and Carmen Aquino, are also not what they seem. Deception masquerades as authenticity and legitimacy, a notion that corresponds to the Ibargüengoitia's treatment of nationalist historiography. The couple resides in a mansion called the Casa de La Loma situated, unsurprisingly, on the hill overlooking Cañada. Rumors abound about the sumptuous life that the Aquinos enjoy within those walls. The house itself is described as the most elegant in the city, but upon closer inspection, the couple does not seem to belong there. Diego frequently gets lost guiding Chandón to his room, a propensity that will mirror his incompetence and inability to keep his bearings in the revolution. When the local bishop stops in for a visit, the Aquinos inexplicably ask Chandón to occupy the administrator's house in town. He accepts without understanding why he is forced to leave with so many rooms in the mansion. Arriving at the smaller house, he finds the shabby home a terrible contrast with the Casa de La Loma. The next day he learns that neither house belongs to the Aquinos: the mayor's home belongs to the government and the mansion belongs to the Marquis de la Hedionda, a wealthy friend of the Aquinos and the target for another one of Ibargüengoitia's snarky wordplays. Thus the Aquinos' wealth and lifestyle are a façade. And Ibargüengoitia invites us to laugh at them when Chandón meets Carmen on the veranda overlooking the city. Carmen romanticizes about the poorer dwellings that inhabit the hill below the mansion, calling them pretty and quaint, observing that each one is neat, orderly, and has a small flowerpot, and exclaiming that "¡Qué dignidad hay en la pobreza!" [There is such dignity in poverty!] (16). Chandón offers a different version of the neighborhood: "Había montones de estiércol, humaredas, hombres dormidos, mujeres cargando rastrojos, niños jugando en el lodo, perros ladrando" [There were dung heaps, smoke, men sleeping, women carrying cuttings, children playing in the mud, dogs barking] (16). The irony, of course, is that the poor people about whom Carmen pontificates have more than she does. The Aquinos' posh accommodations are only temporary and granted at the behest of the Spanish nobility against which they play to revolt and whom they eventually intend to emulate.

All plays must begin with a script, and Ibargüengoitia contends that the insurgents' script was flawed from the outset. *Los pasos de López* has two diametrically opposed scripts: one aspires to peaceful transition through the process of writing, and another sees no way other than full-scale war. Diego Aquino favors a peaceful plan, asserting that independence is a question of bureaucratic paperwork: following a nationwide declaration of independence, the Spanish Crown will recognize the legal right of the American provinces to establish themselves as free and sovereign states and the citizens of the newly freed land will happily receive the news. Violence should be avoided at all costs. However, this gesture toward nation building is weakened by his unwillingness to act. The purchase and manufacture of arms are only *precauciones*, a word that Ibargüengoitia carefully inserts to foreshadow the impending the failure of Aquino's optimistic plan (56). The major obstacle he sees will not be armed confrontation with royalist troops but formation of a postrevolutionary government. While unsure exactly how things will pan out, Aquino expects that Creoles will occupy major administrative posts because independence will offer them "una oportunidad de hacer las cosas a nuestro modo" [an opportunity to do things our way] (50). He also imagines bringing Fernando VII to reign in Mexico without realizing that the ousted Spanish monarch might not look kindly on forsaking the Spanish throne. Beyond mild daydreaming about a utopian Creole future, Diego has no practical plan and sees no reason to develop and no prepare for contingencies. This rose-colored scenario contrasts with Periñón's pragmatism: peace can only be achieved through armed struggle against the Spaniards and their expulsion or extermination. But his fervor for battle plans does not carry over to postwar planning. As far as he is concerned, the new government might be "una república como tienen en el Norte o bien un imperio como tienen los franceses, pero es cuestión que francamente no me preocupa, porque sería raro que llegáramos a ver el final de esto que estamos comenzando" [a republic like they have up north or an empire like the French have. But it is a matter that frankly doesn't concern me because it is unlikely that we will see the end of what we are starting] (85). This sentiment, carried over directly from *La conspiración vendida*, demonstrates a direct link to what might be considered the seed of Ibargüengoitia's independence criticism. Hidalgo's anti-Hispanism is precisely what Alamán decried in his *Historia de Méjico* as primary cause of Mexico's fall into midcentury chaos. Ibargüengoitia does not appear to share this sentiment. Rather, the turmoil that beset Mexico during the nineteenth century was due to bad planning, lack of foresight, and poor execution. Sierra might argue that Hidalgo did not have time to prepare a fully fleshed, postindependence plan, but Ibargüengoitia counters that Hidalgo fatalistically resigned that responsibility to future generations. If Hidalgo is the father of the Mexican nation, he is, in Ibargüengoitia's opinion, a negligent father who only cared for the present.

The inadequacies of the insurgents' script are complicated by directorial problems. Initially, Diego appears to occupy the director's chair. By decree, he is the Crown's representative in Cañada and seeks to derive authority for the newly independent nation from that mandate. Diego's absence from the stage during the rehearsal of *La precaución inútil* might be explained if he is the director, but he is generally a nonentity who wields colonial authority but exercises little power within the group. When colonial officials investigate allegations of a conspiracy, Aquino's feeble attempt to direct them away from the secret meeting place is frustrated by his inability to take charge. He becomes the puppet, not the master, and is eventually arrested. Later, when freed from prison, he attempts to regain control of the insurgency by penning a declaration of independence. Periñón corrects him on two points: "Tienes un error importante, Diego: la independencia la declaré yo el quince de septiembre, no vas a declararla tú hoy... yo soy el jefe del Ejército Libertador, la ciudad está en nuestro poder. Entonces, basando mi autoridad en esta premisa, te nombro corregidor de Cañada" [You have made an important error, Diego: I declared independence on September 15, and you will not declare it today... I am the commander of the Liberating Army and the city is in our power. So, basing my authority on this preimse, I name you *corregidor* of Cañada] (145). Because Diego is unwilling and unable to defend his symbolic right to rule with force, Periñón strong-arms his way to power. If Ibargüengoitia's description of Diego is in any way faithful to the historical Miguel Domínguez, there is little doubt why he disappeared from popular history: he was simply too weak to maintain power.

Nevertheless, Periñón is an ineffectual leader. His charisma attracts the masses, but his permissiveness allows for anarchy in the newly created army. When a soldier steals one of the army's horses, Periñón forbids his execution and orders Chandón to forgive the man. In the absence of discipline, the army becomes a mob, a point most clearly seen during the assault on Cuévano. Cuévano is Ibargüengoitia's cipher for Guanajuato, a mining city in the Bajío that witnessed one of the most spectacular massacres of the insurgency. Spanish loyalists had taken refuge inside a large fortress-like granary called the Alhóndiga. Provisioned with enough food to withstand a long siege, the Spaniards planned to wait until the revolutionary army left. However, the insurgents overran the fortifications and slaughtered everyone inside. The tragedy at the Alhóndiga was later used by conservative historians, especially Lucas Alamán, to demonstrate the uncontrolled, destructive nature of Hidalgo's rebellion. Alamán remembers that Bishop Abad y Queipo had likened Hidalgo's silkworm farm to the revolution: "no seguía orden ninguno, y que echaban la hoja como venía del árbol y los gusanos la comían como querían: ¡la revolución, me decía con este motivo el obispo, de quien originalmente sé esta anécdota, fue como la cría de los gusanos de seda, y tales fueron los resultados!" [there was no order whatsoever, and leaves grew from the trees without pruning, and the worms ate them as they wished: the bishop who originally shared this anecdote, told me that the revolution was like the silkworms and that they had the same results] (227).

Telling the story decades later, Chandón expresses his own impotence during the battle. Defending himself against charges that insurgency leaders had encouraged barbarism among the indigenous troops, he argues that there was no way to avoid it. "Tratamos de detener a la gente pero no nos obedecieron," [We tried to stop the people but they would not obey us,] he argues (133). Chandón recounts that the insurgents attacked the Spaniards "y los hicieron pedazos. En otros lados del edificio había gente que se quería rendir. De nada les sirvió, los mataron igual que a los que resistieron. Un hombre subió corriendo por la escalera, lo persiguieron y cuando lo alcanzaron lo echaron de cabeza al patio" [and ripped them to pieces. In other parts of the building people wanted to surrender. But it did not help because they killed them regardless. One man went running up the stairs, they followed him, and when they caught him, they threw him headfirst to the patio] (133). Periñón does little to suppress this bestial behavior. To the contrary, he justifies it by arguing that, for those who have lived in privation, stealing is no crime (146). Where conservative historians like Alamán denounce Hidalgo for actively encouraging brutality and racial hatred, liberal historians like Sierra blame the inherent savagery of the combatants, but all agree on the criminal results. Ibargüengoitia seems to propagate many of these negative attitudes toward Indians because the novel portrays them as uneducated, violent, and untrustworthy. Ibargüengoitia's representation of Hidalgo is even more problematic. He demonstrates Hidalgo's care for the indigenous community, but it smacks of irresponsible indulgence and raises questions about the paternal responsibility that Sierra attributes to the priest.

Periñón's ineffective use of power unravels the insurgency. Just as with the misshapen cannon El Niño, he has neither the experience nor the foresight to create a useful weapon. At the final battle in Cuijas, the Mexican army appears on the verge of extinction. Ontananza observes that defeat will inevitably lead to dissolution of the revolutionary army, while victory will seal independence. His strategy consists of a controlled series of attacks and retreats: the insurgent forces push out, attack, then pull back, drawing the enemy closer. The gambit is successful, and Ontananza predicts that victory can be achieved by sunset if they patiently continue. Unfortunately, patience is not one of Periñón's defining characteristics. In the heat of battle, he breaks ranks and leads his troops into a massacre. This tactical error destroys the army and ends the insurgency. In a rare moment of self-criticism, Periñón confesses, "Ya sé que metí la pata. Es culpa mía. No les pido perdón porque no lo merezco" [I know I messed up. It's my fault. I do not ask for forgiveness because I deserve none] (167). Ibargüengoitia's antithetical portrait of Hidalgo and the conspirators cuts across the grain of the official history. He shows them as incompetent military leaders, superficial political thinkers, and overly indulgent patriarchs.

Elisabeth Guerrero views this demystification as a redemptive act of historical justice for a character who has long been lost in sanctimonious myths. She argues that Ibargüengotia remains neutral in his assessment of Hidalgo because "*Los pasos de López* does not iconize Hidalgo; nor does it demonize him. Instead, the novel brings the hero down to scale: Periñón fumbles as a military leader and falters as a man of the cloth" ("Plotting Priest" 103). She proposes that his military shortcomings and moral indiscretions make him "an ordinary man" and that "his slips are petty, not the tragic downfall of a hero" (111–12) and that this gesture ultimately demystifies the romanticized official iconography associated with him. I agree that Ibargüengoitia tears down postrevolutionary idealization of Hidalgo, but *Los pasos de López* is far from objective and even farther from neutral. While *La conspiración vendida* maintained a reverent distance, *Los pasos de López*'s expanded historical scope and freedom from the constraints of state sponsorship allowed Ibargüengoitia to criticize Hidalgo's lack of forethought and grave tactical errors that cost lives and delayed independence for another eleven years. As historian Luis Barrón puts it, "Para Ibargüengoitia, quienes fundaron el México del siglo XX fueron quienes utilizaron políticamente la historia para dar legitimidad a un régimen autoritario que los mexicanos tuvimos que padecer. En realidad, la burla—o la crítica, más bien—no era a la Revolución ni a los revolucionarios, sino a quienes hicieron de la historia de México un cuento poblado con héroes de cartón" [For Ibargüengoitia, those who founded Mexico in the twentieth century were those who used history to give political legitimacy to an authoritative regime that we Mexicans had to suffer. In reality, the joke—or better yet, the criticism—was not against the revolution or the revolutionaries, but rather against those who made history a story about cardboard heroes] (10).

The preceding analysis of scripts, directors, and actors is not worth much without mention of the audience that receives these stilted versions of cardboard history. Spectators are first mentioned in Chapter 9, after the performance of *La precaución inútil* has clearly gone wrong: the hero is shackled, the villain is free to pursue the young maiden, and justice has not been delivered. The crowd does not understand what has happened, but either out of politeness for their friends or respect for the colonial administrator's wife, they applaud. Likewise, the citizens of Cuévano who gather on the hill to watch the massacre of their friends and family members in the Requinta proclaim *vivas* and cheer the insurgents' victory. Chandón is dubious about their motives: "No sé qué hubieran gritado si hubiéramos perdido" [I don't know what they would have yelled if we had lost] (134). As in his *Excélsior* articles, Ibargüengoitia criticizes those who applaud the past without really understanding what happened and, perhaps, himself for contributing *La conspiración vendida* to that uncritical history. After more than two decades of refining his story, Ibargüengoitia was able to correct his early contribution to an uncritical nationalist history. Having achieved his own independence, both from financial necessity and from the seamless yet empty narrative of independence, he was able to write about the nation's founding fathers in a manner that fit his vision of Mexico's national idiosyncrasies. If at the beginning of his career he faltered, at the end he exemplified the intellectual who recognizes the value of frank, open, and honest introspection in the successes and failures of a nation. His final novel makes no bones about the faltering steps of Hidalgo or of anyone else associated with independence: what began as a parlor game ended in a national disaster. Ibargüengoitia recognized independence as a massive theatrical flop because the script was poorly conceived, the directors could not provide clear leadership, and the actors could not follow direction or adapt when things went wrong.

There is an epilogue to this story. *Los pasos de López* was the last novel Jorge Ibargüengoitia published, but it was not the last one that he wrote. At the time of his death, Ibargüengoitia was in the process of completing two more: one entitled *Isabel cantaba*, of which we have roughly twenty-three pages that were posthumously published in the literary magazine *Letras Libres* in January 2008, and another historical novel that would have told the story of Archduke Ferdinand Maximilian of Austria, the Habsburg emperor who reigned over Mexico from 1864 to 1867. On November 28, 1983, he reluctantly boarded a plane in Paris to attend a writer's conference in Colombia with the unfinished manuscript of this historical novel. He was close to completing the text and planned to use the travel time to make final corrections. En route the plane was scheduled for a nighttime layover in Madrid. As the Boeing 747 neared Barajas airport, the pilot brought the aircraft in too low and dug the nose into the ground about four miles from the landing strip. Ibargüengoitia and all other passengers, including Uruguayan literary critic Ángel Rama and Peruvian writer Manuel Scorza, were killed on impact. The manuscript was destroyed and no copy appears to exist. Four years later, Fernando del Paso published *Noticias del imperio*, a monumental novel crafted from a decade of meticulous research and analysis of reams of testimonies, biographies, journals, diaries, and sundry historical documents. No doubt, a comparative reading of these two novels would have made for an engaging study in contrasts: Ibargüengoitia, with his characteristic theatrical compactness, would have produced a novel that excelled in its brevity, poignancy, and dramatic tension; Del Paso, on the other hand, immerses readers in a universe of detail, anecdotes, documentation, and elaborate voices. We will never have that opportunity, but the next chapter will undertake a close reading of Del Paso's novel in order to examine another aspect of the rhetoric of failure. Instead of highlighting the flawed nature of personal action, Del Paso writes a recuperative fiction that attempts to incorporate the Second Empire into national history in order to exorcise the uncomfortable hauntings of memory that plague the present.

Chapter 2

Cross-Dressing the Second Empire in Fernando del Paso's *Noticias del imperio*

Fernando del Paso quickly distinguished himself as one of the most promising writers of the midcentury generation when he published *José Trigo* (1966). Structurally ambitious and stylistically innovative, the novel recreates the violent governmental repression of striking railway workers of Nonalco-Tlatelolco in 1959. Excitement for his work continued to grow with the publication of *Palinuro de México* (1977), which follows the adventures of a medical student in downtown Mexico City who dies during a breathtaking climax at the Tlatelolco Square massacre in 1968. Critics and readers anxiously awaited ten years for the publication of his third novel, *Noticias del imperio* (1987), and were not disappointed. It is no less ambitious in its scope than its predecessors and tells the story of the 1861 invasion of Mexico by French forces, the short-lived empire under Archduke Ferdinand Maximilian Joseph of Austria, and the definitive triumph of the liberal faction led by Benito Juárez. Each of these novels can be rightly considered a totalizing novel, which Ryan Long has defined as one that attempts to recreate a single day, event, or nation in its entirety. Each addresses a particular moment of crisis when authoritarianism was thrown into striking relief against the background of democratic institutions and progress. The portrayal of governmental violence employed against peaceably striking workers and protesting students in his first two novels is complemented by the image of European expansionist aggression against an independent nation that had only recently overcome militarism and established a democratic government. By highlighting these fissures in the teleological narrative of power, these totalizing novels create a "site of open-ended negotiation, a space of overlap that helps explain how Mexican novels respond to a period when the representative authority of both state and novel was challenged by the consequences of contradictory historical tendencies" (Long 5). All three can be read as a response to the exercise of repressive power by a national government suffering a crisis of legitimacy.

Throughout his career, Del Paso has combined the highest aesthetic standards with a rock-steady political commitment against totalitarianism and in favor of historical justice. In an interview with Maruja Echegoyen, he admitted that *Noticias del imperio* was written for the express purpose of revealing "todo ese mundo de intrigas, de bajezas, de calumnias y de porquerías" [all that world of intrigues, despicable acts, calumnies, and dirt] that he discovered in European history while preparing the manuscript (Echegoyen 32). Indeed the novel, written during his long residence in London, has regularly been identified for its open opposition to foreign involvement in Latin American affairs. As a journalist working for newspapers and magazines in England, France, and Mexico, Del Paso criticized the Western powers for interfering in the Americas as in the case of the Falkland Island War. During the conflict, Del Paso chided the British for their presumption and belittled their anachronistic imperial pretensions. Beyond a criticism of the political involvement in the region, *Noticias del imperio* can be read as an indictment of any foreign encroachments in Mexico under the programmatic implementation of economic neoliberalism during the Miguel de la Madrid administration. As noted in the previous chapter, José López Portillo, the president who preceded De la Madrid, had pinned the nation's economic hopes on artificially inflated oil prices such that when the petroleum market collapsed in the late 1970s, Mexico was forced to borrow additional funds at exorbitant interest rates. The end result was an economic disaster. De la Madrid was a Harvard-educated banker who believed that opening Mexico to foreign markets and investment was the key to its financial stability. His economic policy was characterized by a heavy reliance on foreign capital; acceptance of International Monetary Fund guidelines and policies for inflation, prices, and debt repayment; and rampant privatization (Camp, "Time" 629). Reflecting this concern for the matter of foreign economic interests in Mexico, *Noticias del imperio* opens with a brief prologue about Benito Juárez's decision to suspend all payments on foreign debt in 1861 which, Del Paso notes, offered the French emperor, Napoleon III, the necessary pretext to launch a full-scale invasion of country and establish a European monarchy in the New World.

What is striking about *Noticias del imperio* is that it completes the arc of Del Paso's denunciation of totalitarianism by doing something altogether unexpected. Embedded within its panoramic critique of empire, the novel paints an endearingly human portrait of the ersatz emperor Maximilian and his deranged consort Charlotte. Instead of vilifying them as tyrannical usurpers, Del Paso narrates their lives, experiences, and deaths with sympathy and grace. What is more, he asks readers to recognize the royal couple's right to a hospitable memory and, in this spirit, then, proposes that Mexico posthumously extend citizenship to Maximilian and Carlota. This recuperative gesture is reminiscent of Edward Crankshaw's *The Fall of the House of Habsburg* (1963), where the author prefaced his history of the European dynasty by recognizing that, though the monarchy had disappeared following the First World War, many of the issues it attempted to solve continue to exist. Without a complete understanding of what the Habsburgs did or tried to do, contemporary society would be unable to understand where and how they went wrong. He then qualified his study with a remarkable caveat: "Understanding calls for the exercise of sympathy (this has nothing to do with whitewashing). There has been overflowing sympathy for the various peoples of the empire but little, if any, for the rulers who tried to hold them together in a dangerous world" (1). Crankshaw's general statement about the fall of the Austro-Hungarian Empire applies to the short-lived Habsburg monarchy that presided over Mexico from 1864 to 1867 because it touches one of the central tenets of this book: that the shortcomings of the present are partly incomprehensible unless a full accounting of the past is made.

In the process of extending posthumous citizenship to Maximilian, Del Paso proposes balancing the scales of a national history dominated by liberal accounts of the past by offering an olive branch to the legacy of conservatism. Accepting its role in Mexico's past, he argues, will allow Mexico to bury it, to make peace with the past, and to move forward. Without this sort of magnanimous gesture, Del Paso suggests that the nation will continue to be haunted by the ghosts of its past. To this end, *Noticias del imperio* is a recuperative fiction that sidelines debating the personal weakness of its main characters in order to rectify a more general failure of historiography. Unlike Ibargüengoitia's critique of the conspirators' buffoonery that we saw in the first chapter, the exaltation of personal ambition over national good that will constitute the main thrust of Serna's depiction of Santa Anna in the third chapter, or Moreno's and Zambrano's diatribe against traitors who weakened national defense during the Mexican-American War which occupies the final chapter, Del Paso does not linger on the archduke's frailties but rather shows him to be an affable, even likeable, character. Del Paso does point out the somewhat incongruous idiosyncrasies of the archduke's personality and, on occasion, examines his policy choices. But even then, the novel mitigates the damning evidence by placing blame on others who pressured an otherwise weak emperor into decisions that ultimately contradicted his love of country. In this regard, Del Paso exemplifies the sympathetic gesture he asks of his readers. This chapter analyzes the argument that *Noticias del imperio* makes in favor of recognizing Maximilian's Mexicanness as path towards recuperating the lost elements of national history. The first part assesses the anticolonial interpretations that studies Del Paso's historical fiction as a sustained critique of empire. These readings are indeed thought provoking, yet they tend to overlook the novel's final invitation to incorporate the Habsburg couple into the national pantheon. The second section lays out Del Paso's rationale and method. Despite his foreign birth, Maximilian should be posthumously considered Mexican because he earned it. To make his case, Del Paso demonstrates how Benito Juárez, the ostensible antithesis of the Austrian archduke, might also be considered a foreigner to nineteenth-century Mexican society. The third, fourth, and fifth sections demonstrate how Del Paso argues in favor of accepting Maximilian by presenting both him and Juárez as cultural transvestites who adopt the cultural norms and values of another society in order to construct and realize a new identity.

Del Paso's Hauntology of Conservatism

The failure to fully incorporate Mexican conservatism into a cohesive national narrative is nowhere more evident than in Mexico City's central avenue, Paseo de la Reforma. It was commissioned in 1864 by Emperor Maximilian I, and completed a year later as part of a beautification project that included the construction of the Alameda Central, the renovation of the Castillo de Chapultepec, and the preservation of other open green spaces in the historic downtown area. Originally named the Paseo de la Emperatriz and modeled after the wide Parisian boulevards and the Viennese Ringstrasse, the avenue was designed to provide adequate communication between the imperial residence at Chapultepec and the city center. After the fall of the empire, it was renamed twice, in each case to honor the triumph of liberal forces. Subsequent governments envisioned further renovations to the downtown area but it was elite of the Díaz regime who imagined a modern metropolis that would be a symbol of order and progress complete with monuments (Hale, Rev. 391). And so, on the eve of the centennial celebrations of independence, Díaz ordered the construction of more than one hundred statues celebrating the liberal heroes of the nineteenth century and the heroes of the ancient Aztec world to line the Paseo. Not surprisingly, conservative figures were summarily excluded from Díaz's pantheon, as if to say that their ideological convictions precluded them from being accepted as authentic members of nation (Krauze 37–39). The transformation of the capital cityscape prefigures the tendency in Mexico's historical imagination to erase the imprint of the Second Empire and, more broadly, conservatism from national history.

The popularity of conservatism, and its more radical variant monarchism, in nineteenth-century politics was due, in part, to the turmoil that followed independence. Between 1821 and 1864, the presidential palace seemed more like the parade grounds for short-lived military presidents than the seat of democratic authority. During that period, thirty-four men had held the reins of the nation and, of those, twenty-four were generals. Four of these general-presidents—Anastasio Bustamante, Antonio López de Santa Anna, Valentín Gómez Farías, and José Joaquín Herrera—took office multiple times. Generals elected themselves by force when the prevailing political winds did not favor their personal interests and pronouncements became the common stock of political discourse. Impassioned patriotic fervor thinly veiled rampant self-interest. The pendulum swung violently between liberal and conservative governments as both factions seemed intent on outdoing the other in extremism. Regardless of a given president's political leanings—whether they supported the church and Hispanism or Enlightenment and Americanism—the early leaders of the new nation were almost universally career military men. This turmoil was exacerbated by the Mexican-American War of 1846, which more than any other disgrace exposed the ambition and dissention that had impeded the establishment of a stable, unified government. The crushing defeat at the hands of US forces and the loss of half the national territory left intellectuals in a quandary about the direction the nation should take. Intellectuals of all stripes began a ruthless self-analysis for the root causes of the failure and, as Charles A. Hale put it, they began to include basic questions about national identity that had previous been approached by only a few exceptional thinkers ("The War" 154). They had intuited that something in the past set the stage for the failure of the present. The question was: What was it?

In searching for a response, Mexican intellectuals scoured the past in search of the problem and, in so doing, touched on some of the most vital questions in the reckoning of national history and character: What was the impact of Spanish colonial influence in Mexico? Whose view of the past more cogently explained the political turmoil of midcentury Mexico? Which version of history could satisfactorily explain the loss of half the national territory? Curiously, the polemic that played out during the 1840s became a vitriolic debate over how to tell the independence story in Mexico. Mexican intellectuals proffered competing versions of the past, one liberal and nationalist, the other conservative and pro-Hispanic. According to liberal historians, Miguel Hidalgo's rallying *grito de Dolores* in 1810 declared emancipation from oppressive Spanish rule and gave birth to a new nation. This version of history framed independence as a struggle that began with humble means, vindicated an authentic indigenous past, and was carried forward by a popular desire for freedom and equality and had enduring power due, in large part, to its portrayal of active involvement by the poor, who had consistently found themselves on the fringes of colonial society. The conservative response offered an alternate story that began by authenticating the colonial endeavor as a peaceful, benevolent process that brought order to an otherwise uncivilized landscape of barbarism and concluded with the near bloodless consummation of independence on September 27, 1821. For many of these conservatives in the 1840s and 1850s, monarchism seemed to be the best option. Seeing the opportunity to advance the monarchist position, dogged conservatives like José María Gutiérrez Estrada offered the crown to a number of European princes. Gutiérrez Estrada had been a lifelong supporter of monarchy and made his feelings clear that the republican experiment had failed. In his 1862 proposition in favor of monarchism, Gutiérrez Estrada recalled his initial dismay at the political situation in 1840, to observe that once again the nation had plunged into "una de esas profundas crisis que está atravesando, casi desde el momento mismo de haberse constituido en República" [one of those profound crises which it has suffered almost from the moment of its constitution as a Republic] (1). As a result, he and other like-minded thinkers determined that the time had come to redeem the country by importing foreign talent. Only a prince of royal lineage could save the nation because monarchism constituted the political structure most suited to the traditions, needs, and interests of the people, who from the beginning had been governed by monarchy.

Mexico's long conservative legacy leads historian Erika Pani to argue that the Second Empire was not, as most post-Reform historians would purport, foreign to the Mexican experience. Though the empire has been perceived as the unfortunate result of French avarice, Austrian ambition, and Mexican treason, she contends that it represents a period of continuity and change during which well-known members of Mexican society attempted to resolve problems that politicians had been wrestling with since independence. In this regard, she argues, the Second Empire is firmly inscribed within the nation's historical process (19–20). Pani is not alone in her recuperation of the Second Empire. Robert Duncan arrives at a similar conclusion when he observes that historians oftentimes misconstrue imperial failures as clear proof that conservatism was destined to fail and, on the basis of such evidence, dismiss Maximilian's reign as a temporary detour from the inevitable triumph of liberalism ("Political" 28). The revisionist work of Pani, Duncan, and other critics amounts to an attempt to overturn the "so-called *liberal* historiographical tyranny" to which Mexican history has been subjected (Fowler, Rev. 636–38) by recognizing that conservatism forms an important part of Mexico's political heritage and that the Second Empire should be interpreted as part of national history.

Nationalist reactions against the historical Second Empire have spilled over into literary criticism, manifesting itself in the form of anticolonial readings of *Noticias del imperio* that focus on textual subversions that explore the discursive gaps in colonial historiography and contrast them with *juarista* liberalism (Jitrik 84), trace lines of symmetry between the novel's portrayal of the past and its concern for present-day imperialism (Menton 82), and invert Eurocentric models of civilization and barbarism (Kurz 21–22). Oftentimes, these readings focus on narratological structures that privilege articulations of "lo irracional de la empresa imperial, el descaro de los emperadores franceses, la total ineptitud de Maximiliano y la relativización (si no la reversión) de la visión histórica que Europa construyó de México y de América Latina" [the irrational nature of the imperial project, the imprudence of the French emperors, the utter incompetence of Maximilian, and the relativization (if not the reversal) of the European historical vision that constructed Mexico and Latin America] (Pons 104). Elizabeth Corral Peña, who, in addition to editing Del Paso's complete works, has written an insightful genealogical study of *Noticias del imperio* that accounts for its primary source material, exemplifies this trend when she argues that Del Paso incorporates a diverse corpus of archival materials into the novel in order to offer readers a complete and complex tapestry in which different threads of the story are woven together into one totalizing whole (17). Many of the texts used to create the novel's framework, she argues, were conservative memoirs such as those written by eyewitnesses who belonged to Maximilian's inner circle. This reliance on insider testimony imbues *Noticias del imperio* with an added air of authenticity and historical equanimity in that it privileges the marginalized conservative voice as much as it does the derisive voices of liberal detractors. Corral Peña then notes that Del Paso shellacs these conservative texts "con un barniz irónico" [with an ironic varnish] that makes that trenchant conservatives like Gutiérrez Estrada appear buffoonish (69). These subtle ironic inversions allow readers to perceive textual hints that reveal the narrator's true opinion about Gutiérrez, an opinion that, for all intents and purposes, coincides with that of almost every historian who has studied the period and especially those that knew him.

It does not require a significant stretch of the imagination to apply this same judgment to most conservatives in the novel. Anticolonialist critics

tend to read *Noticias del imperio* as a revisionist text that satirizes monarchists for their oddness and the monarchist position for its anachronism.
Łukasz Grützmacher has argued that the centrality of this revisionist bent
among literary critics has oftentimes limited analyses to archival readings
that demonstrate how historiographic metafiction subverts the official
story (147–50). These analyses are based on two presuppositions. The first,
based on Hayden White's narratological study of historiographic emplot-
ment, states that historical discourse is no truer than novelistic discourse in
that both are fictionalized constructions of a past that is only available to
us through documents. The second, stemming from a vindicating postcolonial view, supposes that official history was written by hegemonic power
structures for the purpose of self-legitimization and is not only false but
unjust. By metafictionally questioning the basis of these official histories,
traditional critical interpretations suggest that historical novels do justice
to marginalized minorities by upending the official story (163). When one
considers the style of critical analysis that has been performed on *Noticias
del imperio*, this point becomes quite clear. The bibliography on textual
subversions in Del Paso's novel is extensive and most critics seem to point
to the same conclusion: that Del Paso, by means of a meticulous revision
of conservative eyewitness accounts, manages to subvert the colonial discourse of power by means of carnivalesque, parodic, and ironic writing.

While many of these critics have taken their cues from statements that
Del Paso has made regarding the anticolonial bent of his writing, few, if
any, account for what Kristine Ibsen has recently called the "unresolved
ambivalence toward Maximilian" on the part of writers and artists who,
at different times and in different genres, have offered sympathetic portrayals of the emperor (*Maximilian* 118). This ambivalence in Del Paso's
portrayal of Maximilian derives from the dilemma that accompanies the
creation of fully fleshed fictional characters. As Robin Fiddian points out,
Noticias del imperio acknowledges the political considerations that induced
Maximilian to overcome his initial concerns about accepting the role of
emperor, but it also "takes account of the psychological and ideological
factors that may have influenced Maximilian, and it delves into the complex and contradictory character of a historical figure who could be considered the victim of circumstances that he was ultimately unable to control
and who, on the other hand, was undeniably the architect of his own tragic
destiny" (110). This is to say that, while presenting a buffoonish caricature
of Gutiérrez Estrada is relatively simple because he only appears for the
purpose of advancing the storyline, Maximilian slips through narrowly
confined ideological representations because, at some level, writers recognize that he does not fit the prefabricated molds of imperialism. From this
perspective, Juan José Barrientos can rightly claim that Del Paso restores

the emperor's grandeur without divesting him of his humanity (188). This is due, in part, to the ideological indeterminacy that characterizes the postmodern historical novel. The multiplicity of narrative points of view ensures the impossibility of establishing a single truth about the historical event because the novel sets potentially contradictory interpretations of the same historical referent against each other (Aínsa 83). Regardless of a given critic's desire to read an anticolonial message in the novel, or even of Del Paso's own conviction that the novel exists solely for the purpose of revealing all decadence of empire, the protean nature of the postmodern historical novel enables it to evade the strictures of ideological projects espoused by the traditional historical novel. While I agree with these critics regarding the presence of an anticolonial core to Del Paso's novel, what I want to suggest here is that *Noticias del imperio* also revises the hegemonic liberal history about the Second Empire. It subverts the liberal version that demonizes Maximilian and grants him discursive recognition within Mexican history for the express purpose of burying him.

Del Paso explains the rationale for interring the Habsburg couple near the end of the novel in a section entitled "El último de los mexicanos" [The Last of the Mexicans] when he argues that, in the short time that they presided over the nation, Maximilian and Carlota underwent a metamorphosis whereby they became Mexican through the wholehearted adoption of the customs and language of their new homeland. He then asks his readers to accept their honest efforts and posthumously recognize them as Mexicans. The problem is that Mexico never accepted the imperial couple as its own because the imagined community has never properly buried them: "Es decir, ni Maximiliano...ni Carlota...quedaron integrados a esta tierra fertilizada al parejo con los restos de todos nuestros héroes y todos nuestros traidores" (643) [In other words, neither Maximilian...nor Carlota...were absorbed by this land equally fertilized by the remains of our heroes and our traitors] (678). It is noteworthy that Del Paso is not arguing that Maximilian be recognized as a national hero. Rather, his gesture includes the Habsburg couple within a national pantheon that includes stalwarts and turncoats alike. He further suggests that the manner in which Maximilian greeted his demise transformed his execution into a transcendent moment of bravery, into an exemplary Mexican death. I will examine this point more closely near the end of the chapter. Suffice it to say for now that much of Del Paso's explicit argumentation for accepting Maximilian as a Mexican hinges upon the portrayal of the emperor's unflinching bravery at the moment of death and the events that occurred immediately after the shots were fired. Mexico should bury its European emperors, Del Paso suggests, "para que no nos sigan espantando: las almas de los insepultos reclaman siempre su abandono. Como lo reclama y nos espanta, todavía, la sombra de Hernán Cortés" (644) [so they stop haunting us. The souls of the uninterred always cry out against their abandonment. The same way that Hernán Cortés's shadow still cries out and frightens us to this day] (679). As happens with Cortés, who continues to inform Mexico's discourse about nationality and identity despite having no monuments or streets named for him, Maximilian continues to haunt the nation. Both Cortés and Maximilian participated in the formation of the Mexican nation, both are foreigners, both are excluded from the Mexican pantheon, and both have marked Mexican history in indelible ways. But because neither has been metaphorically buried, they continue to haunt Mexico's historical imagination.

Any discussion of ghosts and haunting is, of course, a metaphor for what Runia describes as "presence," or the specific ways in which the unresolved legacies of the past make themselves felt in the present. Spectrality is not, as Fredric Jameson points out, an oracular conduit where the past reveals insight about the future, but rather the revelation "that the living present is scarcely as self-sufficient as it claims to be; that we would do well not to count on its density and solidity, which might under exceptional circumstances betray us" (39). In other words, the epistemological stability that modern concepts of history have attributed to totalizing narratives are, in fact, unstable and likely to reveal gaps where the unseemly elements of the past force their way into present consciousness. In the case of the statuary along the Paseo de la Reforma, then, we can say that the Porfirian attempt create an ironclad (or in this case, bronze-clad) version of the past only serves to underscore the glaring absence of important conservative figures who have not been metaphorically buried by the nation.

In *Specters of Marx* (1994), Derrida argued that the study of the spectrality and haunting is an ethical responsibility toward those victims of war, ethnic violence, genocide, imperialism, or any form of totalitarianism "who are not present, nor presently living, either to us, in us, or outside us" (xviii). Only through exorcising the ghosts of the past can society restore their right to "a hospitable memory" which is borne out of a "concern *for justice*" (175). Jo Labanyi builds upon Derrida's clever neologism "hauntology" when she suggested that ghosts, as the traces of those who have not been allowed to leave a trace, "are by definition the victims of history who return to demand reparation; that is, that their name, instead of being erased, be honoured" (66). She reads Derrida's notion of spectrality for its application to postdictatorial film and fiction in Spain, asserting that his "notion that history occupies in the present a 'virtual space of spectrality' contradicts the notion that postmodernity signifies an 'end of history', suggesting rather that it should be seen as a 'return of history' in the form of the revenant" (80). Avery Gordon summarizes this sentiment when he writes that the haunting we experience is the result of improperly buried bodies, which he interprets both as the missing corpses of those who were disappeared during the brutal military regimes in the 1960s and 1970s as well as those who have been surreptitiously erased from the historical record (16). The ghosts that haunt us are not simply dead or missing people but complex social figures that plague our sense of time and being. Only by investing them can we arrive at "that dense site where history and subjectivity make social life" (8). Hauntology, then, is an ethical and intellectual stance against totalitarianism that proposes recuperating the voices, stories, and legacies of the oppressed as a weapon against future injustices. But the emphasis that all these critics place upon the role of historical justice begs another ethical question because, without exception, these recuperative efforts stand in opposition to some form of conservatism. If, as I have argued, *Noticias del imperio* is a literary burial for Maximilian as the avatar of the conservative legacy, can we properly speak of a hauntology for conservatism? I believe that we can, but in order to do so, we must recognize that that justice, be it historical or legal, is not simply the vengeance of the oppressed upon the oppressor. Rather, justice is only just when its judgment is applied universally. It is important to note that Crankshaw's call, an exercise of historical sympathy for the Habsburg dynasty, in no way meant whitewashing the past or apologizing for empire. If we are to speak of a fair recuperation of the marginalized voices or figures of the past, then we should not simply limit that recovery to the traditional subaltern. The resolution of this spectral haunting is what *Noticias del imperio*, as a project interested in historical justice, undertakes. Regardless of the Del Paso's ideological position, he is willing to exercise sympathy for those who have been erased from national history. Del Paso writes that with a modicum of goodwill, readers can accept the possibility that the royal couple were sincere in their desires to become fully Mexican. And, if they were unable to fully accomplish this goal in life, they might be able to someday if readers are likewise willing to extend a sympathetic historical judgment in their favor.

Two Sides of the Same Coin

While the revisionist work of Pani and other critics ostensibly chips away at unilateral historical accounts, in truth it rejects the historical argumentation that underlies the traditional foundations of Western nationalism that defines an arbitrarily constructed national citizen against an equally arbitrary foreign threat. Benedict Anderson defined the nation as a social construct wherein a group of individuals imagines themselves bound together by a deep, horizontal sense of camaraderie. Those who fail to be included within the imagined totality are regarded as threats to the construct unless they can become acculturated and accepted by the community. Julia Kristeva makes a similar point in her analysis of Rousseau and Diderot's respective definitions of the national citizen in the late eighteenth century when she notes that the figure of the foreigner complicated the discourse of equality caught up in discussions of the rights of man. The foreigner, she argued, constitutes "the *alter ego* of national man" or the "one who reveals the latter's personal inadequacies at the same time as he points to the defects in mores and institutions. The *foreigner* then becomes the figure onto which the penetrating ironical mind of the philosopher is delegated—his double, his mask. He is the metaphor of the distance at which we should place ourselves in order to revive the dynamics of ideological and social transformation" (91). Foreigners, as the taboo others that seduce and repulse members of the imagined community, represent the threat of moral, political, and social disintegration and ultimately become the foil against which national identities are built because the foreign other is the complementary part of the self that brings to the fore our worst fears. The image of the corrupting foreigner is offset by what Bonnie Honig calls the foreign-founder. In a brief but panoramic description of classic political texts of Western culture, Honig underscores the importance of figures like Moses, who appears as an Egyptian prince sent to free Israel and establish a new nation; Ruth, who migrates from Moab to Bethlehem and from whom will spring forth David; Oedipus, who arrives at Thebes in time to solve the Sphinx's riddle and temporarily establishes peace through wise leadership; and Rousseau's lawgiver, who comes from elsewhere to found an ideal democracy (3–4). The task before Del Paso, then, is to convince Mexican readers to accept the foreign-born Maximilian as their own. This is no easy task, however, because the history of the Second Empire has been constructed as a dichotomy that distinguishes between an authentically Mexican president, Benito Juárez, and a foreign usurper, Maximilian. The key to leveling the playing field is demonstrating that both men were considered outsiders by Mexican society and that they both had to cobble together new national identities. By cutting against the grain of liberal Mexican history and highlighting their similarities, Del Paso can then make a stronger argument for incorporating Maximilian into the national pantheon.

This notion of similarity surfaces in the Rodolfo Usigli's introduction to *Corona de sombra* (1943), which was referenced in Del Paso's rationale and serves as one of the main pre-texts for the novel's portrayal of Maximilian. Usigli explains that he wrote the play to repay a debt he owed to historical justice because the imperial couple had been poorly treated by playwrights, writers, film directors, and historians. Mexican writers had employed so little imagination in their portrayals of the Austrian prince who gave up all ties to Europe that he was compelled to reimagine Maximilian in a manner more in keeping with who he was or pretended to be. While it is true that he ordered the death of Mexican citizens, Usigli rhetorically asks how many Mexican presidents and governors, including Juárez, had done the same thing without any condemnation or retribution. To the objection that Juárez and others were Mexicans, the playwright responds that their authentic nationality only increases the brutality of their crimes because they killed their own. Usigli then notes that, while Maximilian was in fact a despot, "su sistema de gobierno pretendió ser de tal suerte mexicano, que el pueblo no pudo ya distinguir entre el príncipe austriaco y el legislador nativo, y el Emperador muere, sin ser mexicano, por la misma razón que otros han caído: por serlo. Cruel paradoja" [his system of government pretended to be so Mexican that the people could no longer distinguish between the Austrian prince and the native legislator, and the Emperor dies, without being Mexican, for the same reason that others had fallen, for being one. Cruel paradox] (66). Usigli states this point even more emphatically thirty years later in an essay where he explicitly delineated a paradoxical conception of Maximilian and Juárez. He imagined them bound in a symbiotic relationship because they were, to use his image, two sides of the same coin.

> Puede ser sacrílego para muchos lo que voy a decir, pero creo—he creído largo tiempo, en toda honradez y simplicidad—que el día en que llegue a registrarse entre nosotros una verdadera *toma de conciencia histórica*, nuestra numismática se enriquecerá con una medalla conmemorativa del advenimiento de nuestra soberanía política que ostente en el anverso la imagen del patricio de la Reforma y en el reverso la del infortunado pero sincero y democrático príncipe austriaco que refrendó las Leyes de Reforma, pasó su primer 15 de septiembre en Dolores de Hidalgo—elegante lección a los anteriores gobernantes mexicanos—, invitó a Juárez a ser su primer ministro—o lo deseó al menos—porque lo había entendido, porque respetaba y compartía su visión política, su sentido de México, y porque al fin y al cabo dio su vida por la soberanía del país que había aceptado, elegido gobernar después de haber rechazado la corona de Grecia. Masones en grado 33 los dos, si bien en sectas rivales. Colaboradores los dos por un destino superior: por el destino de México. (407)
>
> [For many what I am about to say may be sacrilegious, but I believe—and have, in all honesty and simplicity believed for a long time—that on the day we achieve a true historical self-awareness, our numismatics will be greatly enriched by a commemorative medallion celebrating our political

sovereignty that has on one side the image of the patriarch of the Reform and on the other side that of the unfortunate but sincere and democratic Austrian prince who renewed the Reform Laws, spent his first September 15th in Dolores de Hidalgo—an elegant lesson to previous Mexican leaders—, invited Juárez to be his prime minister—or at least desired to do so—because he understood him, because he respected him, and because he shared his political vision, his sense of Mexico, and because when all was said and done he gave his life for the sovereignty of the nation that he had accepted and had chosen to govern after rejecting the throne of Greece. Both were thirty-third degree Masons, even if they were members of rival sects. They were both collaborators for a greater destiny: for the destiny of Mexico.]

Usigli further argues that Mexico owes its political sovereignty to Maximilian because he had accepted the crown that was offered to him, and then gave his life when his service was deemed an impediment to the nation's progress.

Noticias del imperio follows the Usiglian line of numismatic comparison by establishing a number of binary relationships between diametrically opposed elements (Fiddian 107). At the structural level, the novel oscillates between the odd-numbered chapters where we hear the intensely emotive first-person narrative of Carlota and the even-numbered chapters that combine third-person fictional creation with a pseudo-objective historiographic discourse offered by an external narrator who most critics have closely identified with the author. Other binomials appear: America / Europe, Mexico / France, liberal / conservative, history / fiction. However, the most important relationship is between Maximilian and Juárez. This binary conception of the two men is most readily visible when they are found traveling with their personal secretaries. Juárez's secretary, a well-educated white man, provides historical information about the Habsburgs and validates Juárez's comments. Maximilian travels to Cuernavaca with his Indian scribe, Blasio, who never speaks, but constantly copies everything that the emperor says. Both secretaries act as sounding boards for their employer. Both men validate the speaker: one by his agreements, the other by his silence. Chromatically, the roles are inverted: Juárez, the Indian president, perorates to his white secretary while Maximilian, the white monarch, dictates to an indigenous scribe. More than two sides of the same coin, as Usigli imagines, in Del Paso's novel they are mirror images. This binary structure appears to support the anticolonial position that pits Juárez against Maximilian. Moreover, the dual process of demonumentalizing Juárez and creating a more complex portrait of Maximilian serves to highlight their affinities. As we saw in the last chapter, Mexican history tends toward a type of entropy that strips historical figures of their humanity in order to create easily memorable examples worthy of emulation or reviling. *Noticias del imperio* restores that humanity by demonstrating that the Indian president and the Habsburg archduke share more than historians would lead us to believe.

Del Paso demonumentalizes Juárez by appropriating the form of hagiographic biographies and altering their language to emphasize Juárez's otherness. Our introduction to Juárez in the novel, for example, imitates the official history as told to the average four-year-old. The first paragraph of the section entitled "Juárez y 'Mostachú'" [Juárez and Mustachoo] is written in a childlike, fairy-tale lilt: "En el año de gracia de 1861, México estaba gobernado por un indio cetrino, Benito Júarez, huérfano de padre y madre desde que tenía tres años de edad, y que a los quince era solo un pastor de ovejas que trepaba a los árboles de la Laguna Encantada para tocar una flauta de carrizo y hablar con las bestias y con los pájaros en el único idioma que entonces conocía: el zapoteca" (29) [In the year of our Lord 1861, a sallow Indian named Benito Juárez governed Mexico. He had been orphaned at three, and at eleven had become a shepherd who climbed the tress by the Enchanted Lagoon to play his reed flute and talk to the birds and beasts in Zapotec, the only language he knew] (17). The scene evokes a pastoral setting complete with an enchanted lagoon, talking animals, forest, and flute music, reminiscent of the story told by Emilio Abreu Gómez in *Juárez: su vida contada a los niños* (1969) and other such hagiographic historical texts. Del Paso's imitatively simplistic language appears to perpetuate central elements of the myth: the parents' death at an early age, the endearing portrait of Juárez as young shepherd, the enchanted lagoon, the flute, and the primeval Zapotec language. What is exceptional about Del Paso's text, however, is how he undermines this official narrative from the beginning. The first description of Juárez is not that of a glorious, triumphant founding father. Rather, Mexico is governed by a "sallow Indian," an image that contrasts sharply with the robust effigy found in monuments throughout the country. To take but one example, the statue of Juárez that sits atop the Hemiciclo that dominates the Alameda constructed by Maximilian in downtown Mexico City offers spectators a Lincolnesque image. By contrast, in this opening description Juárez's stone-cold, granite features take on the worn look of a man weighed down by exile, calumny, a terrible sense of duty, and the loss of loved ones. Del Paso paints a portrait of insecurity: Juárez, the indigenous president who has been run off by white foreigners, must come to terms with his otherness.

Del Paso notes that, because Juárez was not of European descent, "por no ser ario y rubio que era el arquetipo de la humanidad superior según lo confirmaba el Conde de Gobineau en su *'Ensayo sobre la Desigualdad de las Razas Humanas'* publicado en París en 1854, por no ser, en fin, siquiera un mestizo de media casta, Juárez, el indio ladino, en opinión de los monarcas y adalides del Viejo Mundo era incapaz de gobernar a un país que de por sí era parecía ingobernable" (32) [because he wasn't Aryan or blond (the archetypal qualities of superior humanity according to the Count of Gobineau's *Essay on the Inequality of the Human Races*, published in 1853 [sic]); because he wasn't even a middle-class half-breed, Juárez, the cunning Indian, was—in the opinion of the monarchs and leaders of the Old World—incapable of governing a country that in itself appeared to be ungovernable] (20–21). Joseph Arthur Gobineau was the primary exponent of nineteenth-century racial philosophy and his *Essai sur l'Inégalité des Races Humaines*, became the theoretical framework for racial thought both in the Americas and abroad during a diplomatic mission he grudgingly fulfilled to the Brazilian court in 1869. Gobineau proposed that nature is inherently adverse to miscegenation, but that only those races that overcome this atavistic rejection can improve society. According to his taxonomy, all peoples descended from the white race and, through climatic changes, became diversified; their subsequent differentiation marked a point of departure from which there was no return. These degenerate races, however required the guiding hand of the white race for "a society is great and brilliant only so far as it preserves the blood of the noble group that created it" (qtd. in Biddiss 117). Gobineau argued that the black and yellow races degenerated into apathy, lack of physical vigor, and love of vice, while whites were characterized by their love of life, natural tendency toward political regularity, and organizational skills. He further worried that miscegenation would contribute to the immediate improvement of lower races, but that the long-term result would be "unfavorable to humanity as a whole, by virtue of the enervation of the noblest elements" (117), or in other words, whites.

Concerns about race come to the forefront in the chapter "Así es, Señor Presidente" [That's Correct, Mr. President], the first section of the novel dedicated entirely to Juárez. He and his secretary review a dossier about Maximilian prior to his arrival in Veracruz, and Juárez recognizes the weight that Gobineau's thoughts have on the world's perceptions of race relations. Asking how tall the soon-to-be emperor is, Juárez obsesses over Maximilian's height and physical characteristics as compared to his own. Remembering his childhood, Juárez recalls his indigenous godfather's marriage advice to marry a white woman so that his children would have blue eyes, and then wonders aloud about how white Maximilian is. Color is at the forefront of his mind. He affirms that Gobineau's racial theories should not affect him in the least, but neither can he help noting that some of his children "me han salido bonitos, como se acostumbraba decir... mucho menos prietos que yo" (161) [are quite handsome, as people say—not as dark as I] (161). This ethnic otherness is emphasized by Juárez's interaction with his white secretary who functions as a foil to validate the president's flagging self-esteem. When speaking of race, the secretary assures the president that he and all Mexicans feel pride in their indigenous ancestry, and goes so far as to imagine that he, too, has some Indian blood running through his veins though Juárez derisively retorts that the man is far too white to be a mestizo. Moreover, as if prevailing philosophical arguments about racial inferiority were not sufficient reason for marginalizing Juárez from the upper crust of Mexican society, Del Paso notes that "el Presidente de México agregaba una fealdad física notable, rubricada según afirmaron muchos que lo conocieron y entre ellos la Princesa Salm Salm, por una horrible cicatriz sanguinolenta que nunca apareció en sus fotografías" (33) [the President of Mexico had the added burden of being markedly ugly, this handicap being underscored, according to many who knew him, and among them Princess Salm Salm, by a horrible and bloody scar that never, for some reason, showed up in his portraits] (21). Even his wife, Margarita Maza, a white woman from the upper crust of Oaxacan society, tells their children in the novel that their father is ugly, but is a good man.

Del Paso does not simply reduce conservative objections to Juárez to racial bias or physical appearance, but further underscores how little he fits into Creole society by emphasizing the antiheroic figure Juárez represents when compared with other Latin American foundational figures, who all rode horses and studied the manly art of warfare. When the secretary asks if Juárez if would have liked to learn these activities, the president responds that swordplay never interested him, but that he would have like to learn to ride a horse. He reflects that the inability to ride properly sets him apart from other Spanish-American heroes like Bolívar, O'Higgins, and San Martín—all white or mestizo, of course—who rode well and thinks out aloud that history will remember him as an illustrious man on muleback. But Juárez does find a measure of solace in his customary mode of transportation: "Pero después de todo, las mulas saben andar mejor que los caballos por los caminos muy difíciles sin desbarrancarse, ¿no es cierto?" (147) [Still, mules know how to tread better than horses on very rough terrain without losing their footing, isn't that right?] (145). The mule analogy connotes a number of negative associations that are not applicable to Juárez because mules are hybrid crosses between horses and donkeys and are unable to reproduce; by contrast, the president is a full-blooded Zapotec Indian and had a large posterity. This reflection on fertility and procreation then leads to a conversation about virility, since the archduke had no known offspring and history has recorded that once he and Carlota ceased all sexual activities once they arrived in Mexico due, in part, to an alleged case of syphilis that the emperor contracted during an expedition to Brazil. When Maximilian's possible sterility enters the conversations, Juárez seizes on it quickly because he finds in it a point of strength over his adversary: "¿Estéril? Bueno, ya ve usted por qué a mí no me ofende que me llamen mula, Señor Secretario, si es nada más que por lo tozudo, por lo terco...porque de mula no tengo nada más. Las mulas son estériles y yo no...he tenido varios hijos..." (161–62) [Sterile? Well, now you can see why I'm not offended when some people call me "mule," so long as it's only on account of my being stubborn, obstinate. That quality is all I have in common with mules...I've had several children] (161). Juárez takes great pride in having fathered a bountiful offspring while Maximilian, the product of a culture where procreation means the survival of power and privilege, is unable to have posterity.

If at first blush it seems odd classify Juárez as a foreigner given his canonical status in Mexican historiography, then it might seem equally strange to think of Maximilian as a foreigner, both in Europe and in Mexico. He was a prince of the most powerful empire in the world, raised amid royalty, privileged with education and experience, and yet his biographers almost unanimously portray him as a man who does not fit. He was second in the line of succession to the Austro-Hungarian Empire but showed a patent disinterest in governing. He aspired to glory but lacked the wherewithal to obtain it. He received a military education and rose quickly in the naval ranks but liberally pardoned dangerous opposition generals. He held imperial power but came off to his subjects as a nice, unexceptional man. This good-natured bonhomie contrasts with the austere demeanor of his older brother, Franz Joseph, who presided over the collapse of the Austro-Hungarian Empire, was a career military man, and ran the empire like an ongoing military campaign. By contrast, many portraits of Maximilian reveal him to be a tall, blond, moderately handsome man. Van Oostenrijk painted portraits of Maximilian as a young admiral and emphasized his blue eyes, clear complexion, and flat rosy cheeks, while Winterhalter depicted the newly crowned emperor in military dress with imperial robes. These external features, coupled with his royal lineage and presumably conservative political ideas, are precisely what made him the ideal candidate for the Mexican throne. What conservatives did not realize, however, was that his distaste for administration and his closeted liberal aspirations contradicted this idealized image. Maximilian was much too interested in botany, etymology, history, poetry, and ceremony to be bothered with the practicalities of government. Maximilian made frequent trips to the countryside to collect butterflies, leaving governmental affairs in the hands of his more politically savvy spouse. He would have had a much more fulfilling—not to mention longer-lasting—career as an eccentric humanities professor than he did as an emperor. But he was ambitious enough to desire a throne, and enough of a potential threat to Franz Joseph's line of succession, that the European powers agreed that he should be offered the Mexican empire. As a result, when the Mexican delegation led by Gutiérrez Estrada came to Miramar in 1864, Maximilian graciously accepted their offer.

Within the novel's conscientious depiction of the inner workings of empire, the presentation of Maximilian is a major concern because *Noticias del imperio* "takes account of the psychological and ideological factors that may have influenced Maximilian, and it delves into the complex and contradictory character of a historical figure who could be considered the victim of circumstances that he was ultimately unable to control and who, on the other hand, was undeniably the architect of his own tragic destiny" (Fiddian 110). Del Paso portrays Maximilian as a well-intentioned, hapless romantic with long-standing liberal inclinations whose education in the seat of Austrian power does little to mitigate his love of the arts and his fascination with the natural world. Maximilian does not fit in the empire. Beloved by the commoners of Trieste, he is considered a buffoon by royalty. Del Paso writes that, during the royal couple's trip to Rome to receive the papal blessing for their endeavor, one witness reports that the French surrounded them with adulators "porque sabían que no encontrarían a otro bobo que aceptara la corona de México" (253) [because they knew they wouldn't soon find another simpleton who would accept the crown of Mexico] (260). Maximilian's political alienation in Europe was compounded by his ideological alienation in Mexico. Mexican elites in the nineteenth century had their gaze constantly turned toward Europe, so it is of little surprise that they called for a foreign prince to occupy the Mexican throne. Where Juárez was ostracized for his racial otherness, Maximilian was desired for his. However, his foreignness derived from his politics. The Mexican monarchists wanted a strong, Catholic prince; instead, they got a weak, unproved governor with a penchant for liberal reforms—frequently referred to as *juarismo* without Juárez—that included the universal recognition of all religions and continued restrictions on the Catholic Church's privileges. His liberalism, unknown to conservatives like Gutierrez Estrada and Archbishop Labastida when the invitation was extended in 1862, dashed the hopes of his most valuable supporters. The closer Maximilian moved toward becoming Mexican, the less support he received from conservatives precisely because they did not want a Mexican monarch. Both in Europe and in Mexico, then, Maximilian found himself outcast and unable to fit in.

Del Paso portrays both characters, regardless of birthplace, skin color, political ideology, or religious orientation, as foreigners to Mexican culture. Neither one finds a place within the highly restrictive cultural paradigm of the imagined community. What follows hereafter is a discussion of how both Maximilian and Juárez work against the limitations imposed upon them by society in order to construct a new, authentically Mexican identity through cross-dressing. Cross-dressing is a form of mimicry that, according to Bhabha, exposes the artificiality of symbolic power by placing the repetition of colonial cultural codes at odds with the incomplete assimilation of them, which, by virtue of its very imperfectness, mocks them. This of course follows upon his earlier formulation of pedagogical narratives and dissonant performance that I discussed in the last chapter in that mimicry allows for the emergence of a colonial subject whose very difference from the norms he attempts to model conjures up the fissures that expose the limitation within authoritative discourse ("Of Mimicry" 127). Bhabha's model functions well when considering the cultural transformations that occur when Indian interpreters partially adopt the speech, mannerisms, and cultural values of their English rulers, that is to say, when the colonized subject mimics the behaviors of the master. But it is also worth thinking about the process of mimicry when the colonial master decides to go native. If mimicry is the ambivalent assimilation of cultural codes and behaviors—ambivalent because it is never complete—then we can argue that both characters' mimicry of Mexican culture exposes the fragility of nationalist identity discourse. For the purpose of this analysis, then, I will argue that Benito Juárez and Maximilian of Austria were both cultural transvestites.

Transvestite Performances of Identity

In her pioneering book, *Vested Interests* (1992), Marjorie Garber argued that transvestism constitutes a category crisis that calls attention to cultural dissonances that interrupt the seamless historical narratives that guide Western society. The transvestite figure highlights, through pastiche, parody, and overdetermination the cultural models of identification that should exist within the ideal society. By undermining these narratives, Garber argues, transvestism opens a space for restructuring common conceptions of culture because it becomes "the disruptive element that intervenes, not just a category crisis of male and female, but the crisis of category itself" (17). It is significant that Garber points out that the male / female dichotomy is only one aspect of this greater question of categories because, read more broadly, transvestism embraces a broad range of cultural phenomena that includes race, nationality, socioeconomics, and culture in addition to gender.

Notwithstanding the broad definition that Garber offers, recent studies on transvestism in Latin America typically deal with sexuality more than with the process of cross-dressing. Ben Sifuentes-Jauregui, in his study *Transvestism, Masculinity and Latin American Literature* (2002), defines transvestism as "a performance of gender" but does clarify that the relationship between transvestism and sexual performance is a difficult one: "there is so little known about transvestism as a sexual act because it evades prescribed sexual roles and our imaginary fails to capture the sexual moment with or between transvestites" (2–3). For this reason, he prefers to maintain that transvestism is a performance of gender, or in other words, a performance of traditional categories lumped together under broad banners like femininity and masculinity. Robert McKee Irwin, author of *Mexican Masculinities* (2003), frames his discussion of gendered literary history by referencing Eduardo Castrejón's 1906 novel, *Los 41*, which recounts the police raid on a transvestite ball in 1901. He notes that men dressed as women, dancing with other men threatened the rigid notions of masculinity and male sexuality in Mexican society. The ensuing analysis of major works of Mexican literature highlight shifting constructions of masculinity and nation, as well as the contradictions that emerge in nationalist discourse on race, class, and sexuality. The gendered bent of Irwin's thesis however only demonstrates that transvestism, as a social practice, is strictly associated with sexuality. Likewise, in *Modernity and the Nation in Mexican Representations of Masculinity* (2007), Héctor Domínguez Ruvalcaba proposes that "it is imprecise to call transvestism a sexuality; it is rather a kind of eroticism consummated within an exterior's limits" (34). This tendency toward narrowly restricting transvestism to gendered or sexualized uses only accounts for one aspect of cross-dressing practices.

If transvestism draws attention to the problematic construction of categories in general, then we can conceive of multiple ways, both literal and metaphoric, that a subject might cross-dress as a means of self-realization or self-fashioning. In addition to wearing the other's clothing, any performative behavior that constructs a new identity might, in this manner, be considered transvestism. This follows upon what Jossianna Arroyo terms "cultural transvestism," a process of cultural representation wherein the discourses of race, gender, and sexuality are manipulated to create a form of double identification between the colonized subject and the dominant culture. Through a series of mirror-like games that occur in transvestite texts, writing subjects annul fixed subjectivities by symbolically subordinating themselves to otherness in order to fabricate new identities (20). Arroyo's definition is useful for this discussion of Juárez and Maximilian because Del Paso portrays them as participating in a process of identification that requires them to subordinate their otherness in order to adopt a new culture. Judith Butler's oft-cited formulation that gender, above and beyond any biologically determined characteristic, is constructed through the performance of significant social acts resonates with this discussion of cultural transvestism in that cultural cross-dressers are performing—through mimicry, mimesis, simulacra, costuming, and the adoption of foreign modes of being—a wide variety of socially constructed identity markers for the purpose of establishing their own identity. Just as "gender cannot be understood as a *role* which either expresses or disguises an interior 'self', whether that 'self' is conceived as sexed or not" (528), national identity is not reducible to essentialisms. Citizenry and patriotism are matters of choice and performance. In *Noticias del imperio*, both Maximilian and Juárez adopt culturally significant behaviors designed to help them become Mexican. Notably clothing plays an important role in this transformation but it is not, as I have suggested, the only transvestism present.

In the three studies I mentioned, the critics pay attention to the transformative role that cross-dressing plays in the expression of an internal gendered self that has been arbitrarily restricted by the cultural norms of a predominantly heteronormative society. Sifuentes-Jauregui underscores the emergence of a buried essential identity when he proposes that, for the outsider, the transvestite wears the clothing of another in order to represent, replace, or supplant the other while, for the transvestite, cross-dressing is "an act of self- realization" because it "inaugurates an epistemological shift that locates defines, performs, and erases the fundamental dichotomy" that separates self and other (4). The transvestite subject paradoxically represents, realizes, and recreates the self through the use of another's clothing. In this regard, at its core transvestism is, to use Sylvia Molloy's term, a matter of posing. "Posing," she writes, "makes evident the elusiveness of all constructions of identity, their fundamentally performative nature" because it questions supposedly fixed categories and resorts to exploiting public display as a form of self-advertising or self-fashioning ("Posing" 147). Not surprisingly, Molloy is speaking directly to the matter of posing vis-à-vis representations of homosexuality, specifically in the case of Oscar Wilde and the Irish poet's two trials that were followed closely by Latin American authors. She argues that posing increasingly "problematizes gender, its formulations and its divisions: it subverts categories, questions reproductive models, proposes new models of identification based on recognition of desire more than on cultural pacts, and offers (plays at) new sexual identities" (147). She finds this particularly germane to the Latin American context, because cases of homosexual posing must be considered "in relation to hypervirile constructions of nationhood" such as those described by Irwin, Domínguez Ruvalcaba, and Sifuentes-Jáuregui.

This transformational discourse rooted in cross-dressing surfaces in the opening pages when Carlota, sequestered in Bouchout Castle in 1927, hyperbolically imagines herself changed from a European beauty with white skin into a brown virgin by the gifts brought by a messenger from Mexico. Del Paso plays with the historical Carlota's obsession with cleanliness and her maniacal paranoia about liquids to transform hot chocolate into something that purifies her, that draws out a truer hidden personality. In the repeated references to her whiteness that metonymically tie to her European descent and her foreignness, Carlota sheds the trappings of the imperial past to adopt a new identity, that of the brown, indigenous virgin. Problematically, she continues to think in imperial terms when she crowns herself the Queen of America, suggesting that she assumes the form of the American subject without actually becoming one. Later in the novel, she applies the same transformational logic posthumously to her husband when she plots to incorporate the body parts former Mexican heroes into Maximilian's corpse.

> Y porque también es potestad de los sueños hacer que el espejo sea una rosa y una nube, y la nube una montaña, la montaña un espejo, puedo, si quiero, pegarte con engrudo las barbas negras de Sedano y Leguizano y cortarte una pierna y ponerte la de Santa Anna, y cortarte la otra y coserte la de Uraga, y vestirte con la piel oscura de Juárez y cambalachear tus ojos azules por los ojos de Zapata para que nadie, nunca más, se atreva a decir que tú, Fernando Maximiliano Juárez, no eres; que tú, Fernando Emiliano Uraga y Leguizano no fuiste; que tú, Maximiliano López de Santa Anna, no serás nunca un mexicano hasta la médula de tus huesos. (117)
>
> [Because it's also the privilege of dreams to turn a mirror into a rose, and then a cloud, and then the cloud into a mountain, or the mountain into a mirror; if I want I can glue Sedano y Leguizano's dark beard on your face, or amputate your leg and replace it with Santa Anna's, or chop off the other leg and put Uraga's in its place, or dress you in Juárez's dark skin, or trade your blue eyes for Zapata's, so that no one will ever dare say that you, Ferdinand Maximilian Juárez, are not, or that you, Ferdinand Emiliano Uraga y Leguizano, were not, or that you, Maximilian López de Santa Anna, will never be a tried-and-true Mexican.] (113–14)

There is no coincidence that she begins this process of stitching by suggesting that it can only be performed through the power of dreams. Oftentimes critics reading the novel point to this dreamlike state as the ground where novelistic discourse allows for imaginative recreations of the historical record (Bradu 1988; Castañón 1988; Clark and González 1994; Earle 1996). Let us accept this proposition, but let us also move beyond the simple recognition of the author's theorization of the balances between history and fiction toward a more productive reading of what that means for Carlota's transformational logic. The ultimate goal of this stitching becomes more readily apparent with a literal translation of the last line of this quote. Where the English translation renders the phrase with a colloquial idiom that suggests fidelity and authenticity as a member of the imagined community, Del Paso's original text indicates a subcutaneous change, one that goes all the way down to the "the marrow of your bones." Aided by her surreal imagination, the delusional Carlota hopes to help Maximilian achieve the Mexicanness that he desired by literally incorporating Mexico (or Mexicans) into the remains of her husband's corpse.

Carlota's transformation of her husband is the most radical form of cross-dressing in the novel because she intends to cobble together his new identity through a grotesquely literal form of transvestism. Nevertheless, her fantasy underscores the central role played by costuming in the performative aspect of identity and power and this point surfaces repeatedly, albeit in less Gothic ways, throughout the novel as characters attempt to dress the part they want to occupy. Juárez carefully cultivated an image of republican austerity that has endured in photographs and murals to the present. It is significant that every portrait we have of Benito Juárez is effectively the same: a stone-faced Juarez, dressed in a black frockcoat and starched white shirt, stares impassively into the camera. Sometimes the angle of his body varies slightly, sometimes he wears the presidential sash, but the effect is the same: he projects an image of sobriety and authority. Del Paso ties Juárez's traditional black frockcoat and cane to his liberal readings of Rousseau and Constant and his burgeoning sense of class awareness. His clothing is significant: he does not wear the traditional Zapotec garb. This gesture suggests that, for Juárez, his Zapotec identity needed to be subordinate to the image appropriate for chief executive. Ironically, this decision provides a sharp contrast for the neoindigenist cultural movements and political campaigns across Latin America that have brought Zapatistas in Chiapas or Evo Morales in Bolivia to the forefront of world attention. In both of these movements, indigenism is considered the hallmark of authenticity. In nineteenth-century Mexico, however, Indian blood was considered a strike against a candidate, and Juárez appears to have done everything possible to erase the atavistic problem of his Zapotec heritage. Thus, when Juárez makes the transition from servant to president, Del Paso symbolizes that transition in terms of clothing. He observes that for others—most notably white conservatives—"Benito Juárez se había puesto una patria como se puso el levitón negro: como algo ajeno que no le pertenecía, aunque con una diferencia: si la levita estaba cortada a la medida, la patria, en cambio, le quedaba grande y se le desparramaba mucho más allá de Oaxaca y mucho más allá también del siglo en el que había nacido" (30) [Benito Juárez had taken on the entire nation in the same way that he would always don his black frockcoat: as though it was something that didn't fit him. Moreover, while his coat may have been tailored for him, the nation had not. It was simply too big for him—it spread out far beyond Oaxaca, and also far beyond the century in which he'd been born] (18–19). Though Juárez's overcoat was tailored to fit his body, the nation hangs limply on him because it is too large and unwieldy. It does not fit him and, for white conservatives, he does not appear to fit it.

Maximilian is likewise concerned with the necessity of dressing the part. In a series of well-documented articles on symbolic appropriation and spectacle in the process of nation building, Robert Duncan has argued that Maximilian launched a massive public relations campaign to win over the hearts and minds of his new subjects. The emperor understood "the role that symbolism could play in building new avenues of unity and legitimacy. The creation of an imperial court, the dispensing of awards and medals, and the urban renewal of Mexico City would enhance imperial prestige and foster political cohesion" ("Political" 37). Maximilian's first independence ceremony illustrates his attention to politically sensitive procedural details. In an attempt to curry favor with the liberal faction, Maximilian broke with the tradition of presiding over the celebrations from the national palace in Mexico City and travelled to Dolores Hidalgo, where the first *grito* was issued by Miguel Hidalgo in 1810. Notably, he did so dressed in a traditional *charro* outfit. Additionally, great emphasis was placed on the incorporation of autonomous symbols into courtly insignia, and where possible, Maximilian left as many Mexican symbols unchanged as possible. On the whole, I find Duncan's observations to be an insightful analysis of the pragmatic uses of symbolism in nation-building because he does not simply limit his comments to the Second Empire, but views the matter of statecraft and nation-building through this optic. He suggests, for example, that Maximilian's propagandistic failure was not a product of his ineptitude but of the historical circumstance: "With ardent nationalism still years in the future, Maximilian's appeal to the nation at large ultimately would prove a chimera. Not until later, when technology finally challenged Mexico's physical barriers and class alliances surpassed local allegiances, would national symbols and rituals be truly effective tools in legitimation" (66). He adds that the nation-building projects of the Díaz regime manipulated symbols and rituals in much the same way as had Maximilian, "but this time with greater success. Ironically, the defeat of the empire—and its conservative backers—provided future republican governments with a pantheon of heroes and myths (such as General Ignacio

Zaragoza and Cinco de Mayo) upon which to build their own legitimacy. Even the empire's lasting urban reform, the Paseo de la Reforma, became, as William Beezley states, 'an avenue symbolic of Porfirian centralization'" (66). Del Paso makes the appropriation of symbols and ritual the backbone of his argument in favor of Maximilian's Mexicanization. He portrays Maximilian as one who adopts a foreign identity through transvestite performance in order to become Mexican. In other words, his transvestism is not simply a Machiavellian manipulation of symbol and ritual for the sake of statecraft. Rather, he hopes that outward demonstrations of Mexicanness will somehow alter or reveal his core essence.

The matter of symbolic capital in establishing legitimacy weighed on Maximilian's mind, possibly more than any other concern, as he crossed the Atlantic Ocean in the *Novara* (Duncan, "Political" 38). During those months at sea, he drafted a lengthy procedural manual for the new court called the *Reglamento para el Servicio y Ceremonial de la Corte*, a document intended to establish the courtly procedures that would lend an air of nobility to the Mexican court that was patently lacking in the Parisian court of Napoleon III. The *Ceremonial* is a 330-page treatise that revels in minutia and demonstrates more explicitly than any other document the royal couple's obsession with outward appearances. The first section, the *Reglamento para el Servicio*, outlines the different offices of the imperial court while the second, the *Ceremonial*, lays out the order of operations for all major rituals and ceremonies. In addition to written instructions, Maximilian included twenty-two processional maps for the Imperial Palace, the Cathedral, and the Zócalo. Critics of the Second Empire, guided by the Benjaminian maxim that there "is no document of civilization which is not at the same time a document of barbarism" (256), look upon the *Ceremonial* as a fatuous exercise in frivolity masking the avarice of the French court and a second-rate Habsburg prince. Kristine Ibsen, in her insightfully interdisciplinary treatment of Maximilian, has argued that the *Ceremonial* constitutes yet further evidence that the royal couple was more interested in transforming Mexico into something that it was not than in establishing a governmental structure based on the traditions of the nation. For her the irony inherent in Maximilian's deployment of Mexican symbols is locatable in his attempt to "convince his subjects of his Mexicanness" while simultaneously "attempting to imitate Napoleon III by imposing all the rituals and ceremonies of empire" on his newly founded court ("Dissecting" 718). I want to offer a different reading of the *Ceremonial*, however, because, contrary to what Ibsen and others have seen as the frivolous imposition of foreign courtly procedure on a flimsily constructed faux empire, the *Ceremonial*—both as a historical document and as a major component of Del Paso's novel—demonstrates that Maximilian was seriously thinking about how to bring honor to the Mexican Empire by elevating it above the Parisian court and about how to do so in a way that combined the best of traditional decorum and of Mexico's historical tradition. This gesture, however, can only be recognized if we, as readers, are able to meet Del Paso's challenge to honestly regard the Habsburg's attempt to become Mexican.

While the assertion that Maximilian attempted to imitate Napoleon III is not historically accurate—Maximilian thought very little of his French benefactor and in numerous communiqués labeled him, his wife, and his entire court as nothing less than parvenus—it is clear that even Del Paso, who wants to portray the emperor in the best light possible, cannot help but cast a wry glance on Maximilian's decision to redact a long manual of courtly procedure instead of brushing up on Mexican politics. He hyperbolically notes that, during the long voyage across the Atlantic, Maximilian did not simply dream about the *Ceremonial* but dictated and handwrote a five-hundred-page document with baroque instructions for seemingly trivial matters, such as the 132 clauses dedicated to the presentation of a cardinal's skullcap. Truth be told, no such clause actually exists in the *Ceremonial*, but the exaggeration serves both to poke fun at Maximilian and to underscore his enthusiasm for establishing order in his new empire. As they cross the ocean, Carlota seems more inclined toward a Mexican theme for court dress while her husband, at least at this early point, still prefers the dictates of European fashion. Referring to the garb to be worn by the court advisors, Maximilian wonders, "¿Con casaca azul claro, como en Francia? Nononó, diría Carlota: verde. *All right*, verde, pero verde claro, y con botones dorados, gruesos, en el pecho. Ajá, y con el águila labrada en ellos. *Das ist Recht*" (251) [in light-blue frockcoats, of course, like in France? Nonono, Carlota would say; in green. All right, green, but light-green with thick gold buttons on the breast. Splendid; and the eagle engraved upon them. *Das ist recht*] (257). Carlota favors incorporating Mexican iconography into all facets of imperial life: "Y como concesión a Carlota: ¿te gustaría, *cara*, querida Charlotte, que la levita del medio uniforme de la Guardia Palatina, la Guardia de la Emperatriz, sea de paño verde dragón, y las vueltas de las mangas sean encarnadas para que así, con los guantes de ante blanco tenga los tres colores de la bandera imperial mexicana?" (252) [And as a concession to Carlota he said: "Would you like *cara*, dear Carlota, for the regular frockcoats of the Palace Guard, the Empress's Guard, to be of dragon-green cloth with blood-red endsleeves so that, with the white buckskin gloves, they will have all three colors of the imperial Mexican flag on them?"] (259). Again, these hyperbolic descriptions of courtly dress do not, in fact, exist in the *Ceremonial*. There are only two specific references to colors in the text: one deals with the colors that are considered appropriate for the periods of mourning and the other instructs that national colors be used of fireworks at major national celebrations. But, within the transformational transvestite logic of the novel they make sense. Since these plans are made before Maximilian arrives in Mexico, we might reason that his preference for European fashion is a sort of bet-hedging against the future. Once he crosses the Atlantic, however, Maximilian becomes an ardent defender of all things Mexican.

Beyond clothing, Maximilian attempted to Mexicanize his court by infusing every aspect of decoration and procedure with authentic Mexican symbols. Again, Duncan offers a useful insight into Maximilian's use of symbols when describing the new imperial coat of arms which downplayed Maximilian's ancestral connection to Spain through his Habsburg blood by combining recognizable symbols from the Aztec past, the period of national independence and the present ("Political" 52). In the novel, Maximilian dictates that the butter served at imperial tables should bear the imperial symbols and that the ice swans adorning the tables should be traded for ice eagles devouring ice snakes. These attempts to create a Mexican court seem shallow if one withholds the sympathetic gesture that Del Paso begs of his readers, but they represent an honest attempt to adjust their concept of courtly procedure by integrating as many elements of the newly adopted kingdom as possible. However, it should not surprise us that Maximilian attempted to impose European manners upon his court because his cultural paradigm—one that had been fostered at the feet of the great European monarchs—reflected the imperial belief that decorum, ritual, ceremony, and propriety endowed a court, and by extension a nation, with honor. From this perspective, then, the way to increase Mexico's standing and respectability among the nations of the world to whom he appealed for recognition was to bring culture and refinement to the country. This of course is a strictly colonial perspective infused with numberless prejudices about cultural worth, racial superiority, and political efficiency. However, both in Maximilian's personal writings as well as in Del Paso's portrayal in the novel, this sense of improvement through orderly court proceedings plays an important role in the development of his character. In this regard, Maximilian is not only dressing himself up as part of a process of becoming Mexican, but also dressing up the Mexican court in order to accord it more glory, laud, and honor than what was to be found in the European courts. The *Ceremonial* represents the triumph of form over substance. Given their upbringing, cultural paradigm, and family tradition, Maximilian and Carlota did their best and this is what Del Paso asks us recognize.

What "We" Talk about When "We" Talk about Language

Arroyo locates the practice of cultural transvestism within the spheres of race, gender, and sexuality and how these elements manifest themselves in writing. There is a final component that I would like to explore in this chapter, namely, what we might define as linguistic cross-dressing. In constructing new national identities for these characters, Del Paso pays special attention to scenes that involve the acquisition or use of Spanish as a marker of belonging. Language has long been identified with the construction and performance of national identities: Nebrija's grammar in 1492 and Webster's essays on the necessity of codifying American English in the late eighteenth century stand as prime examples. Recent studies on first- and second-generation immigrant populations across the world attest to central role that language acquisition plays both in retaining original and forging new national identities (Vedder 2005; Chiang and Yang 2008; Dong 2009; Mleczko 2010; Ariza 2010). Bill Ashcroft, responding to Whorf and Sapir's respective assertions that language not only functions as a device for reporting experience but also for defining a speaker's experience, asserts that language is coextensive with reality and consequently inextricable from one's perception of reality because language exists "neither before the fact nor after the fact but *in the fact*" (302). Likewise, W. H. New has observed that, whether "the impulse is to attach oneself to Great Traditions or to sever oneself from them, there is a general agreement...about one thing: language affirms a set of social patterns and reflects a particular cultural taste" (303). It is not coincidental then that, engrained within many of the chapters discussed up to this point, Del Paso frequently mentions the process of language learning that Juárez and Maximilian undergo in order to construct their new Mexican personae. If we accept Wittgenstein's assertion that everyday language "is a part of the human organism and is no less complicated than it" (35), then understanding the logic behind language becomes central to identity construction. Wittgenstein further argues that the limits of language become the limits of perception in that thought, logic, and reason are mediated by language (115) and thus our perception of the world around us is determined by the language we use to describe and interpret phenomenological input (Rao 296–97). When reading *Noticias del imperio*, then, we should ask what is the particular logic that governs their drive to learn Spanish. How does it help them integrate into a society that excludes them or, in the best of cases, relegates them to peripheral positions of citizenry?

For Juárez, language learning functions as a door that leads to educational and professional opportunities. Historian Ralph Roeder informs us that when Juárez arrived in Oaxaca in December 1818, Spanish was a foreign language to him. His adoptive godfather, a devout bookbinder and Franciscan layman by the name of Antonio Salanueva, sponsored the young Juárez in obtaining an education as a pathway to life in the ministry. During his early education at the Royal School, however, he did not learn Spanish grammar so that, when he entered the seminary in 1821, he was still primarily a monolingual indigenous speaker. But within four years he mastered Latin grammar and, in 1825, received excellent marks on his statutory examinations (12). Juárez did not complete his ecclesiastical training, however, and instead chose to study law at the Oaxaca University. Later he taught Spanish grammar in Oaxacan schools. Both the ecclesiastic and legal professions are all firmly grounded in the grammatical and syntactical structures of language. For the priest, language is tied up with the notion of God. Through language, man communicates with God in prayer and the priest brings Christ to the altar in the form of the sacramental host. The language of religion has, for ages, been used as a form of power: those who speak the liturgical language wield the power of God on earth. Likewise, the legal system functions as a grammar of conduct for society. Obeying the laws of social grammar assures good standing in the community while stepping outside the grammatical boundaries of the law incurs penalties. And, for the grammarian, the disposition of words and syntactical elements differentiates the learned from the illiterate. It should be of little surprise then, that Del Paso's depiction of Juárez would be significantly grounded on his mastery of Spanish.

Juárez's control of language affords him the opportunity to establish dominance over others. He does not simply speak the language as an initiate, but masters it and takes pride in correcting those who, like his secretary, fumble with the grammar of their native language. Flipping through his white secretary's report, Juárez notices a misused preposition and corrects it: "Es nutrida *con*, y no nutrida *de*, Señor Secretario....Que debió usted poner 'nutrida *con* una teología' y no 'nutrida *de* una teología'" (149) ["It's nourished *with*, not *by*, Mr. Secretary...you should have written 'nourished *with* her readings', not 'nourished *by* her readings'"] (147). The secretary jokes that the president is always correcting his Spanish, and a humorless Juárez fires back: "Lo tuve que aprender muy bien, Señor Secretario, con todas las reglas, porque no era mi lengua materna. Y lo aprendí con sangre" (149) [I had to learn it very well, Mr. Secretary, with all its rules, because it wasn't my native tongue. And I learned it with blood and tears] (147). Juárez's correction serves two purposes. First, it obeys his sense of legality, feelings of propriety, and love of order. Second, it allows him to establish his superiority over his white secretary. His explanation of his language acquisition is racially charged: Spanish is not his native language, and he was forced, not only to learn it, but also to perfect it through relentless study. These corrective moments sting the secretary's pride. When discussing the romantic liaisons of the European royal families, the secretary comments, "Se me ocurre, de broma, que todos esos adulterios y hijos... e hijos bastardos que han tenido los monarcas europeos, les sirven para limpiar la sangre de vez en cuando" (155) ["I don't know, Don Benito. It occurs to me—it's a joke of course—that all this adultery, all these children... and these bastard children from the European monarchs, that it's all served the purpose of cleaning up their blood once and for all"] (154). In Spanish, the copulative "y" becomes an "e" when the succeeding word begins with an "i" sound, as in the case of "hijos." It is not uncommon, however, in colloquial speech, to hear the copulative "y", as evidenced by the secretary's statement. But the secretary rushes to correct himself before Juárez can do it for him. Thus, we can see that language for Juárez is intimately tied up with identity and power. He forsakes his native language to enter into the hostile world of the racially different other. When Juárez masters Spanish, it becomes a point of honor for him, and one that he is willing to display whenever the opportunity to use language to dominate others or fend off his own insecurities about race and position arise.

Where Juárez uses language as an instrument of power and order, Maximilian uses language to root himself into a linguistic community. It is clear that Maximilian already considered himself Mexican by the time his first Independence celebration came around. During his first year in country, Maximilian presided over the independence celebrations and delivered an address in Spanish in order to "foster loyalty to the empire by engendering a spirit of community" and, Duncan suggests, by promoting a bond with listeners that "ideally would divert attention away from his foreign birth" ("Embracing" 264). During his speech to the citizens of Dolores Hidalgo, he observed that the "seed that Hidalgo planted in this place, must now develop victoriously, and by associating independence with union, the future is *ours... we* must not forget the days of *our* independence nor the men that conquered it for *us*. Mexicans, Long live independence and the memory of its heroes!" (qtd. in Duncan, "Political" 56–57, emphasis added). Moreover, the Mexican imperial court's official language was Spanish and all documents relating to governmental business were written in Spanish. The government "even published decrees in Spanish and Náhuatl, the Aztec language, giving it new political and cultural status. In translation, Maximilian formally became 'Huei tlatoani' (the Great Speaker)" (53). Both Duncan and Del Paso report that the royal couple spoke only Spanish at the dinner table, often providing summaries for visitors who did not understand (61). Early in the novel Maximilian is swimming in a sea of languages. He prides himself on speaking German, French, Italian, English, and Spanish, in addition to some Hungarian and Polish; later he plans to pick up Náhuatl, Maya, Quechua, and Guaraní. Consider the following linguistic jambalaya: "Bravo, sírvame un poco, *per favore*, y venga acá. *Übrigens…à propos*: dígame dónde se hacen en México los buenos vinos…*Et toi, Charlotte, un peu de vin?*" (95) [Bravo, serve some more, *per favore*, and come here. *Übrigens…à propos*: tell me, where are the good wines bottled in Mexico…*Et toi, Charlotte, un peu de vin?*] (90). If language is a national marker, this hodgepodge of Spanish, Italian, German, and French seems to characterize a man who has yet to put down his roots in one linguistic code or, we might argue, one country. When he accepts the Mexican throne, however, he associates himself and his empire exclusively with the language of his new home. Maximilian insists that all communiqués to the French court be written, not in French, but in Spanish. Oddly enough, Carlota, who attempts to integrate Mexican symbols into court procedures, never seems to incorporate the language completely, according to Del Paso. Discussing the translations of *Noticias del imperio* into French, he commented that, while reviewing the French translation of the novel, "me conmovió mucho el monólogo de Carlota, porque si Carlota hubiera dicho eso, lo hubiera dicho en francés, que era su idioma natal" [Carlota's monologue deeply moved me because if Carlota has said those things, she would have said them in French, which was her native language] (Quemain).

This attention to linguistic detail is underlined in the section entitled "El archiduque en Miramar" [The Archduke at Miramare], the novel's first section involving the imperial couple. The emperor- and empress-to-be are meeting with a Mexican professor at their home in Italy for what will ultimately be a very uncomfortable, and revealing, Spanish lesson. While the scene ostensibly deals with language, questions of colonialism, nationality, and identity quickly come to the forefront. The section opens with foreboding portent: "El Archiduque Maximiliano se encontraba esa tarde tranquila y soleada en el Salón de las Gaviotas del Castillo de Miramar en las cercanías de Trieste, la vieja ciudad en cuya catedral, San Justo, fueron sepultados tantos pretendientes carlistas que nunca realizaron su sueño de ser reyes de España" (93) [That tranquil and sunny afternoon, Archduke Maximilian was in the Salon of the Seagulls in Miramare Castle, in the vicinity of Trieste, the old city in whose cathedral, San Giusto—the burial site of so many Carlist pretenders who never realized their dream of becoming rulers of Spain—were entombed] (88). Reminding readers that *Noticias del imperio* is a self-proclaimed tragedy, the evocation of failed aspirants to the throne of Spain alludes to Maximilian's lofty, yet ultimately unfulfilled, aspirations to successfully establish his empire in Mexico. Maximilian stands next to a map of Mexico and a small lacquer box with colored pins; each one represents the mineral or natural wealth of his newfound empire. Selecting a silver-plated pin and sticking it in the state of Sonora, he says:

"Sonora. Si *Herr* profesor me permite una broma, yo puedo...¿yo podría ....?"
    "Sí, Su Alteza: yo podría, tú podrías, él podría..."
    "Yo podría—continuó el Archiduque—decir que el nombre de Sonora es sonoro por la mucha plata que tiene y que la quiere Napoleón. Pero no se la daremos. Es para nosotros los mexicanos." (93)
    [Sonora. If Herr Professor allows me to tell a joke, I can...I could... hmmm?"
    "Yes, Your Highness: I could, you could, he could..."
    "I could say," the Archduke continued, "that the name Sonora is sonorous because of the great amounts of silver its land contains, silver that Napoleon wants. But we won't give it to him. It's for us Mexicans."] (88)

First, the word in question is *poder*. In Spanish, it is both a verb and a noun. As a verb, *poder* means "to be able" and speaks to the individual's capacity to accomplish something. In this sense, it is generally transitive and requires another verb that then indicates one's ability to perform that specific task. As a noun, *poder* literally means "power". Since the ability to assume power and establish control in a foreign land is at stake, the verb *poder* will surface numerous times in the chapter. Second, the verb tenses used indicate a difference of opinions. Maximilian stammers between the present indicative and the conditional, as if vacillating between an affirmation of his calling to establish an empire in the Americas and his doubts about his capacity to govern. The professor provides the correct conjugation of the verb in conditional tense, expressing the potentiality if not the realization of their ability, and will later use the conditional in a manner than infuriates Carlota. Third, the matter of financial gains enters the discussion. There is no doubt that France, aside from grand designs to restore monarchy to Spain's former colonies, viewed the intervention as a worthy investment. Historical ironies being what they are, the intervention in Mexico would eventually lead to the dissolution of the Second French Empire and the transfer of European power from France to Germany. Maximilian's determination to preserve Sonora's silver for Mexico seems at odds with the financial arrangements he made with the French Crown prior to embarking, which entailed bankrolling the entire French expedition in Mexico, including a standing occupational army for seven to eight years, with funds drawn from the Mexican treasury.

Sonora's silver will end up in the French treasury indirectly. And fourth, there is Maximilian's observation that Sonora's silver is for "nosotros los mexicanos" [we Mexicans]. In *Noticias del imperio* there are inclusive and exclusive uses for the word "nosotros." Inclusion in Spanish is generally indicated by tonal (such as emphasis on the antecedent) or physical cues (like hand gestures). Here inclusion is tonal: Maximilian includes himself in the category he designates as Mexican. The first phrase we hear from Maximilian, then, underlines his belief that he is Mexican.

The professor uses this phrase differently, more restrictively. He counsels the empress to adopt the Castilian spelling of her name by dropping a "t", assuring her that it would be "un gesto que nosotros, los mexicanos, apreciaríamos mucho" (94) [a gesture that we Mexicans would appreciate very much] (89). Using the same phrase that Maximilian had previously employed to include himself within the category of Mexican, the professor now distinguishes himself as a Mexican from his employers. There is also a concomitant assertion of cultural values, codes, and mores of which the royal couple is unaware. The professor takes his Mexican identity as license to break courtly codes of behavior and to opine on the political situation in Mexico. The professor further distinguishes himself when he notes that few Mexicans will notice the change in spelling. He says: "habrá muchos de *mis* compatriotas que no se darán cuenta...porque por desgracia, son muy pocos los que *sabemos* leer y escribir, ah?" (94–95, emphasis added) [the change will go unnoticed by most of my compatriots...Unfortunately, we Mexicans who can read and writer are very few, hmmm?] (89–90). The distinction here is double: he first separates himself and Mexicans from the couple using the possessive pronoun *mis*, and then from the illiterate Mexicans, identifying with the first person plural *sabemos* those who know how to read and write. *Herr* professor's subtle exclusions of the royal couple get him in trouble a couple of times. When discussing foreign control of domestic industries, *Herr* professor finds himself in a sticky situation: "Con esto quiero decir que las riquezas de México están en manos de... Sus Altezas no se ofenderán: ustedes no serán extranjeros en mi país. Ya no lo son...las riquezas, decía, están en manos de extranjeros" (96) ["What I mean to say is that Mexico's wealth is in the hands of...Your Highnesses will not be offended as you will not be foreigners in my country? You no longer can be considered foreigners...The wealth, as I was saying, is in the hands of foreigner" [91]. The professor backpedals. He has touched on a delicate subject and speaks before thinking. He points out that foreign intervention in domestic financial affairs, again marking the strong contrast between "extranjeros" [foreigners] and "mi país" [my country]. He recognizes that the individuals he is addressing are foreigners who want to incorporate themselves into a new nation. His first attempt assures

them that they will not—note the future tense's expression of possibility—
be foreigners. His statement suggests that they are not now, but have the
potential to become Mexican. He then corrects himself. They already are
Mexicans, and should not consider themselves foreigners at all. Clearly, the
first Mexican that Maximilian encounters in the novel does not buy into
his assimilation. Neither does he seem to accept a future integration.

To Live and Die like a Mexican

When Maximilian stepped off the *Novara* onto Mexican soil in 1864, he
was greeted with a letter from Juárez informing him that he was not welcome in Mexico and that history would judge them both for their actions.
To this point, I have proposed reading Del Paso's portrayal of Juárez and
Maximilian as a metaphor for a more inclusive way of reading Mexican
history. In both cases, a sense of foreignness led to exclusion that could
only be overcome through performing and mastering essential cultural
elements of society at large. That said, Del Paso is not only concerned
about the way these men lived but also about how they died because it
is Maximilian's death which Del Paso considers "una muerte noble y
oportuna,...una muerte valiente y, en resumidas cuentas,...una muerte
muy mexicana" (643) [a noble and meaningful death,...a courageous
death....a very Mexican death] (678). A consideration of how *Noticias del
imperio* portrays the last moments of each man's life is in order, then, to
round out this discussion. Robin Fiddian notes that the emphasis given
to the Maximilian, Juárez, and Carlota at the end of the novel "underscores the equality of status of the three main protagonists" and "indicates
the importance of their interrelationships within the narrative design and
overall structure of meaning elaborated in *Noticias del imperio*" (108). If, as
I have argued, Del Paso has humanized Juárez to exalt Maximilian, then
the question that will remain at the end will be whether the evidence presented in favor of Maximilian's integration will be sufficient for granting
him his citizenship.

The chapter that narrates both Juárez and Maximilian's death, "La
historia nos juzgará" [History Will Be Our Judge], recalls the president's
self-confident warning about the judgment of history, and the first section, "¿Qué vamos a hacer contigo, Benito?" [What Are We Going to Do
with You, Benito?] fittingly places Juárez on trial for his own actions. The
narration takes place in two states of consciousness: one in which Juárez
is stretched out on his deathbed where a doctor applies boiling water
to the president's bare chest to stimulate his failing heart, and another

in which Juárez imagines himself lying on a table used formerly by the Inquisition and later destined to hold Maximilian's corpse. To one side of the chapel, conservative voices appear, materializing as men in black hoods clutching torches and, to the other, a chorus of liberal adulators dressed in white hoods and holding irises eulogize him as savior of the nation, benevolent father figure, and honest citizen. Directly in front of him hangs Maximilian's naked corpse, which had been suspended from the cupola of the San Andrés chapel to drain his bodily fluids for embalming. As the trial advances, Juárez comes to the conclusion that history's judgment means nothing to the dead because history "sólo podía importarle a los vivos mientras estuvieran eso: *vivos*, se dijo el Licenciado Benito Juárez y recordó que cuando de joven se iniciaba en las lecturas de los enciclope-distas y los autores del siglo de las luces, le había llamado la atención de una frase de Voltaire: 'La historia es una broma', decía el francés, 'que los vivos le jugamos a los muertos...'" (622–23) [could only be of interest to those who were alive, while they were alive, President Benito Juárez told himself, and he remembered when as a young man he was beginning to read the Encyclopedists and the authors of the Age of Enlightenment, one of Voltaire's phrases that caught his attention: "History is a joke," the Frenchman said, "that we the living play on the dead."] (655). The most condemning argument against Juárez, however, is not his abolition of ecclesiastical privilege or the secularization of the Mexican government, but rather, his order to execute Maximilian. The emperor's body hanging from the dome overhead takes on the image of Abel and accuses Juárez "de haber matado a su hermano" (623) [of killing his brother] (656).

In *The Concept of the Political* (1976), Carl Schmitt postulates a political theory based on the antithesis between friends and enemies. Simply put, friends are those with whom we feel an affinity and with whom we can work toward the accomplishment of a given goal while enemies are those who work against us. The formulation seems simplistic but by moving beyond nationalist constructions based on race, creed, or political affilia-tion, Schmitt's dichotomy permits a more thorough understanding of the liquid boundaries that determine coalitions. It is in this manner that Usigli can argue that Maximilian and Juárez were collaborators for the greater destiny of Mexico and Del Paso can suggest through the third person nar-rator who presides over the president's deathbed that Juárez had not simply killed a political competitor but a brother. Before judgment is rendered, however, Juárez stops caring because "sabía que dijera lo que dijera, hiciera lo que hiciera, serían otros, y no él, los que iban a decidir qué había sido, de toda su vida—y de su muerte también—lo más hermoso, lo más desagrad-able, lo más digno de recordarse, lo más vergonzoso. Pero no él: él ya no tendría vela en ese entierro" (626) [he knew that no matter what he said, no matter what he did, it would be others who would choose and decide what he had been all his life—and in death as well—the most beautiful things, the ugliest things, the most important, the most shameful. But not he himself; he had no more to say in the matter] (659). Juárez's judgment scene is important because it establishes the basis on which Del Paso can argue for Maximilian's *mexicanidad*. History only matters to the living. The dead, according to Juárez, have no conscience of history's judgment. Though Del Paso's phantasmagorical portrayal of Juárez's agony evinces a certain dramatic flair, the truth is that his death was a fairly anticlimactic ending for the paladin of Mexican democracy and equality, a point that both Del Paso and Usigli make in their respective writings.

By contrast, Maximilian's death was a sensationally melodramatic event and Del Paso plays this up by making the episodes that occurred before, during, and after Maximilian's execution on the Cerro de las Campanas the central point of the novel's denouement because, remembering his justification for Mexicanizing Maximilian, it is his noble, brave, and ultimately Mexican death that earns him a place within the pantheon of national heroes and villains. A number of plans had been made to help the emperor escape and Del Paso goes into great detail about them. Though he originally agreed to flee, Maximilian recants with a spirit of resignation before the inevitability of death. When his supporters and fellow prisoners contrive a plan to sneak him out of town dressed as a commoner, the emperor responds that under no circumstance will he escape "como tantas veces lo han hecho Juárez y Santa Anna" (518) [like Juárez and Santa Anna have done so many times] (543). In his melodramatic patriotic fervor, Maximilian refuses to run as others before him had: Hidalgo was on his way north when the insurrection failed; Iturbide had exiled himself in England; Juárez was sent to New Orleans, and during the French intervention—though he never left the country—spent most of his time near the border; and Santa Anna had resided in Nassau, Cuba, and Venezuela, waiting for opportunities to return to power. Later, Francisco I. Madero went to San Antonio, Texas, under threat from Porfirio Díaz only to return in 1911 and send Díaz scurrying off to Europe on the *Ypiranga*. Foreign exile has been the common currency of Mexican politics. Maximilian's refusal to leave breaks with this tradition, and this is exactly what Del Paso hopes to emphasize: that Maximilian was more willing to face consequences than were other great Mexicans who, for better or worse, have been clearly identified as Mexicans because of the geography of their birth. The novel portrays this bravery with an ironic tinge of messianism, noting that it was common to associate executions with Christological images of Calvary (586). The commonality of this practice notwithstanding, Del Paso portrays Maximilian valiantly scrambling out of a mired carriage to ascend the Cerro de las Campanas alone. General Mejía requests to change sides because "no deseaba estar a su izquierda, porque a la izquierda del Salvador había estado, en Gólgota, el mal ladrón" (586) [he did not wish to be at his left because at Golgotha the damned thief had been on the left of the Savior] (614). Then the author adds his own comment about Maximilian's death: "Y bueno: cristiana fue, sí, la muerte de Maximiliano en Querétaro, y noble sin duda no sólo por su increíble entereza y su maravilloso estado de ánimo que no flaqueó en ningún momento, sino también por sus últimas palabras que, aunque ingenuas e incluso chabacanas, contribuyeron a dignificar sus últimos momentos" (586) [And yes, Maximilian's death was indeed Christian, and noble no doubt not only because of his incredible integrity and noble state of mind that did not waiver at any time, but also because of his final words, albeit naïve and maybe even simple, served to dignify his last moments] (615). These last words come in the form of a brief speech and, while different versions of what was said circulate, the majority of the chroniclers coincide that the emperor stated his willingness to die for the independence of Mexico, that he hoped that his blood would put an end to the misfortunes of his adopted nation, and that he concluded with a rousing "¡Viva México!"

To this point Del Paso has followed the traditional historical narrative closely, coating the conservative portrayals of Maximilian's messianism with an ironic varnish, as Corral Peña would put it. However, while history records that Maximilian's dying words on the Cerro de las Campanas were "¡Viva México!", Del Paso points out that "los testigos oculares del drama del cerro afirman que después de la descarga, y cuando yacía en el suelo, el Emperador dijo en español: '¡Hombre, hombre!'" (586) [eyewitnesses of the drama on the hill state that, after the discharge, as he lay on the ground, the Emperor said, '¡Hombre, hombre!'] (615). The significance of these final words only becomes clear when we remember that Del Paso prepares readers for this back in the language lesson. The Mexican professor explains to the royal couple that "Hombre es además, en español, y *tal vez sobre todo en México*, una exclamación que puede expresar muchas cosas distintas, según la ocasión: sorpresa, alegría, incredulidad" (98, emphasis added) [And, as you know, *hombre* in Spanish—*perhaps mostly in Mexico*—can express many different things, suitable to the occasion: surprise, happiness, incredulity] (93). It has been argued that Maximilian thought he would escape martyrdom; that his subjects would not murder him. It is possible that his last words—a phrase he had been taught expressed surprise and disbelief—indicate a degree of acculturation that has been previously overlooked. His patriotic declaration may be written off as dramatic flair, but what accounts for this final expression? Why does this Austrian prince bid farewell to life in Spanish and not in German? When Del Paso offers

Maximilian's heroic death as evidence of his Mexicanization, he is not only referring to the well-known "¡Viva México!" but also—and maybe, more importantly—to the "¡Hombre, hombre!"

The novel's treatment of Maximilian's death deserves one more consideration because the emperor's last words are not the final word in the novel. After a lengthy description of how Maximilian's remains were handled and mishandled in preparation for their return to Austria and the argument in favor of posthumously recognizing Maximilian's citizenship, Del Paso complicates what looked like an airtight case by changing the dynamics of the heroic, Mexican death. In a gesture that appears to cater to Maximilian's sense of decorum, ceremony, and pomp, Del Paso writes an elaborate "Ceremonial para el fusilamiento de un Emperador" [Ceremonial for the Execution of an Emperor] modeled after the *Ceremonial* that includes detailed instructions for an execution that would allow Maximilian to die with dignity. Ibsen suggests that this alternate ending can be read as a disarticulation of Del Paso's inclusionary thesis, that Del Paso does not really want to Mexicanize Maximilian but rather mock his pretensions. Yet I cannot help but return to Del Paso's plea for an act of historical sympathy. Yes, the procedure that he writes is exaggerated, minutely detailed, and at some point laughable. But so was Maximilian. If we take Del Paso at his word then we must accept at least the possibility that he is willing to help the emperor along. Ultimately, Del Paso leaves the matter of Maximilian's *mexicanidad* to readers. *Noticias del imperio* represents an exposition of evidence and an invitation to accept them. But Del Paso does not impose a decision upon his readers, nor can he. Rather he allows them to choose. To that end, it doesn't matter what Juárez thought of Maximilian or what Maximilian thought of himself: it is what Mexicans think of these two men posthumously that matters. And successive generations will reevaluate that decision over and over again. The next chapter considers another historical judgment, one that has been levied against the man many consider to be the exemplar of nineteenth-century militarism: Antonio López de Santa Anna. Unlike the recuperative effort of *Noticias del imperio*, however, Enrique Serna's *El seductor de la patria* does not extend an olive branch to the past, but rather uses it as an instructive tool.

Chapter 3

The Voices of the Master in Enrique Serna's *El seductor de la patria*

Enrique Serna is one of Mexico's most popular contemporary writers with seven novels, two short-story collections, and a handful of chronicles and essays to his credit. This popularity is due, in part, to his quick wit, sharp tongue, and low tolerance for hypocrisy. Indeed, everything he writes exhibits a sardonic, almost cruel, criticism of pretense, pomposity, and incompetence that is only attenuated by his use of humor, sense of timing and delivery, and painstaking characterization. Novels like *Uno soñaba que era rey* (1989), *Señorita México* (1993) and *El miedo a los animales* (1995) are populated with social marginalia that oftentimes inhabit sordid underworlds, corrupt centers of power, and impoverished peripheries. There are no privileged spaces and no one is off-limits for Serna. And this is especially true of writers and the literary establishment. In his detective novel, *El miedo a los animales*, the narrator is a failed journalist who goes undercover to investigate the seedy world of law enforcement corruption and becomes the lackey for a police chief who dabbles in drugs, protection rackets, extortion, and the occasional murder. The assassination of a political journalist draws him back to his roots and he seeks to uncover the culprit only to discover that the poets and novelists whom he had previously admired are as corrupt, false, and decadent as the police. At the heart of Serna's cultural criticism lies the conviction that failure is not an extraordinary condition generated by extreme moments of crisis, but rather a fact of everyday life in Mexico.

Serna made his first foray into historical fiction in 1999 with the publication of *El seductor de la patria*. It was hailed as a landmark historical novel at its publication, and the following year it received the Premio

Mazatlán for literature. It continues to be Serna's most recognized work and has fared well in subsequent editions. The novel's enduring commercial success may be directly attributed to its subject: *El seductor de la patria* reconstructs the life of Antonio López de Santa Anna, nineteenth-century Mexico's most representative caudillo. Mixing historical research with narrative imagination, Serna creates a novelized autobiography that challenges readers' perceptions of archive, textuality, authorship, and historiography. The framing narrative occurs between 1874 and 1876, when the former president is allowed to return home from the last of his three exiles. Impoverished, incontinent, disillusioned, and on the verge of senile dementia, Santa Anna spends his final years dictating his memoirs in a series of letters to his estranged son, Manuel, with the help of a former aide-de-camp, Manuel María Giménez. The letters take readers chronologically through the most important events of his checkered military career, including his early years as an officer in the royalist army, his conversion to the insurgent cause, his participation in nearly every major military campaign of the new republic, his embarrassing defeat at San Jacinto, his exiles, his returns, and his poverty and illness during the last months of his life. These letters frame the story of Mexico's formational period, to paraphrase Lucas Alamán, as the history of Santa Anna's revolutions. The switch from the contemporary settings of his earlier work to the historical past appeared to mark a transition for Serna. However, as Vicente Francisco Torres correctly points out, Santa Anna embodies all of the base passions, self-interest, and human frailties that have been the common stock of Serna's work regardless of temporal setting (134). This is to say, then, that Serna invites readers to reflect upon the past in terms of the present by portraying Santa Anna as a self-interested, self-aggrandizing, and self-indulgent charlatan who loves the idea of nation but hates the individual components, not simply because he wants to add one more criticism to an already ample bibliography, but because, encoded within this seemingly straightforward fictionalized biography the author offers a complex portrait of late-twentieth-century politics and a lesson about the way history can be altered for ideological and personal reasons.

Ever the consummate performer who heralded his victories with *Te Deum*s and staged celebrations, Santa Anna appears to take center stage in the novel. But the real story of *El seductor de la patria* happens behind the curtains, where three characters vie for interpretive control over the general's autobiography. Manuel asserts his right as Santa Anna's son to tell the whole story, warts and all, regardless of the damage it might do to his father's already tarnished reputation. Giménez, the ever-faithful assistant, wrestles to ensure a sanitized version of history that will stand as a monument of patriotism for future generations. And an extradiegetic historian, identified only as the compiler, also participates in the contest by supplementing the story that plays out in the letters with a series of documents that correct, modify, or refute Santa Anna's claims. This struggle for control of the historical narrative becomes the main thread that connects the story. By fictionalizing the process of writing an autobiography and weaving into that process a number of voices that compete for authorial control, Serna provides a manual for reading and interpreting historical and political narratives. Readers must sort through biases and concealed intentions in order to sift out historical truth. In this manner, the title of this chapter alludes to *The Voice of the Masters* (1985), Roberto González Echevarría's seminal work on the relationship between language and power in Latin American dictator novels. For González Echevarría it is impossible to think about novels like Alejo Carpentier's *El recurso del método* (1974), Miguel Ángel Asturias's *El señor presidente* (1946), or Augusto Roa Bastos's *Yo el supremo* (1974) without considering the ways in which caudillos have used language to sustain themselves in power, and how novelists have attempted to question the bases of that power through their fiction. In each of these novels the dictator, strongman, or political boss in turn exercises power proximally by his imposing physical presence and distally by the transmission of his words. González Echevarría focuses primarily on the Latin American writer's fascination with the powerful, as in Sarmiento's problematic adoration of Rosas, and only refers to a fictional scribe when discussing Dr. Francia's plump assistant Policarpo in *Yo el supremo*. But he never moves beyond thinking about scribes in the singular. I have pluralized the word "voices" because the voice of the master is not a monophonic melody but a polyphonic chorus made of the scribes who, united behind a central figurehead, have pushed the historical narrative of nation forward.

In this chapter, I examine how *El seductor de la patria* problematizes the relationship between language and power, by introducing multiple voices into what has previously been theorized as a straightforward equivalency. The chapter begins with a consideration of Serna's treatment of failure and its relationship to the declining years of the PRI and the ascension of conservative politics in Mexico. Within his concept of historical continuity, Serna frames Santa Anna as the predecessor of PRI and its paladin, Carlos Salinas de Gortari, in order to chastise Mexico's lagging civil society for not taking a more proactive role in breaking the atavistic cycle of authoritarianism. The second section examines how Santa Anna is presented in the novel. Because it purports to be a fictionalized autobiography, a genre as notorious for what it does not say as for what it does, I argue that while *El seductor de la patria* presents us a man who considers himself a father of the nation, it does so ironically. Despite what Santa Anna may have thought about being self-made, he was utterly dependent upon scribes throughout his life and a significant section of this chapter deals with these secondary intellectual figures. Attachés, aides-de-camp, historians, and novelists have all written in the general's name and, therefore, have entered into his service. The most important scribe for our purposes though, is Giménez, who hijacks the narrative early on and continually works to suppress anything in the biography that might tarnish Santa Anna's reputation. He is not interested in historical truth; he is interested in historical legacies. But it becomes clear that Serna is uncomfortable with the scribe's power in the novel and responds by inserting documents into the narration that contradict Giménez's story. To conclude, I will briefly consider the compiler's involvement and the some of the ethical issues that surface in Serna's treatment of archival material.

The General and His
Twentieth-Century Avatars

In 1994, Serna was contracted by one of the major television networks to write the script for a lengthy historical docudrama on Santa Anna's life. He had written roughly 30 episodes of material before the *telenovela* was canceled. Serna later recalled that "el tema me apasionaba y seguí estudiándola por mi cuenta, con miras a escribir una novela histórica sin las ataduras de los géneros comerciales" [the subject fascinated me and I kept studying it on my own, thinking that I could write a historical novel without all the restrictions of commercial genres] (*Seductor* 9). This comment reveals two points worth mentioning at this juncture. First, it evinces a similarity with the context of Ibargüengoitia's independence history, which I dealt with in the first chapter. Once free from the requirements of a commissioned work—for Ibargüengoitia, a government-sponsored project, and for Serna, a commercial endeavor funded by a major network—both authors felt at liberty to work according to the dictates of their personal interpretations of history. It is should be noted, however, that the nature of their projects differs significantly. Ibargüengoitia was dealing with the venerable founder of the modern nation, while Serna was portraying its greatest villain, which suggests that the freedom to which Serna refers was less ideological than it was structural. Even so the parallel speaks to a system of controls that accompanies commissioned work. Second, and maybe more importantly, the time frame suggests that during the five-year process of research and writing Serna was able to view his character through the historian's optics as influenced by the decline of the PRI and the rise of conservatism in Mexico. In this regard, the novel's treatment of Santa Anna, one of the premier conservative generals of the nineteenth century, can be read as an analogue for late-twentieth-century Mexico because this tension between the past and the present becomes the heart of the novel (Sotelo Gutiérrez 64).

That Serna began his research for the novel in 1994, a watershed year for political turning points in Mexico, may indicate some of the contextual events that influenced his historical representation of Santa Anna. On January 1, NAFTA, a comprehensive economic compact aimed at improving commerce between Canada, the United States, and Mexico, took effect and became the centerpiece of neoliberal economic policy in Mexico. In response, the Ejército Zapatista de Liberación Nacional (EZLN) launched a military offensive against governmental forces in the southern state of Chiapas. Led by Subcomandante Marcos, a university-educated mestizo, the insurgents fought under the banner of indigenous rights and rejected neoliberalism. NAFTA had been the brainchild of Carlos Salinas de Gortari, a Harvard-educated economist who won the presidency in 1988 in what many regard to be one of the most fraudulent elections in modern Mexican history. When Salinas took office, inflation was at an all-time high and, during his six-year administration, he managed to reduce inflation and usher in a new period of economic prosperity for the nation. With that prosperity, however, came an increase in governmental spending on projects designed to boost the PRI's popularity in an election year that drastically raised the national debt and eventually laid the foundation for the December 1994 economic crash. Though the collapse technically occurred during the first months of Ernesto Zedillo's administration, there is little doubt that its causes lie in Salinas's neoliberal economic reforms and mismanagement of national finances. Two more events marred the year: in March, Luis Donaldo Colosio, the PRI candidate favored to win the presidency in the 1994 elections, was assassinated and, in September, José Francisco Ruiz Massieu, the secretary general of the PRI and the next majority leader for the Chamber of Deputies, was gunned down, presumably on orders from Raúl Salinas de Gortari, the president's ne'er-do-well brother. We might summarize all of this by suggesting that 1994, above and beyond anything else, marked the proverbial beginning of the end for the PRI. Economically and politically it was collapsing under the weight of its corruption and fiscal irresponsibility, and six years later its 71-year hold on the presidency and the congress would come to an end.

The parallels between the Santa Anna's omnipresence throughout the nineteenth century and the monopoly of the PRI, which had proclaimed itself the political manifestation of the nation since the Mexican Revolution, were not lost on Serna. In a conference address, Serna made these parallels explicit when he shared his opinion that the general "se había convertido en la patria personificada y, cuando eso sucede, cuando la gente realmente cree que una persona encarna la patria, los defectos y debilidades del personaje pasan a formar parte de la idiosincrasia pop-ular, lo cual puede generar una cultura de autodesprecio" [had become the nation personified and, when that happens, when the people believe that one person embodies the nation, that person's defects and weaknesses become part of the popular idiosyncrasy that can later generate a culture of self-loathing] ("Santa Anna" 181). Serna hoped that the single-party's legacy would fade and that in the future no party would have the opportu-nity to monopolize the nation again. Nevertheless, "lo sucedido durante la época de Salinas de Gortari me hace pensar que por desgracia, la herencia de Santa Anna sigue muy viva en México" [what happened during the Salinas de Gortari years makes me think that, unfortunately, the legacy of Santa Anna is alive and well in Mexico today] ("Santa Anna" 181). Here Serna mentions three noteworthy points. First, he points out the danger of equating the nation with one individual. This is the essential thesis of Thomas Carlyle's historiographic theory, that heroic men metonymically define the nation at given moments, and that their actions summarize the collective will of the people. While a number of Mexican academic histo-rians like Luis Villoro, Josefina Zoraida Vásquez, and Mauricio Tenorio have moved away from this personalist style of documenting the nation, some popular public historians, most notably Enrique Krauze, continue to frame the nation as a cavalcade of great deeds performs by great men. Historical novelists are, to varying degrees, guilty of this same tendency, though possibly more so in the last five years, thanks in large part to the mass consumption of all things historical that has accompanied the bicen-tennial celebrations of independence in 2010, a point that I will discuss more fully at the conclusion of this book. This conflation of the personal and the national leads to a second point for consideration: that the flaws and weaknesses of the caudillo become integrated into a collective pool of cultural idiosyncrasies. Serna further argues that these idiosyncrasies have led to a sense of low national self-esteem and he constructs a series of con-tinuities that link nineteenth-century Mexicans, who felt they deserved no better than Santa Anna, to twentieth-century contemporaries who are unable to break their dependence on the single-party system. The final point Serna makes is that this sense of waning self-esteem had rendered Mexican voters incapable of believing in the availability of other political options, and therefore ready to accept whatever the PRI offered them.

The novel's publication in 1999 also coincides with the ascension of Mexico's political Right. Shortly after *El seductor de la patria* appeared in bookstores, the PAN candidate for the presidency, Vicente Fox Quesada, broke the PRI's 71-year monopoly on national elections by beating the PRI's Francisco Labastida Ochoa by 7 percentage points. Fox, a Harvard-educated businessman and the former president of Coca-Cola's Latin American division, served as a congressional representative from his home state of Guanajuato and later as governor of that state. After a hard-fought campaign during the general elections, Fox assumed the presidency with one of the highest popularity rates on record. During his administration, he pushed the conservative agenda of his party: increased economic ties with the United States, free market economy, privatization, reduced taxes, and continued neoliberal reforms. While the party is outwardly non-confessional, Fox was open about his Catholic faith and worked to increase ties with the Vatican by allowing church doctrines to influence his policies on abortion and birth control. Notwithstanding the promise of political reform, Fox's six-year term proved overwhelmingly lackluster. Opinion polls and newspaper editorials revealed that for the average Mexican, Fox's election did little to improve overall feelings about democracy. The Latinobarómetro opinion poll in 2004 suggested that 67 percent of Mexicans did not care if a nondemocratic government took control of the country, as long as it could solve the nation's economic problems. When asked about overall satisfaction with democracy, an underwhelming 17 percent of the population reported being "very satisfied" or "fairly satisfied," while another 17 percent believed that that democracy was the only suitable government for their country. In like manner, editorial columnists evinced a similar sense of dissatisfaction. Jorge Volpi, novelist turned political commentator, cast a dour forecast for the outcome of the 2006 elections when he wrote that, no matter who won, Mexico would lose (21–22). The elections of 2006 stood to open the door for more democratic reforms. Neither of the two front-runners belonged to the PRI and, what was more, Andrés Manuel López Obrador, the third-party candidate from the populist Left, led in the polls with just weeks left until election day. The Fox administration, however, attempted to tip the scales in favor of its candidate, Felipe Calderón Hinojosa, by raising legal barriers to exclude López Obrador from the elections. While serving as the mayor of Mexico City, López Obrador expropriated private land to build an access road to a private hospital on the outskirts of town. The landowner sued for damages and the Chamber of Deputies lifted López Obrador's constitutional immunity from prosecution. Because Mexican law strips political rights from persons with pending legal actions, López Obrador would be excluded from the participating in the elections as a candidate. Eventually the charges were dismissed, but only after damage to the PAN's reputation had embittered an already contentious presidential race. Mexican novelist Carmen Boullosa denounced Fox's questionable legal footwork in her

New York Times editorial on April 19, 2005, and worried that Mexico's fragile democracy hung by a thread (21). This notion of a "fragile democracy" or a "new democracy" was echoed by other editorialists both in the United States and Mexico and indicated two salient points: first, the general consensus was that Mexico had entered the democratic world only recently with the election of Fox; second, that democracy was threatened by the very individual who ushered it in as he reacted to opposition with authoritarian tactics like those of the PRI in years past.

Serna hyperbolically deforms Santa Anna for the purpose of criticizing this sense of disenfranchisement and the lack of civil society in Mexico. As Raquel Mosqueda argues in an excellent study of the grotesque, Serna does this by purposefully distorting the real-world referents of his literary creations in order to hyperbolically dissect society and expose its corruption and deceitfulness (137). It is true that Serna portrays Santa Anna "as the unpatriotic traitor who deliberately lost the Mexican-American War in exchange for a fistful of dollars and who sold parts of Mexico to its northern neighbor in the Treaty of La Mesilla or Gadsden Purchase, shameless pocketing profits, his signature becoming associated with corrupt and damaging transactions" (Fowler, *Santa Anna* xix), but he does so ironically and in a manner that calls attention to a critical subtext. J. Hillis Miller's defined irony as a style that simultaneously reveals and conceals truths about social reality from readers (qtd. in Villanueva Benavides x). The dark humor, irony, and parody that Serna employs are, as it was with Ibargüengoitia, critical tools used to unmask the pretension and disqualify inchoate justifications for inaction. And so what strikes me as a particularly compelling aspect of the novel is Serna's willingness to criticize his countrymen through Santa Anna. In fact, he reserves some of his most biting witticisms for the Mexican people who placed the dictator and his twentieth-century avatars in power indefinitely. In the first letter to his son, Santa Anna wonders why no one stopped him if he had been such a wicked leader: "Si de verdad arrojé a México en un precipicio ¿por qué nadie me lo impidió? Gran parte de mis culpas le corresponde a la sociedad que ahora me crucifica. ¿O acaso goberné un país de niños?" [If I truly threw Mexico over a cliff, why didn't anyone stop me? The majority of my shortcomings belong to the society that now crucifies me. Or, perchance, did I govern a country of children?] (18). He reasons that Mexico is, by nature, a country of extremes and that he is simply a victim of the bad publicity, because "si bien tuve entonces defectos y a veces defraudé las esperanzas del pueblo, yo solo no pude hacerle un daño tan grande" [if it is true that I have defects and have occasionally betrayed the people's hope, it is also true that I could not have caused so much damage by myself] (18). This vacillation between extremes becomes one of the general's major complaints throughout the novel. "Lo que más detesto de México es la doblez de su gente," [What I hate so much about Mexico is the deceitfulness of its people,] he writes later. "Aquí todo es disimulo, golpes bajos, falsos amigos que murmuran a tus espaldas y a la menor oportunidad te venden por treinta monedas" [Everything here is trickery, cheap shots, false friends who murmur behind your back and, at the least provocation, betray you for thirty pieces of silver] (112). Mexicans prefer to cheer for victims and martyrs, and though no one recognizes it, "tengo por seguro que si [Hidalgo] hubiera tomado el poder no le llamarían ahora padre de la patria, ni su retrato estaría colgado en el despacho presidencial, pues en este país se premia a las víctimas y se castiga a los vencedores" [I am sure that if Hidalgo had taken power they would not now call him the father of the nation, nor would his portrait be hanging in the presidential office, because in this country they reward the victims and punish the victors] (36).

How Serna makes these comments, though, is the key. He surreptitiously weaves them into the novel's presentation of so-called common knowledge about Santa Anna's biography. Will Fowler said it well: "Any legend about him can only be described as a black one" and the idea that all of Mexico's misfortunes can be traced back to him goes unquestioned (*Santa Anna* xix). The matter of common knowledge here is important because collective memory is filled with ideas "that are not labeled, that seem to have no identifiable source, that cannot be referred to in a footnote, and, most important of all, that cannot be connected to how and with what stuff we have furnished our minds" (Runia, "Spots" 312). Runia recapitulates the central argument of a newspaper article written by Dutch writer Karl van het Reve who suggested that slander was the most effective way of implanting negative ideas in collective memory. It is a tricky process, however, because the slanderer must avoid the appearance of settling a grudge with someone. When we have an axe to grind, listeners can cognitively distinguish bias and discard the criticism as a personal vendetta. Van het Reve suggested two ways of covering one's tracks. First, claim that the damaging things being said are common knowledge. The supposed act of just passing on public information removes the speaking subject from the critical limelight and adds credibility through collectivity. Second, instead of compiling every bit of damning evidence imaginable and presenting a logical argument proving the person's guilt beyond a reasonable doubt, slander should be woven into conversations about something else. Covering one's tracks allows for slanderous information to bypass the brain's natural cognitive filters because "only what has not been experienced explicitly and consciously, what has not happened to the subject as an experience, can become a component of the *mémoire involontaire*" (Benjamin 160–61).

El seductor de la patria can be as read as one more literary slander of Santa Anna that paints an unflattering portrait of the prototypical Mexican villain. Indeed, this is how Fowler interpreted the novel's portrayal of Santa Anna's misogyny and corruption in the opening pages of his most recent biography, *Santa Anna of Mexico* (2007). Likewise, literary critic Juan José Reyes understood this to be the novel's intent when he opened his review in *Letras Libres* with the observation that Serna chalks up Mexico's nineteenth-century tragedies to Santa Anna never feeling that his father approved of him (90). Nevertheless, the slander leveled against Santa Anna allows an equally potent indictment of the nation to bypass the cognitive functions of dissociation. In other words, Serna plays upon what readers already "know" about Santa Anna in order to criticize them indirectly. This is how, I believe, Serna can pepper his novel with caustic sound bites like, "En este país la prosperidad es incompatible con el respeto a la ley. La mitad de los mexicanos ha nacido para robar a la otra mitad, y esa mitad robada, cuando abre los ojos y reflexiona, se dedica a robar a la mitad que le robó" [In this country, prosperity is incompatible with the rule of law. Half of all Mexicans were born to steal from the other half, and that half that has been robbed, when they open their eyes and think about, set about robbing those who stole from them] (296) and still have a bestseller on his hands.

Dismantling a Father of the Nation

For reasons that will become clear shortly, Santa Anna is not the most important character in the novel despite *El seductor de la patria* being a fictionalized autobiography. As I mentioned at the outset of this chapter, the novel's main conflict takes place between the scribes who surrounded the general and contributed to the creation of his history and mythos. In order to discuss these scribes, we must first undertake a brief examination of the ways in which the general's story is presented in novel. For all of his faults, Antonio López de Santa Anna was still an exceptional man: a gifted orator, a master organizer, a fearless warrior, and a talented politician. His strengths are often overlooked in deference to his weaknesses for he was at the same time an opportunist, a gambler, a manipulator, and a womanizer. Historians cast Santa Anna in different lights, and none of them are particularly endearing. Lesley Bird Simpson sees him as a vainglorious egotist whose crowning moment of self-aggrandizement was the burial of his now-famous leg. Oakah L. Jones casts Santa Anna as the brilliant, perennial gambler, willing to risk everything in exchange for the big payoff. More recently, historian Will Fowler has striven to shed a positive light on Santa Anna's political career when he argues in *Mexico in the Age of Proposals* (1998) and *Santa Anna of Mexico* that Santa Anna was not a calculating traitor, but rather, a man with honest desires for the welfare of his nation. Nevertheless, most Mexicans and North Americans have decided that Santa Anna was a villain worthy of reprobation, a point exemplified by nearly every any cinematic or historical account of the Battle of the Alamo in the United States or Jorge Volpi and Denise Dresser's decision to strikethrough Santa Anna's name every time it appears in *México: Lo que todo ciudadano (no) quisiera saber de su patria*. Serna shares this vision, and while his bias becomes evident in the novel, he distorts the general's image for very specific reasons.

El seductor de la patria is constructed from a series of letters where the general reflects upon the major events of his military and political career. The novel opens as Santa Anna writes to his estranged son, Manuel, to commission a biography that incorporates his flaws into the narration. "En las memorias de Nassau," [In the Nassau memoirs,] he writes, "recargué deliberadamente las tintas al hablar de mis virtudes, porque me proponía contrarrestar la propaganda del enemigo, pero en tu biografía quiero aparecer retratado de cuerpo entero, como el hombre temperamental y voluble que fui" [I deliberately played up my virtues because I wanted to contradict the propaganda of my enemies, but in your biography I want to be portrayed completely, as the temperamental and fickle man that I was] (19). Since he had already written one defense, Santa Anna sees no reason to do so again. In fact, he finds that taking another, more honest, approach might win more support. He counsels his son to display his humanity while highlighting his victories and achievements. Santa Anna begins with an account of his childhood: his combative relationship with his brother, his search for parental approval, his acquisition of bad habits on the docks of Veracruz, and his enlistment in the royalist army two months prior to Hidalgo's revolution. This period of his life is related in a picaresque mode, where Santa Anna occupies the role of an American Lazarillo de Tormes. His humanity comes to the fore and there is no attempt to suppress his youthful tantrums and excesses. He hopes that this frankness will endear readers to him and help them to overlook his political shortcomings. This redemptive aspect of Santa Anna's project fits Sylvia Molloy's definition of the autobiography as "a form of exposure that that begs for understanding, even more, for forgiveness" (*At Face Value* 6). Santa Anna does not appeal to his contemporaries, but rather to future generations in the hope that the course of historical events will somehow justify his actions.

Molloy points out that a frequent gesture in autobiographical writing is the tendency to fuse the writing subject's *petite histoire* with the broader national narrative. She notes, for example, that Sarmiento's *Recuerdos de provincia* (1850) pretends to be a documental history of Argentina that coincidentally begins with the author's birth nine months after the consummation of independence. The rhetorical implication was that he and the nation were conceived, born, and grew to maturity together. In this manner, Sarmiento, as the remembering subject of an autobiography, imagines himself to be the blank page upon which the history of Argentina is written (148). Santa Anna's autobiography, *Historia militar y política (1810–1874)*, written in St. Thomas during his last exile and published posthumously, displays this same tendency. It is also a testament to just how uncritical Santa Anna could be when describing his own military prowess, bravery, patriotism, and above all, his dedication to family. He portrays himself as the consummate patriot, statesman, and gentleman; he emphasizes his distaste for authoritarianism, his displeasure in the face of cowardice, and his refusal to allow his nation to bow before its enemies. The self-portrait Santa Anna paints is one of a god walking among bumbling, incompetent inferiors. His natural inclination toward self-aggrandizing rhetoric leads him to establish an analogous relationship between home and nation where he presides as a benevolent father figure. But this image is problematic because Santa Anna only rarely mentions his family in the text, and then, only when retiring to his estate after battles to enjoy home life and his garden in Voltairean fashion, or when his first wife dies. He notes that an appropriate time for mourning had to take place before marrying the young Dolores de Tosta, but forgets to mention that this period consisted of just thirty days.

Both in his autobiography and in the novel, Santa Anna attempts to portray himself as the loving husband and provident father in a gesture that suggests that his ability to govern his home enables him to govern the nation. Serna dismantles this image. Remembering Bakhtin's definition of heteroglossia—layers of conflicting voices in a text that create multiple contradictory readings—we should read *El seductor de la patria*'s version of family relationships as an ironic commentary on the general's conflation of home and country. When Santa Anna suggests that he has been a good husband and provided a good life for his first wife, the compiler—whom I will discuss in more detail a little later—interrupts that narrative line with apocryphal letters from Inés to her mother. In these letters, Inés describes the horrible conditions she has to endure at the hands of her spouse. From unsatisfying lovemaking to dealing with her husband's numerous extramarital affairs, Inés' patience and compassion are stretched to their utmost limits. Serna inserts jabs like this to counteract the seemingly oblivious statements the general makes. But that obliviousness should be read with a certain amount of critical malice. For starters, we should recognize that

Santa Anna is writing to his son, Manuel, about Manuel's mother. It stands to reason that he is not going to lay out the panorama of his marital infidelity to the son who would be his biographer. Furthermore, it would be unbecoming of a founding father to engage in such affairs and so he carefully avoids the topic so as to present a more amenable countenance to the nation that might someday read the work.

Part and parcel of the novel's deconstruction of this fatherly image resides in the dictator's concern with virility and paternity. The eponymous protagonist of Carlos Fuentes's *La muerte de Artemio Cruz* contemplates his flaccid penis while lying on his deathbed, and the aging Dominican dictator Rafael Trujillo's impotence impedes his sexual conquest at the end of Mario Vargas Llosas's *La fiesta del chivo* (2000). Samuel Manickam suggests that, by infusing "detailed parodic accounts of Santa Anna's amorous adventures into what is, after all, supposed to be an account of his military career, Serna brings the private sphere onto the public stage where his subject's lack of sexual prowess becomes a metaphor for his public actions. It turns out that Santa Anna was neither a great seducer of women nor of nations" (26). Moreover, Santa Anna is obsessed with being recognized as the progenitor of the new republic, but his imagination introduces a number of dissonant images that dismantle his masculine pretensions. As mentioned before, the general perceives the nation as his offspring. He writes that the "cuerpo de la patria está unido al mío por un cordón umbilical y no consentiré otra mutilación mientras me queden hombres y municiones" [body of the nation is bound to mine by an umbilical cord and I will not permit another mutilation as long as I have men and munitions] (333). In this strangely maternal metaphor—strange because the general is portrayed as a terrible chauvinist and one of the least likely individuals to attribute feminine imagery to his person—Santa Anna envisions the bond between nation and his body inextricably linked by a cord that has not been cut. Mexico is never really born but must remain utterly dependent upon him for nutrition, guidance, and protection. It is eternally engendered but never leaves the (his) womb. At another point, recognizing that his claims to fatherhood will most likely be usurped by Miguel Hidalgo, Santa Anna jockeys for title of obstetrician: "De tal suerte que si no fui padre de la Independencia, por lo menos me corresponde el título de partero" [If I was not the father of independence, at least I should be recognized as the midwife] (94). Again, the birth motif rings clear. In this case, Mexico is born, but only with the help of the provident Santa Anna. If Santa Anna is to be considered the, or even a, father of the nation, there is a sinister, incestuous side to his claim. Though he preserved the nation's liberty on occasion, he did so at the cost of extortion, forced conscription, unlawful taxation, despotic authoritarianism, violations of democratic principles, secret confederations with foreign nations, and schemes to obtain power. In Serna's novel, the scribe Giménez relates that "el general confesó entre sollozos que al perder la pierna se redujo el tamaño de su miembro viril y de ahí en adelante solo pudo cogerse a la patria" [the general confessed through his tears that when he lost his leg, his penis shrank and from that time forward he could only screw the nation] (274). The blatant sexuality of the term "coger" transforms the provident and just father into an incestuous pedophile. On his deathbed Santa Anna confesses to a disguised Giménez that he treated the nation "como si fuera una puta, le quité el pan y el sustento, me enriquecí con su miseria y con su dolor" [as if she were a whore, I took her bread and sustenance, I grew rich from her misery and pain] (503). In each of these scenes, the general's masculinity is questioned. He is connected to the nation by an umbilical cord, he is not the father but the midwife, and his inability to maintain an erection following the loss of his leg means that he can only force himself upon the nation that he treats like a whore.

The location of this final declaration, the deathbed, has been the obligatory start and endpoint for many of Latin America's dictator novels and is significant because it attests to the demonumentalizing effort of the genre. Dictatorial fiction typically offers an archetypal portrait of caudillos, as in *El recurso del método* and *El señor presidente*, or undertakes the biographical reconstruction of a specific individual, as in *Yo el supremo* and Gabriel García Márquez's *El general en su laberinto* (1989). The protagonists are universally masculine and military, and envision themselves as fathers of the nation. As patriarchal figures, the dictator-protagonist draws parallels between his life and the genesis of the nation. Concomitantly, there are explicit links between the caudillo's physical body and the national soil. However, that the story emanates from the deathbed only emphasizes the ephemeral and decrepit nature of the body. Alejo Carpentier's *El arpa y la sombra* (1979) begins with Pius IX desperately pushing through the beatification of Christopher Columbus before he succumbs to old age and infirmity. *El general en su laberinto* follows the exile of Simón Bolívar and his trek north to die in his homeland, with close attention to the liberator's pathological preoccupation with herbal remedies, baths, purgatives, cleanliness, and medicine. *La muerte de Artemio Cruz* narrates the last moments of the oil magnate's life and he ponders the decrepitude of his failing frame including his penis, incontinency, vision, and rotting innards. Illness infects his body as much as he, a pathogen for national ills, leeched the life and vigor from Mexico's burgeoning new society. In each of these cases, the authors draw parallels between body and the nations these men forged or destroyed. The emphasis on physical deterioration indicates a conscientious attempt to undermine the monolithic image of the virile masculine body from which the power of the authoritarian figure emanates. Serna's novel is set during the last two years of Santa Anna's life, when he has been reduced to poverty and illness. The general tells his son in an early letter that, while taking his daily walk through downtown area, his legs buckled and, unable to walk, he lay helplessly, receiving alms from passersby. Humiliated by the indignity of his situation, but attempting to maintain his final shred of dignity, he fights back his tears only to find that "en vez de lágrimas derramé calientes hilos de orina" [instead of tears I spilled warm streams of urine] (15). *El seductor de la patria* dismantles the virility, power, and authority of the dictator by depriving him of control over his body and his voice.

Giménez, the Hagiographic Scribe

Through carnivalesque displacement, *El seductor de la patria* decenters the figure of the dictator and instead focuses on the intellectuals upon whom the general depended as scribes. In the final chapter of *The Lettered City* (1984), Ángel Rama examines the symbiotic relationship that developed between Latin American strongmen and the intellectuals who surrounded and supported them both in the independence period and during the Mexican Revolution. "There was mutual admiration," he writes, "but also lingering mistrust, between the brutal, personalist military commander and the doctor of laws—the manipulator of language, writing, and most importantly, political ideology—and the tension between the two often became extreme" (123). Rama's point is clear: though illiterate caudillos have depended upon their scribes for promoting their political agendas, the relationship is tinged with conflict. Serna recognizes that the corpus of texts we traditionally attribute to Antonio López de Santa Anna is really the product of an army of scribes, who at one time or another wrote in Santa Anna's name. A careful examination of his personal correspondence, for example, reveals that the general used a number of scribes through-out his life, which means that the Santa Anna we read during the Texas campaign is mediated differently than the Santa Anna we read during the Mexican-American War. Because little information exists about the identi-ties of these writers, Serna is left to conjecture about the degree to which they intervene in the general's writings.

Jacques Derrida discusses the symbiosis between master and scribe in *Plato's Pharmacy* when he traces the mythemes associated with the gods of writing from antiquity and suggests that the authority of the master exists in the power of the spoken word and that writing is ancillary. The root of this argument hinges upon a dialectic that separates speech, the primary vehicle by which the master commands respect and obedience, and writing, which he defines as the means by which the master's presence is made manifest in absence of his physical body. The voice emanates from the body and depends upon the proximity of the speaking subject to a listener. Thus, the king is only able to exercise authority over those who are immediately present. All other distributions of his power and influence must be made by proxy. Scribes fill the proximal void by transmitting the master's voice through the written word: letters, proclamations, announcements, cables, and plans. In this manner, the scribe enables the exercise of authorial power by textually standing in for the master. Already Platonic dialectics come into play: the scribe who pens the master's words is a diminished version of the original. He is "a subordinate character, a second, a technocrat without power of decision, an engineer, a clever, ingenious servant who has been granted audience with the king of the gods" only for the purpose of extending the master's power (87). Derrida imagines the scribe as a being without identity, a shape-shifter who "cannot be assigned a fixed spot in the play of differences," a chameleon that adapts his voice to that of the authority figure and, in so doing, obtains a modicum of power through association and appropriation (93). Because writing does not depend upon the master's actual presence, the scribe can represent him in absentia, effectively becoming the master "by metonymic substitution, by historical displacement, and sometimes by violent subversion" (89). This substitution represents the great threat that scribes present to power structures for, by appropriating the voice of the master, they acquire his power by subtle force.

The schema that Derrida offers is useful for this discussion of *El seductor de la patria,* if we add a caveat. Derrida's description of the scribe presupposes the erasure of personal subjectivity and that all scribes can be reduced to a single archetypal writer devoid of personality. The inconsistency in this reasoning is exemplified when the scribe, as a being with no fixed personality, supplants the master through violence. If the scribe is truly an empty vessel, a blank page upon which the master inscribes his dictates, then it is impossible to explain why the scribe would kill the master. A blank slate has no ambition, no aspiration, and no motive. Simply put, this action is unexplainable within the parameters that Derrida defines. We are well beyond thinking that it is possible for an individual to divest him or herself of bias in order to become a pure medium through which information can freely flow. Subjectivity and personal interest will always interfere with the transfer of information when a third party acts as intermediary between the speaking and receiving subjects. The questions that lie before us when speaking of *El seductor de la patria* are how many scribes are involved in the process and to what degree their subjectivity influences the story that unfolds.

Before answering these questions, a word should be said about how the intermediary function of the scribe is emphasized by the epistolary nature of the novel. As mentioned earlier, *El seductor de la patria* is an autobiographical novel that recounts the general's activities between 1810 and 1864. But because he must dictate the letters to his former aide-de-camp Manuel María Giménez and mail the letters to his son, another dynamic develops. The autobiography is a self-representational genre that adopts a certain documentary status and poses as a "true" history to be read by others. The epistolary novel, on the other hand, is a mimetic fictional genre loaded with pitfalls for the uninitiated who are unable to recognize the mechanisms of textual transparency that create an illusion of immediacy. Readers are meant to believe that characters in epistolary fiction are "transcribing uncensored streams of consciousness" that are "seemingly written down without any effort to control their logic or their structure" (Perry 228). This transparency paradoxically creates a blind spot for readers of *El seductor de la patria* because the letters *seem* to be written by Santa Anna, *seem* to be unmediated, and *seem* to be offering an unbiased account. Gerardo Francisco Bobadilla suggests that the epistolary style of *El seductor de la patria* allows the general to express himself and his perception of history directly (92), without ever considering that the textual convention of letter writing is complicated by the introduction of scribes. The directness that Bobadilla imagines is entirely nonexistent. The epistolary form of the novel, above and beyond its subjective self-representational discourse, calls into question the authorship of the letters because Santa Anna does not write most of the letters but dictates them to his former aide-de-camp Manuel María Giménez, a man Serna has described as a "filtro depurador" [purifying filter] ("Santa Anna" 176). Understanding Giménez's role in crafting the narrative is important because it is difficult to know how much of what we are reading is actually Santa Anna and how much is Giménez.

Manuel María Giménez was an intriguing albeit minor player in Mexican history who distinguished himself as one of the few writers to unequivocally defend Santa Anna. Born in Cádiz in 1798, he received minimal formal education and enlisted in the military at the age of 16. At 20, he transferred to the viceroyalty of New Spain with the royal corps of engineers and entered Mexico City in the triumphal procession with Iturbide three years later. He offered his services to Santa Anna in September 1828 by letter, but did not serve as his aide until 1838. Though the corpus of Giménez's printed work is small, its value to the Mexican historical archive is important because it offers an extensive nonliberal perspective on the early years of Mexican independence. It consists mainly of memoirs and letters that clearly state Giménez's identification with conservatism and unwavering devotion to his commanding officer. Over the course of 45 years, Giménez maintained an active correspondence with Santa Anna which is especially noteworthy during the general's exiles. Written on the same day at the end of every month in an impeccably ordered and miniscule hand—almost as if he was carefully carving each word into the page—these letters kept the general abreast of current issues and political intrigues and offer comments about the viability of Santa Anna's return to power. In 1864, he wrote an apology for *santanismo* after Santa Anna was exiled for his support of Maximilian that began with an abbreviated national history from independence to the present wherein the principal actor and hero was Antonio López de Santa Anna. Giménez's defense is a singular document because, in addition to relating one perspective about the general's life, it evolves into a personal diary from which Serna is able to fathom this man's personality. The later journal entries revealed a man embittered by years of adherence to a losing cause.

When comparing the novel to the documents Giménez left behind, it is clear that Serna has recreated Santa Anna's character and personality with an exacting amount of fidelity. Both in his personal writing and in *El seductor de la patria*, Giménez is an acerbic critic of the liberal press, demonstrates a patent disgust for Sebastián Lerdo de Tejada, and expresses a deep-seated dislike for Dolores Tosta, Santa Anna's second wife. We also find that Giménez has a convenient, and at times paradoxical, attitude toward civil and military obedience. When, for example, he was imprisoned by the liberal general Mariano Paredes along with other Santa Anna supporters, he helped plan a revolt against the constitutionally established authority. Not long after, when a subordinate officer criticized Santa Anna's military command, Giménez responded in a conservative paper that the chaos the nation suffered could be attributed to insubordination among the officers. Add to this Giménez's obsessive concern for money and his dramatic flair, and we see that Serna has done his documental research well. But perhaps the most telling moments of the Giménez archive are those where the colonel professes his unconditional adherence to *santanismo* and his belief that he belonged to the general's inner circle and was, in point of fact, the only stable support behind the throne. The historical Giménez frequently repeats that, amid a sea of adulators, "yo seguí siempre a su lado" [I was always by his side] (317) and that, when the general needed someone to lean on, "se agarró de mi brazo, como siempre ha tenido de costumbre" [he leaned on my arm, as he was accustomed to doing] (382). I will return to these points shortly. For the time being, I want to emphasize that Serna found an ideal character—possibly the only one qualified—to defend Santa Anna's legacy.

By means of a simple comparative exercise we can see how Serna takes a text written by the historical Giménez, alters it almost imperceptibly, and incorporates the change into his novel's overall theme, thus creating a credible historical voice based on familiar historical events. An anecdote from the Giménez archive about the Pastry Wars illustrates this point. In 1838, French naval vessels blockaded the port of Veracruz in an attempt to force the Mexican government to pay damages to French citizens residing in the city. President Anastasio Bustamante sent Santa Anna to the port with orders to repel the invaders and to protect national sovereignty. During the battle, Santa Anna lost the leg that, perhaps, goes down in history as the most ostentatiously buried limb of all time. Giménez's narration begins with the nighttime surprise attack by French marines. In the scuffle he was separated from Santa Anna, and does not see him again. He received eight wounds, the most serious to his right hand. The following day he watched the French marines board their vessel as Santa Anna lead a group of two hundred Mexican infantrymen in a counterattack. The French turned their cannon on the soldiers and fired, injuring Santa Anna. The historical Giménez's account and Serna's recreation are nearly identical. The following sets of quotes leave no doubt that Serna both read and incorporated Giménez's writing into his novel. Speaking of the wounds he received:

Si bien ninguna de las *ocho* especificadas *heridas* era mortal de necesidad, no obstante, el conjunto y coincidencia de ellas *puso mi vida en inmenso peligro.* (Giménez 309–10, emphasis added)
[While none of the *eight* specific *wounds* was mortal, nevertheless combined they *put my life in extreme danger.*]
Yo tenía *ocho heridas* repartidas por todo el cuerpo, la más grave en el brazo derecho, que *puso mi vida en inmenso peligro.* (*Seductor* 267, emphasis added)
[I had *eight wounds* distributed throughout my body, the worst was in my right arm, which *put my life in extreme danger.*]
After the attack, Giménez reports enduring twenty days of convulsions:
Las *convulsiones* que *por más de veinte días me acometieron* fueron *terribles* y debieron, por consiguiente, *oponer* estorbos de *gran tamaño* a la naturaleza, para alcanzar la *curación.* (Giménez 309–10, emphasis added)
[The *convulsions which wracked my body for twenty days* were *terrible* and, as a consequence, *presented major obstacles to my recovery.*]
A resultas de la amputación de mi brazo, *me acometieron por más de 20 días terribles convulsiones* que *opusieron* obstáculos de *gran tamaño* a mi *curación.* (*Seductor* 268, emphasis added)
[As a result of the amputation of my right arm, I was *wracked for twenty days by terrible convulsions* that *presented major obstacles to my recovery.*]

Similarly, both accounts of the battle on the pier bear striking resemblances:

cuando *los franceses dieron fuego a la pieza* que habían cargado a metralla. Aquel tiro, disparado *a cien pasos de distancia*, fue bien funesto, pues *sus proyectiles hirieron gravemente al Sr. Santa Anna en una pierna* (Giménez 310–13, emphasis added)

[when *the French fired the cannon* that they had filled with shrapnel. That blast, fired from *a distance of one hundred paces*, was terrible, and its *projectiles seriously injured Santa Anna in his leg*...]

A *cien pasos de distancia*, *los franceses dieron fuego a la pieza* de artillería, con tan buen tino que *sus proyectiles* derribaron el caballo de don Antonio y *lo hirieron de gravedad* en la *pierna* izquierda. (*Seductor* 267, emphasis added)

[At *a distance of one hundred paces, the French fired their cannon* with such accuracy that *their projectiles* felled don Antonio's horse and *seriously injured his left leg*.]

While these comparisons demonstrate how Serna incorporates the Giménez archive into his narrative, we can show significant differences between the stories by the same operation. Brian McHale describes the tendency to modify historically verifiable facts as a key element of the postmodern historical novel. Traditional historical novels obey the "dark area" constraint that relegates fictional invention to those corners of the historical record where little or no information is available making it possible to write about an imaginary encounter between a historical figure and a fictional character without contradicting the existing historical record. Anachronisms and modifications to the historical record allow writers to create more meaningful, imaginative fictions that, while not strictly historical, do allow for a sort of Aristotelian truth to emerge from inchoate historical events (86–93). In this novel, Serna's modifications underscore the near symbiotic relationship that develops between authority figures and their scribes. Returning to the port of Veracruz, the historical Giménez was injured in a nighttime raid, during which French marines "me dispararon un tiro a quema ropa, que por fortuna no salió; pero caí con ocho heridas, la mayor parte de ellas graves, y la pérdida de la sangre me privó del conocimiento" [fired upon me at point blank range, and luckily the gun jammed; but I fell with eight other wounds, the majority of them were serious, and I fainted from the loss of blood] (Giménez 309), while Serna's Giménez escapes with Santa Anna during the fray and accompanies him in the battle at the pier, where he reports that he was struck by the same cannonball that injured the general. There is another major discrepancy regarding the state of Giménez's arm. The historical Giménez relates the miraculous salvation of his right hand from the sawbones' craft (313), while Serna's Giménez purports that

"el mismo galeno que amputó su augusto pie cercenó mi brazo izquierdo"
[the same surgeon who amputated his august foot removed my left arm]
(*Seductor* 81). What accounts for this discrepancy? Why does Serna alter
an otherwise insignificant biographical detail when he works so assiduously to get everything else right?

These alterations emphasize the scribe's undying adherence to and
identification with the general. By modifying some historical data, Serna
allows Giménez to insert himself subtly into the general's biography and,
thereby, to identify himself in a more personal manner with Santa Anna.
He suffers every defeat, glories in every victory, rails against each political
enemy, and unduly weaves himself into the story going so far as to fuse singular and plural verb tenses. While convalescing together in a makeshift
hospital after the battle at Veracruz, Giménez hears the general dictate
what he supposes to be his commanding officer's final words to the nation.
Giménez feels redeemed when this heroic speech is read from pulpits and
reprinted in newspapers because finally "se nos hacía justicia, y hablo en
plural, porque la gloria de don Antonio se extendía por contagio a todos los
que participamos en su intrépida acción, sobre todo a los heridos como yo"
[they had done us justice, and I speak in plural because the glory of Don
Antonio extended to all those of us who participated in his intrepid action,
especially those who were wounded like me] (*Seductor* 268). Giménez
shares the general's victory with all veterans of the war, but he is careful to
carve out a special niche for those who, like himself, were injured in battle.
Later Santa Anna receives a personal letter from the president commend-
ing him for his valiant service. Santa Anna asks Giménez to read the letter,
which reveals that he has been granted a jeweled cross in recognition for
his valor. "Más que un golpe de suerte, el hecho de que yo leyera esa carta
me parece un acto de justicia divina, pues a todas luces, el Señor quiso
decirme que la cruz también me pertenecía, si no materialmente, al menos
en forma simbólica" [More than a stroke of luck, the fact that I read that
letter seemed an act of divine justice, because in all ways, the Lord wanted
to tell me that the cross also belonged to me, if not materially, at least
symbolically] (269).

Symbolic union is not enough, however, because Giménez demands
a more literal identification with the general focusing specifically on
Santa Anna's amputated foot and his own mangled hand. Historians
have often commented that the excesses of Santa Anna's regimes can
be best exemplified by the attention given to his severed limb. In the
novel, Giménez informs readers that it was his idea to bury the limb
with fully military honors in 1838 as a remedy for the general's postwar malaise. Declaring that no one knows an injured man like another
injured veteran, Giménez proposes "rendirle honores fúnebres a su pie

amputado, y darle cristiana sepultura en una ceremonia militar" [rendering funeral honors to his amputated foot, and giving him a Christian burial with military honors] (289). But the ceremony appears to have less to do with Santa Anna than with a vindication of his own injuries and to solidify what Giménez views as an unbreakable bond with Santa Anna. The night before the ceremony he deposits his amputated arm into the urn where Santa Anna's leg is stored and reseals it. Giménez tells us that he is not motivated by pride or the desire to share in the general's glory, but rather because, "solamente quise rubricar la unión consustancial de nuestros destinos. No valgo nada ni merezco la inmortalidad. Siempre fui un mozo de estoques, el actor cuyo nombre no figura en la marquesina, pero me ilusiona que los mismos gusanos que royeron su pie también mondaron mis pobres huesos" [I only wanted endorse the consubstantial union of our destinies. I am worthless and do not deserve immortality. I was always the sword bearer, the actor whose name never appeared on the marquee, but I was excited by the thought the same worms that chewed on his foot would also peel the flesh from my poor bones] (289–90). This continual fusion makes disentangling the scribe from the general one of the most difficult tasks in reading the novel. *El seductor de la patria* attests to the problematically fuzzy boundaries that constitute the master-scribe relationship, especially regarding the coexistence and codependence of language and power. But it is imperative that this distinction be made if we are to understand the biases in historical discourse and the motivations of those who write.

For the most part, Giménez is careful not to reveal himself in the novel, but when Santa Anna's son Manuel, the official biographer, accuses Giménez of gold digging, the secretary takes special offense. His response is worth quoting extensively because it underscores how entwined these characters have become:

Tu falta de tacto me ha causado un serio disgusto. ¿Cómo pudiste calumniar así al buenazo de Giménez, si sabes muy bien que revisa toda mi correspondencia? El pobre me leyó tu carta con la voz entrecortada por el llanto, cuando bien hubiera podido romperla, si fuera tan granuja como crees. Me vi obligado a pedirle disculpas, pues quería renunciar en el acto. Te equivocas de cabo a rabo al dudar su honestidad…Giménez es un amigo a carta cabal. ¿Quién más soportaría el trato que le doy sin cobrar un centavo? Con Dolores ya no puedo ejercer el hábito de mandar: sólo Giménez obedece mis órdenes, aun cuando son un tanto enérgicas, porque los años me han agriado el carácter y a veces lo regaño por fruslerías. Pero él nunca se queja: es el último soldado bajo mi mando, el cirineo que me ayuda a cargar mi cruz. Si lo perdiera me sentiría más mutilado de lo que estoy. De manera que te aconsejo retirar tus acusaciones sin fundamento y pedirle disculpas. (126)

[Your lack of tact has made me very upset. How could you slander dear Giménez in such a way when you know that he goes through all of my correspondence? The poor man read me your letter through his tears with a faltering voice when he could have easily destroyed it, if he were as awful as you believe. I had to ask his forgiveness because he wanted to resign immediately. You are completely wrong to doubt his honesty... Giménez is a true friend. Who else would put up with the treatment I give them without asking a cent in return? I can no longer control Dolores: only Giménez obeys my orders, even when they are too energetic, because the years have made me bitter and sometimes I rebuke him for nothing. But he never complains: he is the last soldier under my command, the Cyrene who helps carry my cross. If I lost him, I would feel even more mutilated that I already am. So I counsel to retract your baseless accusations and ask his forgiveness.]

Who exactly is speaking here? Is Santa Anna upset about an insult to a subordinate? Or is it Giménez speaking in the name of the general to defend himself? For reasons that should be clear by now, I would argue that Giménez's pen is at work again. The self-critical remarks are out of character for Santa Anna. Nowhere in the text or in the historical record does Antonio López de Santa Anna ever recognize his short temper, his heavy hand, or his indebtedness to others. It seems more likely that the servant uses the master's voice to vent frustration and to affirm his dedication. This, of course, represents a double displacement of historical fact. Serna alters Giménez's history to create a fictional character for his novel. This fictional character then alters Santa Anna's history to offer a fictional Santa Anna to history. And then we must account for the ambiguity of certain statements. The recrimination for Manuel's lack of tact, for example, does not identify the speaker. Stating that losing "him" would cause the writer to feel more mutilated than he already is shares this same ambiguity. While disentangling the ambiguity may be problematic, textual clues from the letter indicate that Serna's Giménez is tampering with the historical record.

Up to this point, Giménez's conflation of the first person singular and plural, in addition to his penchant for writing as the general, have been tactics to defend himself from calumny and obtain the honors that he feels he deserves. He takes credit, for example, for writing the Plan de Tacubaya, the tripartite proclamation against President Bustamante by Santa Anna and Generals Paredes and Valencia (284). Manuel questions Giménez's authorship of the plan, accuses him of seeking the limelight, and chastises his identification with Santa Anna. He writes that "sus vacilaciones entre el yo y el nosotros revelan una identificación con mi padre que llamaría enfermiza si no fuera francamente abusiva. Que yo sepa mi padre nunca tuvo un hermano siamés" [your vacillations between "I" and "we" reveal an identification with my father that I would call unhealthy if not down-right abusive. As far as I know, my father never had a Siamese twin] (292). He then instructs the scribe to distance himself from the biography's true subject and to let him make the decisions about what should or should not be published. Giménez responds that this would not be an easy task because the general always delegated the writing of his correspondence and reports to trusted advisors. The Santa Anna that everyone knows—or thinks they know—is in fact "una creación colectiva de todos los que alguna vez hablamos en su nombre. Prescinda usted de los documentos apócrifos en la confección de la biografía y se quedará con un muñeco de relleno de paja. Le guste o no, su padre es nuestro invento, y aun si decide reinventarlo tendrá que partir de un modelo más o menos ficticio, mucho más elocuente y pulido que el original" [the collective creation of all of us who at some time spoke in his name. Leave the apocryphal documents out of your biography and you will be left with a straw man. Whether you like it or not, your father is our invention, and even if you decide to reinvent him you will have to start with a more or less fictional model that was much more eloquent and polished than the original] (293). This statement summarizes the dilemma that Giménez and other scribes present in the biographical process. It also marks a change of tactics because, instead of delineating an affinity with Santa Anna, Giménez differentiates himself from the general and sides with the scribes and asserts that Santa Anna is a collective, fictional creation. Giménez argues that the extant documents composing Santa Anna's archive were never written by him. And indeed, many letters—even those from similar periods—evince a different hand. Santa Anna's refusal to write his own story subjects his legacy to the good or bad will of others. Giménez paints Santa Anna as the summation of all the underlings, subordinates, and lackeys who carried him on their shoulders and who spoke in his name. This theme seems consistent in Giménez's writing: subordinates enjoy prestige by fictionally creating Santa Anna without ever becoming the leader. Furthermore, Giménez stresses that any attempts to clean up or denigrate the general's biography will only contribute to the ever-growing mass of scribes and secondhand documents. And finally, Giménez suggests that the flesh-and-blood Santa Anna is less polished and less eloquent than the historical creation.

Giménez's participation in the autobiographical process is, as I have pointed out, highly suspect. So much so, in fact, that even Santa Anna begins to question his objectivity and instructs Manuel to carefully inspect the content of each letter for places where the scribe inserts himself. Apart from this, Giménez attempts to supplant Manuel as the biographer by censoring information that the general wants to include. As mentioned earlier, Santa Anna originally intended for his new biography to portray his youthful misdeeds and humanity in order to curry favor with posterity. But the full disclosure that characterized the original letters ends as soon as Giménez takes over the transcription of the general's memoirs. Immediately following the account of the general's picaresque childhood, the next letter opens with a brief introduction: "Te escribo con una caligrafía más clara, pues ahora tengo un secretario que se ha ofrecido a ayudarme sin cobrar un centavo. Es el coronel Manuel María Giménez. ¿Lo recuerdas?" [I write to you with a clearer handwriting, for now I have a secretary who has offered to help me without asking for payment. It is Colonel Manuel María Giménez. Do you remember him?] (33). This innocuous entrance, related almost as a curiosity, does little to arouse suspicion. Santa Anna describes his first military campaign and recounts a gambling debt contracted with a local doctor and cardsharp. Giménez then adds a postscript to the letter stating that he has no idea how the debt was paid, and that it really does not matter because such information would only serve the interests of the liberal press. There is no mention of the liberal press in the original letter because Santa Anna considers that the autobiography he wrote in Nassau sufficiently refutes the accusations of his enemies. This biography serves a different purpose and is intended for a different audience. Santa Anna does not worry about his enemies as much as he does about posterity. Far from censuring all elements that could be used as a weapon against the general, the first letter explicitly advises the biographer to put his weaknesses in the forefront in order to win over future readers. We can assume that Giménez is unaware of Santa Anna's original instructions because he was not present to write them. What appears to be an innocent comment at the end of this letter already indicates that Giménez is interfering in a manner contrary to the wishes of the biographical subject.

The instructions to suppress increase as the biography addresses more controversial issues. Santa Anna's first governorship of Veracruz, for example, was tainted by corruption scandals, forced loans, exorbitant taxes, and illicit love affairs. The narration Giménez provides Manuel tells the story of a benevolent patriarchal leader, worshipped by the local population. This fond remembrance of a bucolic past serves as counterpoint to bitter recriminations against liberal conspiracies, traitors, and false friends. Realizing that this bitterness might tarnish the history, the letter writer advises, "Para efectos de mi biografía solo debes recalcar que mientras fui un rey en pequeño, mientras pude gobernar como Adán en el paraíso, conté con la aprobación unánime de mi pueblo" [for the effects of my biography you should only emphasize that though I was but a small king, as long as I could govern like Adam in paradise, I enjoyed the unanimous approbation of my people] (*Seductor* 73). "For the effects of my biography" becomes a reoccurring motif that precedes instructions to withhold information that might damage the general's image in order to cast Santa Anna in the most positive light possible. In this case, Manuel is instructed to overlook potential moral, ethical, and political transgressions and to present Santa Anna as a provident patriarch. Another instruction to suppress appears when Giménez relates the general's physical and emotional health. As dementia and illness set in, discouragement replaces the general's former optimism. He is a bitter old man telling stories, but because weakness is not appropriate for the story that Giménez wants to craft, he advises Manuel to clean up the story of his father's old age by not allowing "que el recuento de su vida se empañe con el salitre de la amargura. A veces el general increpa a la patria como un amante despechado. Está en su derecho, pues tiene motivos de sobra para guardarle rencor, pero los mexicanos del futuro no deben saber que su patriotismo ha flaqueado con la edad y los desengaños" [the retelling of his life story to be muddled by the residue of bitterness. Sometimes the general rebukes the nation like jealous lover. He has earned the right, for he has more than enough reason to hold a grudge against her, but future Mexicans should not know that his patriotism has diminished with age and disappointment] (156). Near the end of his life, Santa Anna lost some of the political instincts that had kept him afloat in Mexico's turbulent waters. Exiled yet again, the general looked for another way to return to Mexico and to the presidential palace. But at the time of his final adventure, he had squandered most of his political capital. Unable to rally generals to his cause, he gambled on a financial venture to secure troops of his own accord by signing exorbitant loans with a con artist who left him in debt and to face ridicule. Giménez plays on Manuel's filial sympathies, letting him know that his father is dying and counsels him to end the story before the disgraceful episode with the loan shark.

Giménez's main tool in preserving his version of history is suppression. When historical facts challenge the story that he wants to project, Giménez attempts to erase youthful mistakes like gambling debts from the record, writes off uncomfortable realities like the general's multiple love affairs, hides information like Dolores's letters, covers up mistakes like the defeat at Cerro Gordo, and calls for filial piety in deference to Santa Anna's debilitated mental state. He includes everything that is worthy of history—all that supports an immaculate image of the general—and suppressed all that is not—all that detracts from that image. We have seen that he is willing to interfere in the official biographer's work when the questions are too pointed and we have little information indicating how much Santa Anna participates in the biographical process. We are left with Giménez's version of the story, a story he claims to be "el más fidedigno y autorizado" [the most faithful and authorized] (*Seductor* 274). The scribe's obsession with preserving the saintly portrait he has created is so strong that, whenever given the choice between the real Santa Anna and his fictional creation, Giménez chooses the latter.

The novel closes with a final letter from Giménez that relates the general's demise. Giménez reports that the only two present are himself and Santa Anna's oldest daughter, Guadalupe. To assuage her fear that her father will die without receiving last rites, Giménez disguises his voice, dresses up as a priest, and goes in to hear Santa Anna's final confession. Santa Anna confesses to having uselessly sacrificed his men for personal gain, betrayed friends and political allies, ruined the lives of his wives and his children, and given in to the excesses of vanity, cowardice, and pride. He closes his confession stating that he had treated the nation like a whore and that "México y su pueblo siempre me han valido madre" [Mexico and her people have never meant anything to me] (503). These declarations threaten to upend the story that Giménez has attempted to build and the scribe attempts to staunch the hemorrhaging mea culpa. While playing the priest, he acts the same way he does as biographer. First, he masks his suppression with religious patriotism, alternately telling Santa Anna there is no need for repentance and then subsequently forgiving the general's sins in the name of God and country. When Santa Anna refuses absolution, Giménez appeals to his vanity, asserting that national heroes have no need to incriminate themselves. But this strategy likewise holds no sway over the dying man. The only way Giménez can stop the general's confession is by smothering the general to death. The scribe reports, "Al poco tiempo dejó de jadear, se aflojaron los músculos de su cuello y expiró con serena grandeza. Ahora está sentado a la derecha del Padre" [He soon stopped panting, the muscles of his neck relaxed, and he expired with great serenity. Now he sits on the right hand of the Father] (503). Because he cannot manipulate the general's words and protect history from reality, Giménez murders the Santa Anna of flesh and blood because the historical image is ultimately more important than the man.

Manuel María Giménez parodically recreates the role of Don Quixote's faithful squire, Sancho Panza. Santa Anna's harebrained adventure in Texas lacks the comic resonances of Quixote's battle with the windmill or wine flasks, but evinces a similar illusory pathos. Don Quixote's evocative imagination draws Sancho Panza into his madness and the squire begins to have his own illusions, first living through the errant knight's fantasies, then inspiring them, and finally attempting to control them. His conversion to Quixote's way of thinking moves in opposition to Quixote's awakening sense of reality during the journey home. Traveling together, they move apart. On his deathbed, the agonizing Quixote condemns his madness, rescinds his illusions, and attempts to make his mistakes a cautionary tale of bad behavior. He seeks reconciliation with society, renounces his alter ego's name, and takes his societal name, Alonso Quijano. Sancho, however, refuses to accept the impending end of their adventures. Farm life pales when compared to the wild rides, the swashbuckling, the danger, the adrenaline, the chance to relive the glory days of yore. Likewise, Santa Anna's deathbed confession seems divested of his initial illusion. Occasionally stirred to ideas of political insurrection, for the most part he realizes that his days are over. He forsakes the pension the government has offered him, recognizes that he is unable to control even the most basic of bodily functions, and roils in his cynicism and hubris. On the other hand, Giménez refuses to let the illusion fade and pushes desperately to preserve *santanismo*. He is willing to suppress truth, modify facts, cast blame on others, and ultimately, to kill the very individual whom he hopes to deify, in order to create a pristine narrative of the general's life.

Call and Response

Unchecked, Giménez's version of history would land this novel in the category of fanatical apologetic writing and would, like the actual biography written by the historical Manuel María Giménez, find itself lost on musty bookshelves. There is a second voice, however, that methodically works to counter Giménez's narrative. The only reference we have to this character is a curious footnote, and it stands out because there is none other like it in the entire novel. Santa Anna's son, Manuel, requests that the general respond to a questionnaire and an asterisk that follows the sentence leads us to the following: "* Nota del compilador: el cuestionario no fue hallado en el archivo de la familia Santa Anna" [* Compiler's note: the questionnaire was not found in the Santa Anna family archive] (125). This annotation calls attention to the presence of an intelligence who works behind the scenes to provide documents for the reader. The function of this compiler is akin to what Hugh Kenner describes in Joyce's *Ulysses* as "the Arranger." The Arranger is not a narrator per se because he does not move the story along, reveal new explicit information about the characters, or do any other function normally associated with narration, but rather, sits on the sideline and treats the reader with "the sour xenophobic indifference Dublin can turn upon visitors who have lingered long enough for hospitality's first gleam to tarnish" (23). Unlike the indifferent Joycean Arranger, Serna's compiler cares deeply about the reaction of his audience and furnishes additional documentation that is used to correct "what is said in one text by comparing it with another, and offers other pertinent information" (González Echevarría, *Voice* 78) that dismantles the dictator's self-aggrandizing narrative and contradicts Giménez's epic historical representation of Santa Anna's life.

In the preceding chapters, I argued that Ibargüengoitia and Del Paso undermine the widely accepted stories told about independence and the Second Empire by revising central national myths. *Los pasos de López* portrays the conspirators as irresponsible, disorganized, and incapable of creating a stable independent nation while *Noticias del imperio* demonstrates that national identities are not inherent or even contingent upon the place one is born, but rather one's desire to be included within the imagined community, as well as the nation's willingness to accept evidence of that desire. Likewise, *El seductor de la patria* is an archival novel that engages in a systematic reassessment of archival documents as a means of exposing the epistemological and ontological gaps presents in a seemingly monolithic national history. For Michel Foucault, the archive is not simply a repository of information, but rather a system of organization and censorship that is intimately linked to the power structures that determine the limits of what can be said by privileging certain parcels of information, while suppressing others. Taking cues from Foucault, González Echevarría views the archive as a colonial institution that governs knowledge through the propagation of official myths and argues that contemporary Latin American literature is tied up with anthropological investigations into these foundational stories. He views the self-reflective nature of Latin American writing as a natural by-product of literary attempts to dismantle the mediating force of the archive (*Myth* 28–29). This metafictional modality shows that "the act of writing is caught up in a deeply rooted mythic struggle that constantly denies it the authority to generate and contain knowledge about the other without, at the same time, generating a perilous sort of knowledge about itself and about one's morality and capacity to know oneself" (29). For González Echevarría, archival fictions consist of three elements: the presence of a history that is mediated through a series of legal, scientific, or other documents; the presence of an internal historian who reads and interprets the existing documents and then, in turn, contributes to the existing corpus by writing another version of the past; and the presence of an unfinished manuscript that the internal historian attempts to finish (22). All three of the characteristics are present in *El seductor de la patria*.

All told there are more than 90 documents that serve as counterpoint to the scribe's seductive narrative. They include journal entries, newspaper articles, speeches, reports, personal letters, and legal documents. They punctuate, and often contradict, claims made by Santa Anna's biography. The dynamic is not unlike the kind of call-and-response relationship that develops between blues guitarists on stage: one lays down a musical phrase and the other develops it by adding additional flourishes. We see this when Giménez, giving voice to the general, speaks about all of the sacrifice of personal wealth that Santa Anna placed on the mythical altar of the nation in defending the rule of law against foreign and domestic foes. It sounds convincing and there is a moment when readers might feel that, for all the slander mounted against him, Santa Anna was still in many regards a major national hero worthy of a little more historical mercy. It is at these moments when the heroic narrative presented by the scribe begins to woo the sympathies of the reader that the compiler responds with financial documentation about how many haciendas the general had purchased, how much he earned from his crops, how many thousands he received in bribes and kickbacks, and how little he paid his employees. The reason for these insertions is clear: the compiler fears the discursive seductiveness of the heroic narrative and does not trust the reader to come up with the correct interpretation.

The primary triggers for the appearance of historical documents are attempted suppressions. When Giménez hides damning information, the compiler provides a contradictory view. For example, as noted earlier, Giménez portrays Santa Anna as a good husband and father. He believes that the general gave his first wife, Inés, a happy life. The obvious intent here is to establish Santa Anna as a provident father, an attentive husband, and a man capable of governing his home and, therefore, the nation. The compiler inserts a series of five letters from Inés to her mother in response to the colonel's story. In the first letter, written shortly after their wedding, Inés complains to her parents that marrying her off at the age of 14 was cruel and inhumane. "Ni en mis peores pesadillas me imaginé que el matrimonio fuera algo tan espantoso. ¿Por qué me hicieron esto?" [Never in my worst nightmares did I image that marriage was so horrific. Why did you do this to me?], she asks. "¿Te parece muy cristiano haberme casado con un hombre que podría ser mi padre? ¡Y qué hombre, Dios mío! Cuando me pretendía era todo lindezas y caravanas; apenas me trajo aquí empezó a portarse como una bestia. Viene todo sudado de montar a caballo y se me echa encima para hacer sus porquerías, como si fuera un mueble o un animal doméstico" [Does it seem very Christian to have married me to a man who could be my father? And what a man, my God! When he courted me everything was beautiful and chivalrous; as soon as he brought me here, he began treating me like a beast. He comes in covered with sweat from riding his horse and throws himself on me to do his filthy things, as if I were a piece of furniture or some animal] (137). We also learn that in her new hacienda the only person Inés cares for is her servant, Nazaria. The second letter relates Santa Anna's refusal to visit their first daughter's crib. The implication—which will be made more explicit in future letters—is that Santa Anna wants male offspring and cares little for females. Inés also mentions Nazaria's sudden disappearance. The third letter opens with the revelation that Santa Anna has forced himself on Nazaria and impregnated her. Inés is called to help birth an indigenous woman's child and finds out about her maid's secret. When she confronts Santa Anna with her discovery, he recognizes the child and instructs her to forget the matter. From this point on Inés resolves to keep her bedroom door shut to him. In the fourth letter, Santa Anna uses his political influence to enter his wife's chambers again. Inés' father, a Spaniard, is in danger of being exiled under the 1827 law ordering the expulsion of all Spaniards. When she asks her husband to help, he responds that she must let him return to her bed and provide him with a male heir. Inés accedes to his demands, but the fifth letter shows how little things have changed. When news arrives that a second girl is born, Santa Anna refuses to leave the cockfight he is attending to visit the child. The appearance of these letters has a clear intent: to discredit Santa Anna's claims to being a good husband and father. They demonstrate, with the authority of a firsthand witness, the general's arbitrariness, cruelty, disrespect for women, lust for control, and willingness to abuse political power for personal gain. These letters are not simply a comment on his domestic life. These letters openly contest an affirmation intended to bolster the image of a benevolent patriarch, foreshadowing the monster that Santa Anna will become.

These letters also underscore the problematic nature of the compiler's use of external documentation, because most, if not all, of his insertions are apocryphal and therefore entirely subjective. The problem that Inés's letters present for the sake of historical documentation is best summarized by Fowler when he notes that, as a general rule, Mexican women of the period did not typically write diaries and what few documents we have written by them do little to shed light on their concerns. To date there are no documents available from either of the general's wives ("All the President's Women" 59). What is more, the letters that Serna includes present Inés as a sexual slave, demoralized by a misogynistic and depraved husband, whose concern is for a male heir, and who neglects his fatherly responsibilities toward his daughters. By contrast, Fowler notes that testimonies from the period offer a completely different portrait of Inés, that of a confident, well-mannered, stable woman who took the lead in domestic life. Inés enjoyed a substantial amount of freedom, was actively involved in society, and managed the president's largest and most cherished hacienda, Manga de Clavo. After her death in 1844, Manga de Clavo and other properties fell into disrepair because his second wife, Dolores, disliked the countryside. Inés was well loved by citizens and, upon hearing that she had died prematurely, twenty thousand people marched to Mexico City to pay their respects (63). For Linda Hutcheon, apocrypha allows for a healthy reorganization of the archive by dismantling the official story and supplanting it with a poetically truer version that stands in opposition it. While this is germane to discussions of heroic stories like what we saw with Ibargüengoitia's treatment of the independence story in chapter 1, *El seductor de la patria* is a novel about and against the perennial villain of Mexico's nineteenth century. In this case, though, the apocryphal documents support a negative view of the general. The problem arising from the faux apparatus of historical documentation used by the compiler is that it is not accountable to any form of external check or balance. Its only referee is the character that offers it and it, therefore, opens up a number of questions regarding the reliability of apocryphal data in these historical fictions. Thus *El seductor de la patria* pits two falsified histories against each other without any recourse to verifiable information. The compiler's discourse checks Giménez's story, but there are no checks or balances for his own. In this manner he is, as González Echevarría comments about the editor in Roa Bastos, "the final authority in this collection of texts... no matter how weak an authority he may appear to be" (*Voice* 78). In this manner the scribe and the compiler are both shape-shifters who use dissimulation to strike and then hide their hand.

What is sure, however, is that the compiler is terribly uncomfortable with the leeway that the novel affords the general's story. Let us be clear: the subject of the novel is a man who wooed his way to power no less than eleven times, who participated in every major event between 1820 and 1864, and who, despite numerous exiles, still maintained the hope of regaining power. Santa Anna was the premier political Don Juan of the nineteenth century, and Serna knows this, perhaps even fears this. *El seductor de la patria* should be read, then, as a text intended to immunize the Mexican reader against the seductive rhetoric of authoritarian power (Mosqueda 121). The historical novel pertains to what Jacques Rancière has called the ethical regime of art in that it maintains a curiously didactic tension between artistic integrity and social responsibility. The ethical regime for Rancière arranges images that relate to a given community and establishes a system of values and hierarchies with the intent to educate the moral sensibilities of citizens. Plato expelled poets and playwrights from his utopian republic not because art as a product leads to improper imitation but because it arranges social images in such a manner that the system of hierarchies is destroyed, leaving a chaotic distribution of the sensible as the foundation for community (*The Politics of Aesthetics* 20–21). Thus, if we consider the ways in which the historical novel arranges images as a means of educating a national sensibility—Walter Scott's dialectical oppositions of authentic Saxon characters, modes of speech, customs, and local traditions against an array of unnatural Norman traits and behaviors—then it becomes clear that, seated within its design, the historical novel is essentially didactic in nature. If the main function of the novel is to allow readers the opportunity to understand the way another individual thinks, feels, acts, and responds, then the terrible danger is that readers might fall under Santa Anna's seduction.

Some critics have argued that Serna offers an objective portrait of Santa Anna. César Antonio Sotelo Gutiérrez writes that the objectivity of Serna's historical research allows him to present a multifaceted rendering of the general's personality. The general is not demonized and his actions can only be judged when one takes into account the circumstances of mid-nineteenth-century Mexico. Sotelo Gutiérrez does clarify, however, that the novel does not attempt to vindicate the general "pues la ficción, fundamentada en un concienzudo estudio histórico, no excluye las traiciones y corruptelas en que éste incurrió. Olvidando el tradicional maniqueísmo de la historiografía mexicana, el texto presenta una visión de la historia más objetiva, sin apasionamientos partidistas o doctrinarios" [because fiction, based on a conscientious study of history, does not exclude the betrayals and corruptions that he was involved in. Setting aside the traditional Manichaeism of Mexican historiography, the text presents a more objective vision of history, without party or doctrinal passions] (65). I disagree. Serna is not, nor can be, objective because he carries with him the weight of more than a century of negative myth. Just as the scribe cannot divest himself of identity in order to faithfully and dispassionately transmit the master's language, Serna cannot distance himself sufficiently from the culturally transmitted legends that have come to characterize the general's biography. What is more, the prime material that Serna uses to build his narrative—the histories written by Sierra, Jones, Callcott, and Muñoz—are inherently biased against Santa Anna and, therefore, imbue Serna's novel with their bias. Serna does not allow readers to judge for themselves because Mexicans, he argues, have demonstrated a lack of good judgment in matters of the political heart for nearly two centuries. In the end, the presence of the compiler demonstrates how little Serna trusts readers to correctly interpret the past. He spoon-feeds them the "real" story that, like Giménez's, is based on subjective fictions and suppressions. The faux apparatus of documentation that contradicts the hagiographic narrative is falsified. Inventions, no matter how real seeming they may be, continue to be fiction.

Giménez and the compiler are not Santa Anna's only ghost writers. Historians and fiction writers have also, either by design or by accident, joined the ranks of those who took up the pen in Santa Anna's service. *El seductor de la patria* is only the most recent novel written about the general's life and deeds. Indeed, some of the nation's most consecrated authors have written about him in an attempt to understand who this man was and why the nation was pathologically drawn to him. One of the first was Victoriano Salado Álvarez's *Su alteza serenísima*, published in 1853 as the first volume in a series of popular novels called *Episodios nacionales mexicanos*. Hailed as a perfect balance between historical investigation and tasteful writing by prominent Mexican historian José Luis Martínez, Salado's novel embodies the mid-nineteenth-century ideological rift between liberals and conservatives that I discussed in the last chapter (Jiménez Marce 102). Ireneo Paz, a contemporary of Salado and the grandfather of Octavio Paz, wrote a novel with the same title that was published nearly 60 years after his death. Rafael F. Muñoz wrote two books on the general's life: *Santa Anna: El que todo lo ganó y todo lo perdió* (1936) and *Santa Anna: El dictador resplandeciente* (1945). Agustín Yáñez, most well known for his novel *Al filo del agua*, began working on a biographical manuscript in 1932 but only after his death did *Santa Anna, espectro de una sociedad* (1982) come to light. The works of Muñoz and Yáñez tend more toward historiography than toward fiction, but nevertheless included humorous fictional dialogues for the general. By contrast, Leopoldo Zamora Plowes inclined more toward the literary in his picaresque novel *Quince Uñas y Casanova aventureros* (1945) about adventures of dashing young man who courts one of Santa Anna's many love interests. Historian José Fuentes Mares penned and produced a historical drama in 1969 using the already traditional title *Su alteza serenísima*, which would again be used for Felipe Cazal's feature-length film in 2000.

Many of these works laid the foundation for *El seductor de la patria*. In the prologue Serna observes that any approximation to a historical figure must necessarily depend upon the collective efforts of previous writers and that Santa Anna's biography is no different. Santa Anna never wrote anything himself. The documents that we typically assign to him are in reality the work of an army of secretaries that accompanied him through his career. Their writings mold our perception of the man because we have no direct access to him. Moreover, every major history written about Mexico's nation-building period must necessarily create its own vision of the general and his involvement in national affairs. Serna carves out a niche for himself in this tradition when he notes that *El seductor de la patria* does not compile all that has been written about the general, but rather, it attempts to reinvent him as a fictional character and explore his personality based on the historical record. Serna inserts himself into a tradition of historians, not fiction writers. These initial lines propose that the book we are about to read is not fiction but biography. However, he inverts this position in the most common practice of historical novelists when he admits to renouncing historical objectivity in order to free up his imagination. Nevertheless, Serna recognizes his indebtedness to the classic texts of Mexican historiography, a debt he qualifies as "la misma deuda de gratitud que un fabricante contrae con sus proveedores de materia prima" [the same debt of gratitude that a manufacturer owes to the providers of raw materials] (9).

At first glance the prologue appears to be a perfunctory disclaimer about artistic license. Yet it reveals several noteworthy points. Serna inserts himself into a historiographic discourse by outwardly adopting the role of historian while maintaining his right to literary creativity. Thus he proposes to recreate Santa Anna based upon information contained in the aforementioned classics of Mexican historiography while rejecting "historical objectivity" in order to give free rein to his imagination. In essence he reiterates Hayden White's proposal that, while nineteenth-century historians claimed the prestige of both the scientific and artistic traditions without adhering to the formal precepts of either, contemporary historians "must be prepared to entertain the notion that history, as currently constituted, is a kind of historical accident, a product of a specific historical situation, and that, with the passing of the misunderstandings that produced that situation, history itself may lose its stature as an autonomous and self-authenticating mode of thought" (*Tropics* 29). White warned that historians might be called upon to "preside over the dissolution of history's claim to autonomy among the disciplines, and to aid in the assimilation of history to a higher kind of intellectual inquiry which, because it is founded on an awareness of the similarities between art and science, rather than their differences, can be properly designated as neither" (29). This higher historical inquiry is exactly what Del Paso proposed in *Noticias del imperio* and what Serna attempts to achieve in this novel. He also recognizes that, in spite of poetic license, he must still adhere to the historical framework Santa Anna's life imposes upon him.

In an essay entitled "Vidas de Santa Anna," Serna recounts that the general's biographers have taken as many liberties with their subject as have the fictional writers. He notes that Oakah L. Jones, one of the most frequently cited biographers, misses an important bit of irony in Karl Marx's estimation that the Spanish never produced a genius like Santa Anna. While Jones employs the idea of Santa Anna's genius to frame his entire narrative, Serna points out that Marx—whose dislike for the Spanish knew no bounds—was not praising the Mexicans or Santa Anna. Instead, his left-handed compliment was a slap in the face for both nations. Serna then briefly describes Callcott's biography and the novelized biography that Octavio Paz's grandfather wrote. He concludes discussing Rafael F. Muñoz's novel, *El dictador resplandeciente* (1976), where Muñoz generates a psychological profile that traditional historiography had been unable to create. He also throws in some scintillating details that are not historically verifiable, such as Dolores de Tosta hiring homeless street urchins to visit Santa Anna in his dementia to entertain the general with falsified memories of important battles. Serna writes: "Para traducir la vida de Santa Anna al lenguaje de la novela moderna es preciso tomarse libertades mayores que las de Rafael F. Muñoz. Pero hasta yo, que pensaba alejarme lo más posible del método historiográfico, me vi obligado a deslindar la ficción de la realidad en biografías, memorias y testimonios viciados de origen, para no plagiar a los novelistas embozados que me antecedieron" [In order to translate the life of Santa Anna to the language of the modern novel it is important to take greater liberties than those of Rafael F. Muñoz. But even I, who thought to distance myself as far as possible from the historiographic method, was obligated to separate fiction from reality in the biographies, memoirs, and testimonies, all of which were tainted from the beginning, so as not to plagiarize the shrouded novelists that preceded me] (81). What Serna does not mention, however, is that these historian-novelists, including himself, are nothing more than the latest recruits in general's army of copyists. When writers appropriate the general's voice and use it to express their own perspectives on the events of the past—as Serna does here in a scathing critique both of the PRI and his fellow citizens—they ironically join the ranks of Santa Anna's scribes. Three more of those scribes will be the subject of the final chapter of this book.

Chapter 4

Paralysis and Redemption in Three Novels about the Mexican-American War

In the days prior to the terrorist attacks on the World Trade Center in 2001, the United States and Mexico were making headway on comprehensive reforms to immigration law. President Vicente Fox had made an official visit to Washington a week earlier and urged a joint session of Congress to grant legal rights to millions of undocumented immigrants who were working in the United States, arguing that they had brought and would continue to bring large economic and cultural benefits to the United States. His performance impressed US legislators and reporters alike and President George W. Bush appeared to share Fox's sentiment. The attacks on the World Trade Center, however, brought negotiations to an abrupt halt. Despite Fox's best attempts to push through guest-worker programs and amnesty, analysts in the immediate aftermath believed that the issue had been moved to the back burner while the White House focused its attention on recovering from the attacks and combating future threats. One year later, as the Bush administration was making its case for launching a full-scale ground war in Iraq, the talks had all but fallen off the Washington agenda. Though Fox insisted that Mexicans residing in the United States posed no terror threat and called to resume talks aimed at giving legal status to some of the more than four million undocumented workers living north of the border, the White House kept its distance. Distance was further created by Washington's insistence that Mexico support its war effort. Warning that relationships between the two countries would deteriorate if Mexico did not side with the United States, Bush held numerous conversations with Fox in person and by phone, and announced to the media that he expected Mexico's unequivocal support of the war effort. Eighty-five percent of Mexicans, however, opposed the war and resented Washington's strong-arm politicking. Fox refused to support the invasion, and Bush retaliated by cutting off all immigration talks and approving a wall to secure the border. Outraged by Washington's arrogance and the unjustified invasion of a foreign country coupled with its less-than-diplomatic attempts to coerce cooperation, Mexican intellectuals worked to find diplomatic and artistic ways of denouncing Washington's aggressive behavior. Journalists, political cartoonists, public intellectuals, and novelists expressed nearly unanimous denunciation of the Bush administration's aggressive foreign policy.

This political impasse was only the latest in a long series of conflicts that have characterized the relationship between Mexico and the United States. Military, political, economic, and cultural interventions by the United States have engendered a longstanding sense of distrust between the two nations. The loss of Texas in 1836, the expropriation of the remaining northern provinces in 1848, the deployment of Marines in Veracruz in 1914, and Pershing's punitive expedition in 1916 still linger in the nation's consciousness. Following the Mexican Revolution, governments worked to foster a strong nationalist sentiment by encouraging anti-America sentiment. The nationalization of the Mexico's petroleum industry, for example, was popular among Mexicans because it put the nation's rich subsoil mineral wealth back in the hands of the government and, more importantly, because it was viewed as a strike against American economic interests. In the 1980s, a new crop of conservative bureaucrats and policymakers, in strengthened social ties with the United States and, during the Miguel de la Madrid administration, implemented a series of neoliberal economic reforms that brought concerns about the growing interrelatedness of the two nations back into public discourse. Throughout the early 1990s, public opinion in Mexico toward the United States changed. Despite a lingering distrust created by 150 years of political and military intervention, on the whole, the nation seemed more amenable to an integrated, interrelated society and economy. Politicians and academics adopted a modernist political narrative that stressed Mexico's openness to the outside world and reduced the Manichean rhetoric that constructed the United States as a lurking and manipulative enemy (Morris 108). Nevertheless, Steven Morris points out in an insightful reading of political cartoons and op-ed columns from a broad swath of major Mexican newspapers that, despite indications that Mexico had nurtured a more collaborative view of the United States, "perceptions of the United States as power-hungry, hypocritical, and anti-Mexican still inform public discourse," thanks in part to the passage of a new immigration law in the United States and the drug certification process in March, Bill Clinton's first official visit to Mexico in May, and the execution of a Mexican national in Texas in June 1997 (106). These tensions were understandably exacerbated by the failed immigration talks of 2001 and the political fallout that accompanied the United States' decision to invade Iraq. Indeed, the parallels between the nineteenth-century military intervention in Mexico and the twenty-first century invasion of the Middle East resurrected the dangers posed by the spirit of American expansionism for many writers.

Since the invasion of Iraq, three bestselling novels about the Mexican-American War have been published in Mexico: Francisco Martín Moreno's *México mutilado* (2004), Ignacio Solares's *La invasión* (2005), and Guillermo Zambrano's *México por asalto* (2008). A close reading of these three novels reveals, in addition to acerbic criticisms of the United States, a conscientious attempt by authors to identify the unresolved shortcomings of national character. Just as Serna wrote his biographical novel on Santa Anna as a manual for understanding the complex relationships between voice and truth that are inherently part of social discourse, the novels I address in this chapter attempt to identify national character flaws that led to past defeats and continue to cause problems in the present. What is striking about these representations is how they differ in their respective social projects. The first two that I will discuss, *México mutilado* and *México por asalto*, get caught in creating an awareness of failures and limitations without ever moving to a lessons-learned attitude or suggesting a new course of action. In this sense, their use of failure stymies the political implications of their writing. What is more, the way that these novels communicate the pain of the traumatic past through writing indicates the degree to which the war has not yet been fully assimilated. This is to say that, at the textual level, we can see these authors violently reacting to or compulsively repeating the traumas of the past. By contrast, *La invasión* attempts to work through national trauma through confession and writing.

In order to understand how these novels reflect upon and seek to better understand the effect the war had on the nation's historical imagination, I will couch this analysis within the broad framework of trauma studies. The psychoanalytic turn in critical theory that followed on the heels of cataclysmic world events like the Holocaust gave rise to a theoretical caucus that studies the effects of traumatic experiences on individual and collective memories and identity constructions, and frequently focuses on writing as a therapeutic exercise intended to help victims work through the past. Studies in trauma surge on the heels of crises, such as wars, natural disasters, genocides, and terrorist attacks but tend to recede once the initial shock subsides. This may be precisely because, as Judith Herman points out, to speak of trauma is "to come face to face both with human vulnerability in the natural world and with the capacity for evil in human nature" (7). Herman observes that there is an implicit need for trauma theory to be linked to active political movements that legitimate alliances between researchers and victims and that counteract normal social processes of silencing and denial. Not being actively involved in the processes of remembering and bearing witness of atrocities "inevitably gives way to the active process of forgetting. Repression, dissociation, and denial are phenomena of social as well as individual consciousness" (9). An analysis of the processes of repressing, dissociating, and denying, together with their concomitant resolutions of remembering, repeating, and working through lays at the heart of this chapter because, if as Ernst Renan suggests "griefs are of more value than triumphs" for binding nations together (53), then the Mexican-American War might be rightly considered a foundational trauma, which Dominick LaCapra has defined as an cataclysmic event that paradoxically becomes "the valorized or intensely cathected basis of identity for an individual or a group rather than events that pose the problematic question of identity" (23). According to historian Antonio Castro Leal, who recommended that every Mexican schoolchild study this disgraceful period of national history, a correct understanding of this foundational trauma will help Mexicans "adquirir una conciencia plena y valiente de nuestros vicios y defectos, de nuestras fallas y limitaciones, de nuestros desmayos e incapacidades, de la desproporción entre lo que soñamos ser y la estatura que nos impone la realidad" [to acquire a clear and complete awareness of our vices and defects, of our failures and limitations, of our discouragements and handicaps, of the disparity between what we dream ourselves to be and the stature that reality imposes upon us] (ix). Strikingly Castro Leal's recommendation to make the war an obligatory course of study does not include an impotent denunciation of the invading army but views correct historical understanding of the nation's weakness as an opportunity to constructively engage with the past as an object lesson for future generations.

México mutilado: "My Voice is Sufficient"

The first novel published about the Mexican-American War following 9/11 was Francisco Martín Moreno's *México mutilado*, a bestseller that sold more than one hundred thousand copies in its first 90 days on bookstands (Haw 4). Moreno is a lawyer, journalist, and one of Mexico's most prolific historical novelists with more than ten hefty volumes to his credit. His brand of fiction is conspiratorial, that is to say that it is dominated by a discourse that imagines webs of governmental complicity in the nation's ills and captures "a sense of uncertainty about how historical events unfold, about who gets to tell the official version of events, and even about whether a causally coherent account is still possible" (Knight 3). Each book is an exposé on the grimy underworld, backroom deals, and self-interested maneuverings that have exacerbated existing social disparities, undermined the democratic process, and maintained the nation in a somewhat premodern feudal state. *México negro* (1986) places the struggle for control of petroleum at the center of the first forty years of the twentieth century; *México sediento* (1998) reveals the intrigues behind the distribution of water rights from independence to a period in the immediate future; *México secreto* (2002) undertakes an analysis of foreign espionage and focuses primarily on the Zimmerman letter; *México ante Dios* (2007) chastises the Roman Catholic Church for its obscurantism and reactionary meddling in national politics; and *México acribillado* (2008) is an Oliver Stone-style investigative novel about the assassination of Álvaro Obregón. Though not the most recent of Moreno's conspiracy novels, *México mutilado* is the most representative of the group in that it attempts to provide a coherent narrative exposing "una cadena de traiciones sin nombre, tanto por parte de los militares como de los políticos y de la iglesia, apostólica y romana, institución, esta última, no sólo la más retardataria de la nación mexicana, sino también aliada al invasor, al igual que el propio Santa Anna" [a chain of nameless betrayals by the military, the politicians, and the Catholic Church alike, the last one being not only the most repressive institution in Mexico, but also an ally to the invaders, as was Santa Anna] (10).

The narration begins as Santa Anna, exiled in Cuba, considers the impending hostilities between the two nations as an opportunity to restore his honor. Understanding that the United States will only be content with the acquisition of Mexico's northern territories and that Mexico will never voluntarily relinquish them, he proposes to collaborate with the US government in a military operation that will force the Mexican congress to sell the lands as a way of staving off a complete takeover. Santa Anna sends a secret emissary to the White House, and the newly elected president James K. Polk, and after cautiously weighing the general's offer, accepts the deal and opens the naval blockade of Veracruz. Once in the country, Santa Anna takes control of the army and carefully dismantles the national defense in order to lose strategic battles. American troops under the command of Zachary Taylor and Winfield Scott then sweep across the country, suffering minimal losses and receiving aid from traitorous Mexicans who, rather than sacrifice their lives in defense of the sacred motherland, aid and abet the invaders. The novel closes with the ignominious Treaty of Guadalupe Hidalgo and a brief epilogue about how each of the historical actors lived out the rest of their lives. These novels pull no punches in assessing damages, naming names, and pointing fingers. Moreno fashions himself as a crusader for good amid a host of evildoers, and this literary vigilantism has allowed him to cash in on a niche market: angry fiction that affixes blame for Mexico's current social ills. In all of his novels, and in *México mutilado* in particular, Moreno chooses the furies for his muse instead of Clio. He asserts that his historical representations are inspired by the indignation that the traumatic past demands. *México mutilado* reopens the traumatic experience of the past to the present in an attempt to engender a sense of sense of righteous historical indignation and operates on the same logic that underpins Cathy Caruth's notion that traumatic experiences can only be explored by reopening the original wound because "trauma is not locatable in the simple violent or original event in an individual's past, but rather in the way that its very unassimilated nature—the way it was precisely *not known* in the first instance—returns to haunt the survivor later on" (4). The significance of this openness for Moreno's novels, however, is that it never allows for a sense of healing. There is no possibility of closure in Moreno's writing. Instead, history is presented as a continual scene of outrage and perennial violation that demands vengeance.

Moreno's concept of the novel hinges on the omniscience and the authority of the narrator, who is privy to the thoughts, ambitions, secret conversations, and intimate thoughts of every character. As with the other historical novels we have examined up to this point, *México mutilado* pits the poetic veracity of its historical account against a contrived pedagogical history foisted upon the nation by the hegemonic state apparatus. In the prologue, he writes that the time has come to make all the nation's dirty little secrets public, "de divulgar, de gritar con la escasa fuerza que aún me queda, de exhibir, de decir, de hacer correr la voz con mi propia versión de los hechos sin contemplaciones, con la esperanza de que alguien, en el futuro, me desmienta o me corrija, aporte más luz y entonces sólo entonces nos vayamos acercando a la verdad, una verdad, que por el momento, sólo yo poseo" [to divulge, to scream with what little strength remains, to expose, to speak, to spread my own version of the facts without contemplations, with the hope that someone in the future might refute or correct me, or shed more light and only then will we draw close to the truth, a truth that, for the moment, only I possess] (20). Moreno takes his criticism beyond the limits that moderation imposed upon Ibargüengoitia, Del Paso, or Serna by asserting that that all history is not simply a misrepresentation of facts but patently false. Academic and state historians—inseparable for Moreno—cannot be trusted. Because

Moreno couches historical narrative within the discursive practices of testimonial literature, a genre that privileges the subjective experience of personal memory, he posits his novel as a truth-bearing counterfactual account that "refuses to view that only history has a truth claim" (Hutcheon, *A Poetics of Postmodernism* 93). But, unlike Hutcheon's postmodern theorization of the constructive process that occurs through "questioning the ground of that claim and by asserting that both history and fiction are discourses, human constructs, signifying systems, and both derive their major claim to truth from that identity" (93), the narrator in Moreno's novel does not derive his claim to truth from the epistemological construct of historiography or fictional discourse, but rather as the product of a first-person, subjective account of what *really happened*. This goes beyond the Aristotelian argument for poetic truth offered by most historical novelists in that they recognize that there is at least some value in the historical record that can then be embellished upon by the effects of the fictional imagination. Moreno, in true conspiracy-theory style, rails against what he considers to be the fabricated lies of official and academic historians, effectively discarding the entire body of scholarship in existence. And yet, he protests too much. This overtly antiacademic stance regarding historical documentation is paradoxically undermined by a textual reliance upon external sources. "No necesito de muletas ni de recursos documentados aportados por terceros ni de elementos probatorios," [I do not need any crutches, third-party documentation, or proof,] he tells us, both at the beginning and end of his narration, "baste mi voz y mi memoria, además de mi amor por la verdad y mi deseo de hacer justicia de una buena vez por todas y para siempre" [my voice and my memory are sufficient, in addition to my love of the truth and my desire to see justice done once and for all] (*México mutilado* 20–21). Nevertheless, he includes hundreds of footnotes that refer readers to a corpus of external documentation that makes no distinction between historical fictions like James Michener's novels, propagandistic pamphlets, academic histories, and eyewitness accounts.

As might be expected, the primary villains of *México mutilado* are, unquestionably, the Manifest Destiny-loving gringos who, inspired by an expansionist imperial philosophy that justified pillaging others in the name of deity, manufactured a rationale for war and unjustly despoiled Mexico. John L. O'Sullivan, a New York journalist and staunch supporter of Jacksonian democracy, coined the phrase "Manifest Destiny" in an 1845 editorial that favored the annexation of Texas. He wrote that Mexico had meddled in American politics "in a spirit of hostile interference against us, for the avowed purpose of thwarting our policy and hampering our power, limiting our greatness and checking the fulfillment of our manifest destiny to overspread the continent allotted by Providence for the free development of our yearly multiplying millions" (5). Robert Johannsen observes that this phrase went relatively unnoticed at the time of its first use because of overwhelming support for annexation from within and without Texas. It was the subsequent occurrence, in an editorial published six months later, that made Manifest Destiny a permanent fixture in American political discourse. The subject of this article, "The True Title" was the hotly contested Oregon territory, equally claimed by the United States and Great Britain. O'Sullivan was more outspoken on this occasion than he had been previously:

> Away, away with all these cobweb tissues of rights of discovery, exploration, settlement, continuity, etc. To state the truth at once in its neglected simplicity, we are free to say that were the respective cases and arguments of the two parties, as to all these points of history and law reversed...our claim to Oregon would still be the strongest. And that claim is by the right of our manifest destiny to overspread and to possess the whole of the continent which Providence has given us for the development of the great experiment of liberty and federated self-government entrusted to us. (qtd. in Johannsen 9)

But Johannsen points out that O'Sullivan's concept of Manifest Destiny differed from the political manifestation we normally associate with the term because he "employed *Manifest Destiny* with reference to the annexation of Texas and the adjustment of the Oregon boundary dispute, the phrase has been narrowly applied to territorial expansion alone," when in fact, it had much broader application (10). He purports that Manifest Destiny

> drew sustenance from the pervasive currents of a popular Romanticism, and credibility from the dynamic political, social, and economic changes in American life that were spawned by a new spirit of optimism and self-confidence. Manifest Destiny combined a fervent, idealistic, even mystical expression of Romantic nationalism with the realistic, practical consequences of extraordinary technological and economic developments as well as an unprecedented movement of Americans to distant parts of the continent. Indeed, it was the latter that gave the former its credibility. The dramatic expansion of the United States in 1840s, the realization of the long-sought-for "ocean-bound republic," marked the apogee of American Romanticism; and it was the war with Mexico that seemed to win a place for the United States in the sweep of world history. (12–13)

Manifest Destiny, then, was a philosophy that fed into the burgeoning sense of American exceptionalism and sprang from the notion that the

United States had been blessed by providential hands to carry out a great mission. This concept of a chosen people with a divinely sanctioned mission was not new to midcentury Americans. Puritan colonizers expressed similar visions for the unborn nation. But O'Sullivan's phrase, nurtured with Emersonian philosophical vigor, summarized this overall sense of uniqueness.

The representative American in *México mutilado* is, not surprisingly, James K. Polk who, more than any other president before or after, embodied Manifest Destiny's political application. An early adherent to Jeffersonian democracy, which argued among other things for the establishment of the "Empire of Liberty," Polk was attracted to Andrew Jackson's vision for America. Polk ran for Congress in 1824, the year Jackson first ran for the presidency. Jackson lost that campaign, but won the election of 1829, and Polk would remain one of the president's strongest supporters. When Martin Van Buren lost Jackson's support for reelection in 1844, Polk was chosen to fill the ballot. Polk promised, among other things, to serve only one term as president, to settle the Oregon dispute with Great Britain, and to acquire California from Mexico. Despite the overall success in fulfilling these promises, historians generally paint a dour picture of the man. Even Justin Smith, a staunch defender of the American cause, characterizes Polk as "very wanting in ideality, very wanting in soulfulness, inclined to be sly, and quite incapable of seeing things in a great way." The president willfully "deceived men or permitted men to deceive themselves" (qtd. in Price 102). Dean Mahin, who has authored an exceptionally good historical appraisal of President Polk's machinations, which attempts to cast him in the best of possible lights while recognizing his numerous faults, observes that Polk had been itching for a fight with Mexico for months, planning out possible contingencies that might lead to conflict and the destabilization of the Herrera administration (70–71).

The synecdochical relationship between Polk and the American people as a whole in *México mutilado* is exemplified in a discussion between Polk and future president, James Buchanan, when Polk states with a Mephistophelean sneer that:

> Nosotros, los americanos, los anglosajones, constituimos una raza superior destinada a llevar el buen gobierno, prosperidad comercial y buen cristianismo a las naciones del mundo. En nuestro espíritu de laboriosidad no caben los sujetos improductivos. Nuestro deber es rescatar a quienes han caído en la perdición o se han extraviado para conducirlos al mundo de la prosperidad, llegado el caso, inclusive, a la fuerza.... Usted coincidirá seguramente conmigo...en que nosotros los americanos somos los elegidos de Dios y

como prueba de ello está nuestra victoria sobre la gran Inglaterra...Claro que teníamos derecho a hacernos de los territorios del sureste, como igual lo tenemos para apropiarnos ahora de los del suroeste. (143–44)

[We, the Americans, the Anglo-Saxons, are a superior race destined to take good government, commercial prosperity, and good Christianity to the nations of the world. There is no place in our hardworking spirit for unproductive souls. Our duty is to rescue those who have fallen into perdition or have lost their way and to guide them to a world of prosperity, and if need be, by force. ... You will surely agree with me...that we the Americans are the elect of God and the proof of this is our victory over England...Of course we had the right to take the southeast territories, just as we do to appropriate the southwest territories.]

Speaking collectively in the first person, Polk alludes to the sense of racial superiority derived from Gobineau's philosophy that I discussed in the second chapter. Inherent within this discourse was the redemptive mission of the white race to take prosperity and civilization to lesser peoples through miscegenation and force. He also invokes the religious undercurrent of Manifest Destiny, that divinity had chosen the American people for this redemptive mission, and that this privilege was made manifest in their victory over the world's primary imperial power, England. It is, of course, Moreno's omniscient, truth-bearing narrator who allows us to eavesdrop on a conversation that, in many ways, recycles central themes from anti-American thought like José Enrique Rodó's *Ariel* (1900). He also allows us access into the intimate corners of Polk's life to fathom the crassness of his soul. When news arrives that hostilities on the border had begun, Polk dedicates hours to crafting his appeal to congress for a declaration of war, including the now-famous assertion that American blood had been spilt on American soil. Feeling content with his draft, he enters his wife's bedroom wearing a questionably Freudian nightcap that his mother knitted for him and quickly and unceremoniously mounts her without "caricias ni besos ni arrumacos ni insinuaciones ni palabras obscenas ni advertencias lujuriosas ni respiración perdida ni sudores ni invocaciones ni contracciones ni lamentos ni apelaciones" [caresses, kisses, sweet-talk, insinuations, obscenities, lusty warnings, shortness of breath, sweat, invocations, contradictions, laments, nor appeals] (237). As soon as the act is consummated, Polk clambers out of bed, lowers his nightshirt, and walks out whistling "Yankee Doodle" while his wife glares hatefully at his receding figure. The portrayal of Polk's coldhearted, self-congratulatory sexuality is intended to further construct a negative portrait of an enemy, who is worthy of hatred both at home and abroad.

In addition to these criticisms of the American government, and in keeping with Castro Leal's assertion that the war should serve as a heuristic tool for understanding Mexico's shortcomings, *México mutilado* offers an equally critical introspective condemnation of the traitors who undermined the nation and paved the way for the Yankee victory. Moreno flatly rejects any sociological, military, or political reason for why Mexico was destined to lose the war, asserting that sheer numbers and patriotism should have been sufficient to devastate a ragtag band of invading highwaymen. The true source of Mexico's defeat, he argues, is entirely locatable in the destabilizing effect of Santa Anna's personal ambition and the unpatriotic actions of the Roman Catholic Church. Both are guilty of having colluded with the enemy, Moreno suggests: Santa Anna worked secretly with the White House to pass through the naval blockade of Veracruz in order to broker a deal to sell the northern provinces for thirty million dollars and, in exchange for a guarantee of its economic interests, the church aided the invaders by threatening excommunication for anyone who attacked the Yankees. Moreno condemns those whom he considers traitors, and imagines painful, ignominious deaths and punishments for them. Moreno notes, for example, that the citizens of Puebla, which has long been a conservative bastion of the church in Mexico, welcomed Scott's army with open arms. He then revels in visions of machete-wielding mobs brutally beating and executing the poblanos for their effeminate and traitorous acts. Setting aside the historical inaccuracy of its portrayal of Scott's reception, this sequence in the novel synthesizes a number of other brutal episodes, where murder is offered as the only reasonable punishment for citizens who do not toe a retrospectively created heroic nationalist response to the American invasion. In these scenes, violence is enacted upon so-called bad Mexicans in a manner that suggests that Mexico's inability to defend it itself from foreign invaders should be recompensed by inflicting pain and punishment upon citizens who did not react appropriately. In this sense, *México mutilado* functions as an ideological text, in that it describes not only the proper allocation of loyalties but also the appropriate manner for dealing with those who break faith with a system of nationalist sentiments.

Historian Jesús Silva-Herzog Márquez recoils from this "patriotismo vengador frente a lo que [Moreno] considera una deslealtad imperdonable" [vengeful patriotism faced with what Moreno considers to be unpardonable disloyalty] when he suggests that betrayal is a common part of the human experience and that, far from being an issue for moralists to take up, it should be recognized as part and parcel of the political process (16). Traitors are considered disloyal because they betray a transcendent, sacrosanct principle such as the family or the nation, but Silva-Herzog argues that they are in fact choosing between two coexisting, divergent loyalties. The requirement to choose means betrayal, no matter which path an individual takes, because at some point he will betray one of his loyalties. He views Moreno's call for vengeance against the poblanos as a dangerous proposal with serious implications. As indicated by the work of Charles A. Hale in the *Mexican Liberalism in the Age of Mora* (1968) and Will Fowler in *Mexico in the Age of Proposals* (1998), the political situation in midcentury Mexico was much more complex than Moreno would have readers believe. The ideological divisions that split the political realm and were sustained by military arms left Mexico in a state of political and social chaos that generated little confidence in the national leadership. Recalling Mariano Otero's acerbic statement that "en México no hay ni ha podido haber eso que se llama espíritu nacional, porque no hay nación" [in Mexico there is no, and never has been, what we might call national spirit, because there is no nation], Silva-Herzog argues that the cohesive imagined community that populates contemporary conceptualizations of the Mexican nation did not exist and could not, therefore command or demand the type of self-sacrificing patriotism that Moreno finds lacking (16).

The a posteriori reduction that Silva-Herzog finds in Moreno's novel reflects the trend described by British scholar Nicola Miller when, in the concluding chapter of her compelling intellectual history of Spanish America, she observes that the tendency to write history for the sake of gaining political advantage was carried out "at the expense of critical enquiry and analysis by the interventions of 'cultural *caudillos*'" (210). These cultural caudillos were not simply state functionaries, she points out, but also fiction writers who hijacked historical narratives, discarded uncomfortable social and cultural complexities, and reduced the practice of history to a question of ideology. *México mutilado* is rife with such unreflective, historically inaccurate reductions that oftentimes divert attention away from social factors that allowed for political corruption and onto political actors. But the most clear example of this style of simplistic reduction comes near the end of the novel when the narrator rhetorically asks how Mexico could have withstood the brutal onslaught of "un gigante goloso, salvaje, soberbio y brutalmente asesino" [a colossal, savage, proud, and brutally murderous giant]. He then answers his own question with righteous indignation by appealing to traditional nationalist principles:

con unidad nacional, con convicciones y amor patrióticos, con lealtad, con valentía, con honestidad, con la suma incondicional de esfuerzos, con instrucción militar y armamento adecuado, con la aportación generosa de recursos económicos y con la certeza de que tendrán el destino establecido y, además, con un fraternal compañerismo, con audacia, astucia, inteligencia y determinación insertados en el marco de un sociedad herméticamente

sellado con principios mexicanos, los mismos que el líder de la coyuntura
histórica para enfrentar la adversidad, habrá de explotar con lealtad, talento
e imaginación en el marco de una democracia. (550)
    [with national unity, with convictions and patriotic love, with loyalty,
with bravery, with honesty, with unconditional effort, with military training and adequate armaments, with generous contributions of economic
resources and with the certainty that their destiny will be sure, and moreover, with brotherly companionship, with daring, shrewdness, intelligence,
and determination with the context of a society hermetically sealed with
Mexican principles, the same principles that the leader who confronts such
a historical moment should exploit with loyalty, talent, and imagination
within the framework of a democracy.]

Playing upon the existing distrust for institutions and the readers' "relaxed
fascination with the page" (Kavanagh 310), Moreno elides a serious consideration of the social and political complexities of the war by reducing everything to a matter of what Slavoj Žižek would call ideology at its purest. For
the Slovene philosopher, ideology is not simply the reduction of complex
ideas to simple, unimpeachable axioms without reference to the historical
background that complicate the black-and-white statements the speaking
subject makes, but is rather a complex system of written and unwritten
rules that allows for these seemingly unimpeachable abstract axioms to be
passed from the realm of pure theory and renders them livable for others
(*Living in the End Times* 3). What makes these ideological rants so appealing, of course, is the emotional manner in which they affect the audience.
It is impossible to argue against communism, Žižek suggests, when the
speaker reduces the complexity of its philosophical and economic notions
to a defense of human rights and equality; by the same token, critiques of
liberal market economies fall by the wayside when discussions are whittled
down to the unassailable freedom of personal choice. In both cases, ideology appeals to universal standards without taking into consideration the
ramifications of these ideas beyond the narrowly constructed discourse of
its enunciation. Something similar occurs with Moreno's novel. There is
no opportunity to question Polk's avarice, Santa Anna's personal ambition, the pettiness of Mexican military officers, and the collusion of the
poblano elites because Moreno's narrator is incapable of offering a nuanced
portrayal of social, political, and economic complexity.
    It is at this juncture, then, when what is taken for commonsense his-
torical truth is uncritically accepted, that the political implication of this
novel comes to the fore. If ideology is the complex way in which social
interactions are portrayed and managed through cultural representation,
the problem inherent in Moreno's rant is best summarized by historian
Josefina Zoraida Vásquez's review of the numerous errors, discrepancies,

misinterpretations, and shortcomings in the novel, when she pointed to the potential dangers that historical fiction presents in supporting narrowly conceived negative foundational fictions. Recognizing the novel's success on the bookstands, she writes that "desasosiega la versión y el mensaje que trasmite este libro a un público desconcertado y lleno de incertidumbres ante las dificultades que la nueva transición nos presenta. Me queda el temor de que sirva para abonar el cinismo o la decepción. Eso es algo que le quita el sueño a cualquier educador que sigue confiando y no se rinde a la moda de hablar mal de México" [this version of history and the message that this novel transmits to a disillusioned public makes me uneasy. I am afraid that it will only lend credibility to cynicism or disappointment. For educators who continue to maintain hope and refuse to give into the tendency to speaking badly about Mexico, this is something that keeps us up at night] (32). Her concern, above and beyond historical inaccuracy, is the overwhelmingly pessimistic, defeatist message that this novel communicates at a moment when the nation was refashioning itself politically and culturally.

Indeed, despite the appeal to common patriotic values of courage, honor, self-sacrifice, and integrity, at the ideological level *México mutilado* works against any sort of social action by engendering a sense of social rage that is cathartically exhausted by the novel as it demonstrates, time and time again, the futility of social action. The novel suggests that the common citizen will be continually depredated by elite classes, that this has always been the case, that this will continue to be so, and that Mexico might as well get used to the idea. Moreno's message, then, is one of inevitable victimhood where the everyday Mexican will always be a slave. As a vehicle for cathartic anger, the novel allows the reading public to exhaust its indignation upon the usual suspects of Mexican history: the United States, the church, and Mexican politicians. But this catharsis is inherently impotent because it produces nothing more than a self-gratifying sense of righteous indignation not unlike the sense of uncritical satisfaction that Žižek associates with charity or almsgiving. Those who contribute money to disaster relief or hunger projects are ultimately alleviated of the burden of dealing with the causes of injustice, poverty, and inequality because they are able to assuage their sense of guilt by contributing money; in essence, they have done their part and no further action is required (*First as Tragedy* 52–55). The vitriol present in Moreno's novel allows readers to vicariously vent their anger but does not connect that feeling with any programmatic system of change. This is to say that *México mutilado* ironically undermines its own project: in its expository anger, the novel enables a sense of hopelessness that defeats any form of constructive action.

México por asalto: The Paralysis of Trauma

Four years after Moreno struck bestseller gold with *México mutilado*, Guillermo Zambrano, a correspondent for the BBC in Miami and occasional crime novelist, published *México por asalto* with the powerhouse Random House Mondadori. *México por asalto* tells the dramatic tale of the St. Patrick's Battalion, a group of roughly three hundred Irish conscripts that deserted from the American forces, took up arms with the Mexican army, and participated in nearly every major battle during the Mexican-American War. It follows the battalion's exploits by focusing on John Riley, an Irish immigrant to Michigan who, having previously deserted from the British army, is conscripted into the American army and sent to the US-Mexico border with Zachary Taylor's army. When Protestant US officers savagely mistreat the Irish Catholic infantrymen, Riley encourages the troops to cross the river and join forces with the Mexicans under General Ampudia. Their knowledge of American tactics and armaments make them valuable assets to the Mexican army and they are gratefully received. As confrontations between the Americans and the Mexicans increase, the St. Patrick's Battalion fights alongside the Mexican regulars in all the major battles: Monterrey, Angostura, Cerro Gordo, Churubusco, and Mexico City. Zambrano shares Moreno's acrimony when he opens the novel by reminding readers that between 1846 and 1848, "durante la arbitraria guerra contra México ordenada en Washington por el presidente James K. Polk, y facilitada en México por un hombre presuntuoso llamado Antonio López de Santa Anna—un criollo sin arraigo nacional que fue presidente en varias oportunidades—y respaldada además por la actitud egoísta de una Iglesia católica rapaz y nada solidaria; se registró la pérdida de la mitad del territorio nacional" [during the arbitrary war against Mexico, President James K. Polk ordered from Washington, and aided in Mexico by a presumptuous man named Antonio López de Santa Anna—a Creole with no national sentiment who was president on numerous occasions—and backed by the selfish attitude of the greedy and unsupportive Catholic Church, half of the national territory was lost] (15). In fact, the similarity between the bitterness of these two novels almost invites one to read the novels as companion volumes, though written from distinctly different narrative points of view. Where Moreno focuses on the politicians and military officers who conspired to plunder the nation, Zambrano takes up the everyman story by introducing us to the lives of infantrymen who are swept along by the decisions of others.

Zambrano's portrayal of the Irish immigrants of the 1840s responds directly to the increasingly divisive cultural discourse that cropped up in

US politics following the 9/11 attacks. Concerns that al-Qaeda operatives were planning to launch biochemical attacks against the United States hardened the resolve of anti-immigration proponents to erect a security wall and inspired a number of paramilitary vigilante groups to patrol the borders. Immigrants were portrayed as threats to public peace, drains on welfare resources, and unproductive members of the society. Legalized Mexicans who maintained their Hispanic cultural and linguistic identities have been portrayed as stubbornly un-American. Since 2003, a number of legislative bills have been passed to crack down on immigration, but none as controversial as the Arizona SB 1070, which criminalized the failure to produce documentation of legal status and granted broad enforcement powers to state law enforcement officials. Critics claimed that the bill constituted an open invitation for harassment and discrimination against Hispanics regardless of their citizenship status. Zambrano placed the immigration front and center in *México por asalto* when he dedicated it to "los mexicanos de ayer, hoy y mañana, y a todos los irlandeses amigos de México" [Mexicans past, present, and future, to all the Irish friends of Mexico]. In the opening pages, Irish Catholic immigrants are portrayed by the dominant Protestant population as illiterate, drunken, criminal, shiftless, lazy, and racially inferior. Their neighborhoods are off-limits to good society, except for the brothels where impoverished Irish women prostitute themselves to Protestant men in order to survive. Police brutality against the Irish is rampant and the government turns a blind eye to the needs of these new immigrants, who are not considered authentic citizens. Social marginalization does not preclude them from being considered worthy cannon fodder by military officers intent on preserving the lives of Protestant soldiers by putting Irish conscripts on the frontline. Thus, in the novel, when a group of dockworkers begins rioting in response to the rape and murder of two popular local Irish girls, the police arrest and beat the rioters and sweep the investigation under the carpet. Denied due process and trial by jury on the basis that the Irish are not citizens and therefore unprotected by constitutional law, the dockworkers are given a choice of serving out a sentence in federal prison in New York or joining the military.

The very notion that nineteenth-century Irish Catholics formed an excluded group within the body politic of the United States makes the St. Patrick's Battalion ideal for this style of criticism because of the peripheral sensibility that they bring to American culture. Borges provides the most succinct explanation of this phenomenon when, writing about Argentine writers and the Western literary tradition, he notes that Jewish cultural critics offer the most insightful interpellations to Western culture precisely because they exist on the periphery, neither fully integrated in the West by virtue of their religious ties nor fully on the outside through years of cohabitation (*Obras* 272). He makes similar observations about Irish when speaking of Joyce within the realm of English literature. In *México por asalto*, John Riley, as the military and spiritual leader of the Irish conscripts, is given extraordinary access to the Protestant military leadership and, because of his good soldiering habits, is offered a battlefield promotion to the rank of an officer. He inhabits the Protestant world, while being constantly reminded that his situation is extraordinary and that he does not fit in among the real Americans. Again we see Bhabha's formulation of mimicry: the colonized subject is given the opportunity to adopt the dress and standards of the imperial masters without ever being fully recognized or accepted by them. Thus, Riley is a privileged outsider: he is able to weigh the revealed thoughts and intents of the Protestant officers against his own values and loyalties. Something similar happens when he crosses over to the Mexican side. He already speaks some Spanish and is therefore able to communicate with the Mexican military command, where he gains insight into the petty rivalries between Mexican officers that undermine the national defense effort. As with the American army, Riley can perceive what others do not. Through his eyes, through the gaze of the privileged outsider, readers are able to understand the "truth" about the war: that both sides were equally arbitrary in their treatment of the common soldier, that personal interest was more important than the lives of men.

Beyond the story's plot, what makes *México por asalto* so interesting for this discussion of trauma is the seemingly unconscious and violent way in which the historical aspects of the novel surface during the development of the story. For Freud, the traumatic past interrupts the present through violent explosions of images and flashbacks. In *México mutilado*, the political backstory forces its way through fissures in the narrative structure and reconstructs the events that condition each character's reaction. During the opening scenes of the novel, an argument between Irish laborers and Protestant military officers in a pub leads to a tense confrontation of interests: the army needs recruits to fill its ranks for the upcoming war and the Irish, many of whom had served as infantrymen in the British army, recognize that their contribution is to be cannon fodder, thus sparing the lives of young Protestant Americans. When Riley argues that the invasion would constitute an immoral act, the officer violently cuts off the conversation with the invective that a foreigner should not proffer opinions on national matters. The bar's clientele follows the conversation closely and a hush falls over the place. At this point something inexplicable occurs. Zambrano disrupts the dramatic tension by interjecting a lengthy and unnecessary digression about Abraham Lincoln's address to Congress questioning the legal justification for the invasion, and declaring that the contested territory between the Nueces and Bravo rivers did not belong to the United States, before resuming the story. This historical *ex abrupto* might be overlooked as the overzealousness of a young writer, if Zambrano did not have so much experience under his belt. Instead, this clumsy interruption resembles the unconscious acting out that Freud described in patients who do not remember repressed traumatic experiences but act them out: "He reproduces it not as a memory but as an action; he *repeats* it, without, of course, knowing that he is repeating it" (150).

LaCapra argues that the "undecidability and unregulated *différance*, threatening to disarticulate relations, confuse self and other, and collapse all distinctions, including that between present and past, are related to transference and prevail in trauma and post-traumatic acting out in which one is haunted or possessed by the past and performatively caught up in the compulsive repetition of traumatic scenes—scenes in which the past returns and the future is blocked or fatalistically caught up in a melancholic feedback loop" (21). This pathological acting out manifests itself in Zambrano's novel as a series of compulsive repetitions in phraseology and ideas. The most obvious illustrations of this repetition are the epithets Zambrano applies to the major characters like Zachary Taylor, the general who commanded the northern army for the United States, who with very few exceptions appears as "el viejo Taylor" [old Taylor], "el astuto Taylor" [astute Taylor], and "el viejo y astuto Taylor" [old and astute Taylor]. On one page, the first description appears no less than five times. We might argue that this is simply the mark of an inexperienced or unoriginal author who, lacking sufficient poetic gift, falls into sloppy repetitive patterns. It could also be an editorial problem at Random House Mondadori. But the consistency with which these three adjectives appear throughout the entire novel suggests something else is happening here. Zambrano is locked into a certain frame of reference where the two defining characteristics of the general are his age and his craftiness. The adjectives also carry a certain religious value that construct a satanic image of the American general which fits well, both with the notion of the ungodly invasion of Protestant forces against a Catholic nation, as well as with the religious struggle that Riley undergoes. We see this pattern emerge again when Zambrano ends two consecutive paragraphs with the exact same phrase attributing the moral decline of an Irish soldier to drinking mescal (204), the pathological repetition of the phrase "el poblado mexicano de Corpus Christi" [the Mexican town of Corpus Christi], and the verbatim duplication of Lincoln's protest against the invasion (39, 119).

The enduring anger and resentment present in both Moreno and Zambrano might be interpreted as a truncated process of grieving. In psychoanalytic terms, neither author is able to work through the traumatic past and help orient their readers toward the possibilities of a renewed future. They are caught in a melancholic feedback loop, a continuous recycling of the past that has no end primarily because they are unable to withdraw their nostalgic longing for a lost utopia. We can, of course, argue that the object of desire in this case is the expropriated territory, but a similar case can be made for the sense of national pride and sovereignty that were violated by the invasion. These novels do not represent mourning in the Freudian notion of closure because, at the end of each, the characters and, metonymically, the nation are unable to find peace with the defeat. Both communicate a sense of outrage that has not been ameliorated in the ensuing 160 years, activating Anzaldúa's definition of the border as an open, bleeding wound. And it is precisely in the exploration of that wound that Caruth articulates her notion of trauma as an experience that can only be understood by regressive reflection. Only by returning to the site of damage can the victim make sense of a violent act that was, in the moment of commission, unable to be assimilated. In both novels this sense of openness is made present both by the sense of outrage that the narrator feels and by each novel's conclusion. Both end precisely at the close of the war, as Yankee troops pull out of Mexico City. The final image in both cases is that of a defeated, broken people watching their conquerors walk away, leaving them amid their ruins. There is no time to heal and the shock of defeat still lingers near the surface. This unresolved and open-ended sense of victimhood constitutes the primary pitfall for the rhetoric of failure. Instead of being used as a critical tool it creates a sense of pessimistic paralysis.

La invasión: Confessing the Nation's Sins

Where both *México mutilado* and *México por asalto* are burdened by a debilitating sense of anger and are ultimately unable to channel the rhetoric of failure into a productive current of righteous indignation, Ignacio Solares's *La invasión* deals with the same historical material and the same historical problems, but does so in a manner that invites reflection and action. He overcomes the temptation to read the apparent repetition of the past as an indicator that the future is atavistically doomed to failure and uses failure as an "unusual means toward self-knowledge" (Ochoa 6) that therapeutically helps the nation work through the traumatic past. This change in tone is evident from the first page of the novel, which opens as a sniper's bullet kills an American soldier attempting to hoist the Stars and Stripes over the National Palace in Mexico City in 1847. The act of defiance ignites a riot among the Mexican citizens, who had passively watched the Yankee army occupy the plaza. Stones, teeth, and fingernails are used to attack the invading forces. These events are recorded by Abelardo, a melancholic prophet figure who sees premonitions of impending destruction in heavenly signs and associates them with the invasion. For fifty years Abelardo ruminates on the riot and his meager participation in it, until his wife finally convinces him to piece together his memories of days leading up to the war, including his failed love affair with a young socialite named Isabel, his participation in the Zócalo uprising, and his support of rebellious insurgent forces. As with all the novels we have studied up to this point, *La invasión* is a metafictional novel in that we watch the chronicle being assembled by Abelardo and he frequently directs his addresses to the reader as a means of explaining why he writes the chronicle. The ostensible reason he offers is to make an attempt to account for what happened, to try to explain why Mexico was so miserably defeated by the invading Yankees. Yet, as the story progresses, Abelardo's tone becomes less journalistic and more confessional. It is this religious confessional attitude that I want to focus on throughout the remainder of this chapter because, maybe more so than any other Mexican writer in the twentieth century, Ignacio Solares has placed an honest metaphysical preoccupation at the center of his examination of Mexican history.

This is not to say, however, that Solares is alone in his metaphysical musings. A strong metaphysical current runs through twentieth-century Mexican literature, but rarely does it ever form the thematic background of an author's entire oeuvre. Instead we find isolated incidents where spiritual or messianic motifs contribute to portrayals of ideological zealotry, structure a sociopolitical criticism, or establish a narrative framework for exploring what Borges once defined as the aesthetic beauty behind philosophical ideas (*Obras* 775). For instance, Ricardo Flores Magón's second revolutionary short story "El apóstol", published in January 1911, portrays a political activist drumming up support for the *maderista* cause as a martyr bringing the good news to the benighted countryside. The Mexican Communist Party expelled José Revueltas in 1949, in part, because he portrayed members of the party as zealots suffering from various messianic complexes in *Los días terrenales*. In *El llano en llamas* (1953), Juan Rulfo portrays post-Revolution Mexico as a land bereft of redeeming grace, mocked by heaven. Juan José Arreola parodies Christian parables to decry North American imperial encroachments in "En verdad os digo" from *Confabulario* (1967). In *El evangelio según Lucas Gavilán* (1979), Vicente Leñero rewrites the life of Christ in contemporary Mexico City as a commentary about urbanization, agrarian reform, and the public good. René Avilés Fabila dedicates a section of *Borges y yo* (1991) to the task of rewriting the Bible as a challenge to traditional readerly reception and interpretation. Carlos Fuentes' *La campaña* (1992) tells the story of an Argentine man who participates in all the major battles of the independence war and finally arrives in Mexico where he meets a priest who bears a striking resemblance to José María Morelos. The novel ends with a long religious statement of political belief wherein the priest expounds that true independence stems from good government founded on the bedrock of religious piety.

By contrast, Ignacio Solares has made spirituality the unifying element in novels like *Madero, el otro* (1989) and *La noche de Ángeles* (1991) and historical dramas like *El jefe máximo* and *Los mochos*. A Catholic by birth, he considers himself a spiritual man and a connoisseur of all faiths. "Estudié con los jesuitas," [I studied with the Jesuits], he admits, "aunque tengo un rechazo absoluto a la iglesia. Muchas veces he pensado que el gran reto de los católicos es convertirse al cristianismo" [though I absolutely reject the church. Many times I have thought the greatest challenge for Catholics is to convert to Christianity] (Rodríguez Marcos). His texts encompass spiritual journeys, question the relationship between life and death, probe the limits of the good within the realities of political power, challenge traditional Christian cosmologies, and argue for a strong sense of the divine. Douglas Weatherford references the spiritual current in Solares's work, but does so tangentially (73–92). In a bolder tone, Rafael Hoyle argues that Solares writes against the grain of Mexican literature by foregrounding the spiritual in a world imbued with tension between secularity and religiosity. He explains that, despite a sustained criticism of the church as an institution, Solares encourages readers to seek out religious discipline as both a means toward spiritual salvation and social progress (28). Social progress here is not simply defined in political terms relating to access to governmental services and participation in the electoral process, but more organically as the physical, emotional, and spiritual welfare of the nation.

The religious foundation of the novel is clearly defined in the prophetic function that Solares assigns to the protagonist, Abelardo. Though we can speak of prophets as revelators or those foretell future events, biblical prophets are primarily historians and literary authors. The book of Genesis has more to say about the how the nation of Israel came to be than it does about the geology, hydrology, and biology of the earth's creation, and the Pentateuch is equal parts Jewish history and religious law. Prophetic writings transcribe significant events from national history and preserve them for the didactic uses of future generations. They are punctuated by phrases that invite recollection of past divine interventions and couch these admonitions within literary tropes and structures that are formulaic enough to facilitate memorization and transmission. This formulation follows upon the Enrico Mario Santi's conceptualization of the poet-prophet as one who speaks or writes on behalf others. Whether that other is perceived religiously as a divine being or secularly as the collective sovereign people, power emanates from a source external to the speaking subject and endows the prophet with the ability to "present absolute knowledge in poetic form" (15). Santi continues:

> At its etymological root, to prophesy means to speak on behalf of someone or something, be it an inspiring god, nation, or muse. The prophet is the one who speaks, yet his speech derives its authority not from an inner reservoir, but from an outside and sometimes alien source. Our sense of drama tells us that the prophet must be a self-assured, inspired spokesman. And yet both of these key adjectives (self-assured, inspired) subvert from within the very stability that they seemingly promote. Prophecy dramatizes, above all, a lack in the intentional speaking subject who is reduced by an overpowering external discourse to a mere agent or instrument. (16)

As a prophet, Abelardo feels compelled to record his nation's sins. He began writing in the days leading up to the invasion, but only finishes it 30 years later at his wife's insistence: "Lo que rehúyes es escribir sobre tus culpas y tus alucinaciones, insufribles para la gente que vive contigo, te conozco...Si no lo escribes ahora, te van a llegar de golpe en el momento de la muerte, y va a ser peor, créemelo" (30) [You're trying to run away from writing about your guilt and hallucinations, which are insufferable for the people who live with you...If you don't write your story now, all those images will haunt you at the moment of your death, which would be much worse, I assure you] (15). Magdalena hopes that by recalling the past and writing it down, Abelardo will be able to clear his conscience.

Note that Abelardo follows in a long tradition of reticent prophets and that his chronicle is not simply a personal journal entry but rather a public confession of the nation's guilt. His own subjectivity is partially suppressed as he becomes the medium who writes on behalf of his people. Additionally there is an apocalyptic aspect to the prophetic figure that merits mentioning. When societies fall from grace, prophets are called to bring them back into line. If the people repent, as in the case of Nineveh, destruction is abated. If, on the other hand, the people persist in their ways, God unleashes turmoil upon the people. The Old Testament prophet Jeremiah warned that Jerusalem would be leveled by invaders from the north, and Isaiah recriminated the nation of Israel for being a "sinful nation, a people laden with iniquity, a seed of evildoers, children that are corrupters" because "they have forsaken the LORD, they have provoked the Holy One of Israel unto danger, they are gone away backward....Your country is desolate, your cities are burned with fire: your land, strangers devour it in your presence, and it is desolate, as overthrown by strangers" (Isaiah

1:4, 7). Though apocalyptic prophets like Jeremiah, Isaiah, Malachi, Jesus, and John did speak at length about the destructions that would precede the coming of the Son of Man, revelation is not solely a voice of warning (Ehrman 145–47). In a broader sense, prophetic revelation communicates truth intended to bring people closer to the divine. Abelardo's chronicle intends to unearth the secret truths that will help fin de siècle Mexico avoid the instability that characterized the first years of independence.

Earlier I characterized Abelardo as a melancholic prophet, in part because LaCapra and Caruth allude to an open dialogue with the traumatic past that allows survivors to dialogue with their pain. Their observations echo Freud's 1917 essay, "Mourning and Melancholia," where he defines mourning as the process by which the libido is surreptitiously disassociated from an object of desire that has been lost. This distancing renders the object dead to the individual, or in other words, transforms it into a preterit object. Freud differentiates melancholia from mourning because the former does not distance the patient from the object of desire, but rather reinforces the empathetic bond. Whereas mourning brings closure, melancholia opens the subjective conscience to the loss and reinforces the individual's bond with the absent object. If melancholia is, as Freud suggests, an open channel to one's traumatic past—differentiated from mourning in that mourning involves the withdrawal of the libido from the desired object, rendering it dead and preterit, while melancholia reinforces the libidinous desire—then David Eng and David Kazanjian may rightly assert that melancholia allows for a positive constructive dialogue with the past. A number of studies have postulated that the gift of prophecy may in fact be linked to melancholia, depression, and an overactive limbic system (Dudley 90). Just as Eng and Kazanjian have conceptualized melancholy as an open conduit that allows for open dialogue with the traumatic past (2–5), Solares and others point to the possibility that melancholia or depression or a hyperactive amygdala "appear to...provide the foundations for mystical, spiritual, and religious experience and the perception, or perhaps the hallucination, of ghosts, demons, spirits, and sprites and belief in demonic or angelic possession" (Joseph 106). As his chronicle opens, Abelardo relates that "Por aquellos días me sucedía con frecuencia que durante un ataque de melancolía viera—o entreviera—unas llamitas errantes en el cielo, danzarinas, que llegaban y se iban, y a veces bajaban a posarse, por ejemplo, en lo alto de una iglesia—les encantaban las iglesias, en especial las churriguerescas" (19) [Around that time, during my episodes of melancholy I would frequently see—or catch glimpses of—flames flickering in the sky. They would come and go, dance about, and sometimes descend and alight upon, for instance, the tower of a church—they loved churches, especially baroque ones] (7). The flames he sees accompany his bouts with melancholia and visions of things to come. Abelardo's friend, Doctor Urruchúa, thinks that Abelardo's visions are premonitions of impending danger: "esas llamas en el cielo podrían ser signos agoreros de desastres que se ciernen sobre el lugar en que aparecen, lo que tiene sentido por la situación tan grave que atraviesa hoy nuestra pobre ciudad" (20) [those flames in the sky might be ominous signs of disasters looming over the places where they appear. It would only make sense given the grim circumstances our poor city currently faces] (7). He attributes Abelardo's visions to a heightened spiritual sensitivity brought on by his psychological problems and wonders if the melancholic are not also visionaries capable of discovering "señales premonitorias en el cielo para las que nosotros—pobres seres normales—estamos incapacitados" (74) [warnings in the heavens which we—poor normal beings—are unable to perceive] (48). As prophet of a fallen Mexico, Abelardo makes an account of the nation's sin. Twice the notion of purging national or collective sin is addressed: once, when Magdalena insists that he write the chronicle so his guilt does not overwhelm him at the moment of his death and because, "la ciudad misma, para purgar su culpa igual que tú, necesita que lo recuerdes y lo escribas" (30–31) [the city itself needs you to remember and write] (15); and again when Doctor Urruchúa, alluding to Abelardo's role as spiritual messiah, asserts that Abelardo's visions and neuroses atone for the nation's errors: "Está usted purgando la culpa de quién sabe cuántos capitalinos con sus sueños y sus visiones, amigo mío" (60) [With your dreams and visions, my friend, you are purging who knows how many inhabitants of this city of their guilt] (39). The sins most prominent in the novel are those of idolatry and passivity.

The first commandment of the Decalogue warns the children of Israel against idolatry, proscribing the manufacture and worship of other gods. This law was given in response to the nation fabricating the image of a golden calf and prostrating themselves before it. Solares proposes that nineteenth-century Mexico's golden calf was Antonio López de Santa Anna when Abelardo asserts that "la relación de Santa Anna con *su* pueblo me resultó reveladora para empezar a entender eso que llamamos 'mexicanidad', y que con tantos esfuerzos y sobresaltos intentábamos construir por aquellas fechas" (38) [ever since Santa Anna rose to power, I think that understanding his relationship with *his* people is fundamental to understanding the phenomenon of 'Mexicanicity,' which at that time we put so much effort and care into trying to construct] (22). It bears repeating that Santa Anna, the premier caudillo of the nineteenth century, was involved in practically every major event from the first insurgency to the French intervention of the 1860s, and that his role in the American invasion has been the subject of much speculation. Some argue that Santa

Anna's participation in the war was duplicitous. Others, including the general himself, suggest that his feigned complicity with the invading army allowed him to know the position and troop strength of the enemy and to use that information to mount a defense. Still others maintain that Santa Anna, true to form, switched his intentions of dealing with the Americans when he perceived the possibility of fending them off. Whatever the case may be, Santa Anna's participation in the conflict was less than admirable on many accounts and has tarnished his already besmirched image in the eyes of Mexican historiography.

Solares' interest in Santa Anna has less to do with his military engagements and more with the ongoing love-hate relationship with the Mexican people that led Justo Sierra to famously designate him the seducer of the nation. In what seems to be a reoccurring theme, Solares emphasizes the theatricality of the general's life and career. Paying special attention to the parades and fanfare, Abelardo relates that despite everything "sus múltiples caídas y descréditos, de lo acerbo de las burlas y de las maldiciones, cada vez que el héroe regresa al poder, se le organiza una nueva entrada triunfal a la capital y todo el mundo sale a la calle" (40) [his multiple falls from grace, his public disgrace, the harsh jokes of which he was the butt, the bitter curses breathed against him—each time the hero returned to power, a new triumphal entry was organized for him in the capital and everyone attended] (23). He observes that the motivation was twofold: the people loved parades and the well-to-do society anxiously awaits a protector. Moreover, the wealthy were enthralled by "el boato que Santa Anna imprime a la vida oficial, a pesar de los constantes quebrantos económicos" (41) [the ostentation which Santa Anna impressed upon official life, despite the constant economic downturns] (24). Solares' description of this infatuation with the decorum that Santa Anna brought to Mexican society is, of course, undermined by the reminder that they were always accompanied by economic hardship. Socialites are caricatured by their pretentious jewelry and overly enthusiastic applause; military officers wear their dress uniforms for no particular reason. Solares suggests that the upper crust of Mexican society bartered the long-term welfare of their nation for superficial and extravagant comforts. The essence of this adoration is distilled from the massive earthquake that punctuated Santa Anna's 1845 incarceration in the prison at San Juan Ulúa. Solares relates that many *capitalinos* began spreading the rumor that the heavens were punishing the nation for threatening the life of a chosen leader. Worshipping Santa Anna, then, is tantamount to idolatry. But it is symptomatic of a broader issue: Mexico's willingness to forego stability in lieu of temporary physical comfort and luxury. This theme will play out numerous times in the text. It is tempting, for example, to draw parallels between Mexico's love affair with Santa Anna and Abelardo's ongoing infatuation with his girlfriend's mother. Both should be taboo. And yet both Abelardo and Mexico are inextricably attracted to persons whom they know should be off limits.

Idolatry is essentially a sin of commission, that is, it requires willing action. The second national sin, passivity, is a sin of omission. The novel begins with Abelardo's account of the flag hoisting at the city center. The narration is repeated later, but with more detail. Abelardo writes that the Mexicans submissively followed the invading army through the streets toward the Zócalo "como un gran animal torpe, por su tamaño, por su pesantez" (204) [like a huge, uncoordinated animal] (152). The multitude congregates in the city center and watches as General Scott offers his triumphal speech in English. The crowd responds with insults and threats, but there is no action. Solares observes that, as emotive and poetic as the insults might have been, no one dared move against their newly arrived conquerors. A moment of change comes, however, when Próspero Pérez, a beggar, challenges Mexicans to do something. "Estoy preguntando, ¿qué, aquí no hay hombres? Porque supongo que los hombres, los de veras hombres, no soportarían que los pendejearan como ustedes lo soportan. Lo pendejean y algo peor. ¿O no ven la mierda que les echa encima, con su pura presencia, cada yanqui que entra a esta ciudad?" (208) [I'm asking, are there no men here! By my way of thinking, men—real men, that is— wouldn't allow themselves to get screwed and just stand by and do nothing. You're getting screwed and then some. It's as if every single Yankee entering this city is throwing his crap at you. Their very presence does it. Can't you see?] (155). Following this passionate call to arms, the multitude attacks the American army. But the resistance is short-lived, and the insurgency is put down within a matter of weeks.

The counterpoint to this passivity is Father Domeneco Celedonio Jarauta, a Spanish priest who led a guerrilla rebellion against Scott's forces in Jalapa but never enjoyed much success. Solares places him in Mexico City for the raising of the American flag and credits him with shooting the soldier who tried to raise the banner. Jarauta is an interesting footnote in the pages of Mexico's religious fanaticism. A Spaniard by birth, Jarauta fervently supported the Catholic Church and condemned Protestantism. His objection to the North American invasion had little to do with politics and everything to do with protecting the church's rights in the Americas. Abelardo relates that, "Así como la lucha contra el Islam ocupaba la mente de San Ignacio de Loyola durante su juventud, en la de él se volvió obsesión ayudar a los mexicanos a pelear contra los *infieles* yanquis, para lo cual tenía que ser jesuitas y nada más que jesuita" (223) [Just as the fight against Islam had occupied the thoughts of St. Ignatius during his youth, it had become the priest's obsession to help Mexicans fight against the Yankee

infidel, something only a Jesuit would do] (167). Jarauta tells Abelardo
that the North Americans' mission was clear: "apoderarse de México,
exterminar a sus habitantes, luego conquistar el resto a América Latina,
imponiendo el mismo dominio bárbaro, con la bandera de las barras y
las estrellas como único símbolo; brincar a Europa, someterla también,
acabar con su cultura y sus tradiciones, y concluir su larga y siniestra marcha...en el Vaticano" (226) [to take control of Mexico, exterminate its
inhabitants, then conquer the rest of Latin America, imposing the same
barbarous domination, with the flag of the stars and stripes as its only
symbol. Then they would jump to Europe, subdue it also, do away with
its culture and traditions, to conclude its long and sinister march in...the
Vatican, which they would invade] (168–69). Jarauta's role in the novel
should be interpreted as a defense of Catholicism. As I have pointed out
earlier, Solares bears no special love of the church and, in fact, criticizes its
adherents for their lack of Christianity. But Solares certainly does roman-
ticize Jarauta's zeal. There is a definite sense of appreciation for the Jesuits
and their contributions to American civilization. Again, Solares has commented that the Jesuits left an indelible impression upon him. Much like
James Joyce, whose experience with the Irish Jesuits left a similar distaste
for the institution, Solares is unable to distance himself from Jesuits and
the achievements of that order. Solares prefers the Spanish priest's energy
and willingness to fight over the passivity of his own people.

The key moment for Solares's use of the rhetoric of failure comes after
the American forces occupy the city, when Abelardo enters a small parish
to hear Mass. The priest offers a scathing sermon that hits at the heart
of the novel's message. He proposes that the US army is a plague sent by
God to punish Mexico for its numerous sins. The devil is not to blame,
but rather, the very God that liberated Israel from Pharaoh, that destroyed
Jericho, to whom they dedicate their prayers and against who "son inca-
paces tanto el Ayuntamiento como el general Santa Anna o el mejor de
nuestros guerrilleros" (245) [our city government, General Santa Anna,
and the best of our soldiers are nothing] (183) brought the invading forces
as punishment. He continues:

> Durante mucho tiempo esta ciudad tuvo su oportunidad de salvación, como
> todas las ciudades del mundo, como cada uno de sus habitantes en particu-
> lar. En su eterna misericordia, Dios nos dejó la oportunidad de elegir, de
> encontrar nuestro camino. Pues bien, esto no podía durar. ¿Qué hemos
> hecho con este país a partir de que se proclamó independiente? Díganme,
> ¿qué hemos hecho de él? ¿A quién hemos permitido que nos gobierne? Dios,
> cansado de esperar a que fuéramos más cautos y más responsables, qué digo
> cansado, harto, decepcionado de todos nosotros, Él ha tenido que tomar
> cartas en el asunto. Tenía que hacerlo, no tenía más remedio. Y entonces nos

mandó a los yanquis como castigo. Por decirlo en una palabra: los mexicanos nos ganamos a pulso esta invasión. (246–47)

[For a long time this city had the opportunity to have salvation, like
every city in the world, like each inhabitant in particular. In His eternal
mercy, God gave us the chance to choose, to make our own path. But this
could not last forever. What have we done with this country since it was
declared independent? Tell me: what have we done? Whom have we allowed
to govern us? Tired of waiting for us to become more careful and responsible, and although I said 'tired,' I could have well said 'fed up' or 'exasper-
ated' with each one of us, God has had to take matters into his own hands.
He had to! He ran out of options! So He sent the Yankees to us as punishment. In summary, we Mexicans earned this invasion.] (184)

The priest's words resonate with biblical foreboding, but they also communicate the possibility of redemption if Mexico is willing to accept its own
role in the paving the way for defeat. In what may be the starkest use of the
rhetoric of failure, the parish priest declares that, "nosotros mismos llamamos a nuestros invasores. Acéptenlo, asúmanlo, vívanlo como una realidad
ineludible, con todo lo que implica de vergüenza y de dolor pero también
de posible redención" (248) [we called and invited our invaders. Accept
it. Let it become part of you. Live it as an unavoidable truth, with all
that it implies—shame, pain, but also the possibility of redemption] (185).
Mexico's inability to lay aside its ideological divisions and work together
for the common good set the stage for the American invasion, and yet,
the clear recognition of guilt offers a modicum of hope for redemption.
This redemption rests upon the nation's willingness to remember and to
act. The priest closes: "He aquí, hermanos míos, la reflexión que quería
traerles para que esta invasión norteamericana no quede sólo como un
suceso más en nuestra historia, sino como un medio para la penitencia y
la posible salvación de nuestra alma. Quizá del alma de la ciudad entera"
(248) [My brothers and sisters, may this American invasion not be just one
more event in our history, but a means to our penitence and the possible
salvation of our souls. And perhaps of the soul of our entire city] (185). It is
at this point that the difference between Solares and Moreno or Zambrano
becomes clear: Solares engages the public in a frank discussion of failure,
but does so without becoming mired in cynicism.

The priest's words imply that Mexico can break the atavistic cycle of
failure by applying the familiar adage: those who fail to learn from history are doomed to repeat it. The novel's structure builds upon this con-
flated temporality by playing up parallels between Hernán Cortés and
Winfield Scott. Cortés arrived at Tenochtitlan (present-day Mexico City)
in November 1519. By July 1520 he had worn out his welcome, and the
Aztecs drove the Spaniards from the city. Cortés retreated to the coast,

regrouped, and convinced the Tlaxcalan Indians to help him overthrow
the Aztecs. With their aid, Cortés was able to subdue Tenochtitlan in 1521.
Scott, inspired by William Prescott's *The Conquest of Mexico* (1843), followed Cortés's route to the Aztec capital: he landed at Veracruz and met
little resistance as his troops traversed the path across the lowlands, up
into the mountains of Puebla, and into the valley of Anahuac. Like Cortés
before him, Scott recognized the value of dividing to conquer. American
forces arrived in Puebla to open arms and stayed there comfortably for
three months while planning the final assault on Mexico City. Puebla has
always been a Catholic stronghold in the nation, and the poblano elite did
not look kindly on the acting president Gómez Farías's liberal encroachments on ecclesiastical privileges and church properties. They were also
displeased with Santa Anna's forced loans which were frequently aimed
at the clergy's pockets. So when Scott agreed to establish order and protect the church's interests, Puebla rolled out the proverbial red carpet. It
is significant that Abelardo thinks about both men while witnessing the
American troops parading in front of the national palace because the building and its location are key to this theme of repetition. It lies in the heart of
downtown Mexico City, near the ruins of the Aztec Templo Mayor, on the
same plot of land that Cortés had used to build his residence in 1523. This
is, and always has been, the center of Mexican political and ecclesiastical
power. All of Mexico's conquerors—the Aztecs who settled the valley, the
Spaniards who overthrew the Aztecs, and the Americans who defeated the
Mexican army—go to this place, and Solares suggests the same problem
that proved the undoing of the Aztec empire allowed the Americans to
overrun the nation. Scott and Cortés exploited Mexico's instability and,
consequently, their victories were not due to their own strengths but to
Mexico's weakness.

The key to breaking this cycle is confessional writing. Solares' philosophy of historical writing can be summarized by the concept of confession
as an articulatory practice that allows one to "distinguish between past
and present and to recall in memory that something happened to one (or
one's people) back then while realizing that one is living here and now with
openings to the future" and, thus enable "survival or a reengagement in
life" (LaCapra 21–22). Both LaCapra and Caruth agree that the exploration of repressed experience can be carried out through the therapeutic process of writing even though they differ about the possibility of effectively
finding closure because writing constitutes a blank space wherein victims
can explore and work through their trauma. In *The Writing of the Disaster*
(1988), Maurice Blanchot explained that while traumatic experiences may
elude full comprehension and demarcate the limit of writing, this does not
mean that "disaster, as the force of writing, is excluded from it, is beyond

the pale of writing" but rather exceeds the already flawed capacity of language to codify human experience (7). Solares shares this vision when he stated that "Carl Gustav Jung, en 1913 dijo: 'no hay mayor terapia que la escritura.' Esa escritura que describe Jung abre zonas insospechadas; si uno se pone a escribir, encuentra sus *yo* secretos. Básicamente, escribo para conocerme" [In 1913 Carl Gustav Jung said, "the best therapy is writing." The writing that Jung describes opens unexpected zones: if one begins writing, he finds his secret I. Basically I write to know myself] (Garduño). Abelardo's wife, Magdalena, encourages him to write his chronicle as a type of public confession. Her husband's memories are not his alone, but metonymically those of the entire city. He, however, is reticent to commit these shortcomings to paper because he considers them unworthy. But these unworthy memories are precisely the ones that she thinks best embody the period: "Son las mejores para recrearlas y reflejar la condición humana, me parece. La memoria indigna y la memoria chusca. ¿No también andabas con ganas de hacer un recuento de los pasajes chuscos de nuestra historia, hasta llegar por lo menos a Maximiliano y Carlota? ¿Qué pasó con eso?" (22–23) [It seems to me that's the most important kind for reflecting upon the human condition. Humiliating memories and droll memories. Didn't you want to write a retrospective on all the droll episodes contained in our history, up at least to Maximilian and Carlota? What happened with that?] (9). In what follows, I turn my attention to these confessional elements. Solares styles the novel's protagonist, Abelardo, as a melancholic prophetic figure whose mission is to purge the nation of the painful war memories. To do so, he must likewise purge himself of personal misdeeds: he must personally confess to cowardice and infidelity. This allows him to tackle the political and ideological dissensions that plague Mexico and allow foreign invaders to take advantage of Mexico.

If Abelardo's chronicle is his confession and the means by which Mexico's guilt is to be purged, then to conclude, we might wonder to whom he confesses. Textual evidence supports the hypothesis that Abelardo is confessing, at least on a very personal level, to his wife, Magdalena. She inspires him to finish his chronicle as a therapeutic device for working through his traumatic past. Magdalena also takes an active role in questioning Abelardo about his past and prodding him to write. She makes laconic criticisms of his historical narrative and his decision to include Doctor Urruchúa's notes. But her real interest is in his romantic past. Numerous times she feigns disinterest in the chronicle, telling Abelardo to let her know when he gets back to the love affair. This suggestion is strengthened by the narrator's closing words when he confesses that he wrote so explicitly about the love affair precisely because he knew that she was reading it: "Pero sabía que tus ojos estaban ahí, siguiéndome, alentándome a hacer una confesión completa, fuera cual fuera el precio y el resultado. Finalmente, tú lo sabías, lo estaba escribiendo para ti y en consecuencia para eso Otro, o Espejo, o Rey de la Muerte, o Conciencia Universal, o Dios, o como quieras llamarlo" (297) [But I knew that your eyes were there, pursuing me, encouraging me to make a complete confession, whatever the cost or the result. Finally, as you know, I was writing it for you, and consequently for that Other, or the Mirror, or the King of Death, or the Universal Conscience, or God, or whatever you want to call it] (226). So at one level the chronicle clears the air with his wife. At another, however, it attests to the "angustiosa necesidad de *rendir cuentas*" (162) [the anguishing need to *make an accounting*] (118) to a higher power. After stating that man's necessity to make an accounting surpasses mere religiosity, Abelardo asks to whom man aspires to account.

¿Ante quién? ¿Ante un amigo que ya murió, como es el doctor Urruchúa? Estoy seguro de que tengo su perdón anticipado. ¿Ante un punado de posibles lectores? Dudo de que llegue a tenerlos. ¿Ante el soldado al que apuñalé? Estábamos en guerra y yo no tenía opción. ¿Ante mi familia? Mi mujer chasqueó la lengua cuando le dije que también ella debía perdonarme. ¿Ante la posteridad? En fin, todo junto puede ser. Pero, ¿no se tratará también, aunque involuntariamente, de anticipar el encuentro con Aquél que nos dio el alma y que la reclamará de vuelta en cualquier momento? Nada que atempere ese encuentro puede resultarnos banal. En especial si, como he pensado siempre, es a través de la escritura que se hace más posible el encuentro. (162–63)

[To whom? To a friend who died, like Dr. Urruchúa? I am certain that he has given me his forgiveness. To a handful of possible readers? I doubt I'll have many. To the soldier I stabbed? We were at war and I didn't see any other option. To my family? My wife clicked her tongue disapprovingly when I told her that she should also forgive me. To my posterity? Anything is possible. But might it not be related, in an involuntary way, to anticipating that meeting with Him who gave us our souls and who could take them back whenever He pleases? Anything that could temper that meeting cannot be considered trivial, especially if, as I have always thought, it is through writing that the meeting becomes possible. (118)

He discounts family, friends, and potential readers. But most importantly, Abelardo posits that people's urge to confess prefigures our ultimate encounter with deity. Writing becomes a rehearsal for that meeting wherein we perform a preliminary cleansing. Or we might suppose that, in Solares' conception of writing that the act of confession itself is enough to satisfy the demands of conscience. This might fit the metafictional style of narrative fiction that surfaced in the 1960s and continued through the

1980s. Unfortunately, it amounts to little more than historical solipsism. These two options cannot preclude another possibility. The ultimate goal of confession is absolution and, yet, in neither case is there any evidence that Abelardo or—by extension, Mexico—is forgiven for his misdeeds. The novel closes with Abelardo lying next to his sleeping wife, who at no point deigns to receive him. Instead, he speaks to her back, suggesting that she is either unwilling or unable to forgive his transgressions. Nor is there any indication of divine forgiveness. To some degree, then, we must read *La invasión* as a truncated story of confession. The priest invites parishioners to learn from the mistakes of the past but nowhere in the novel do we see the fruits of this sermon. The act of contrition has been completed, but the reward has yet to be granted.

These three novels about the Mexican-American War underscore the disparity that separates the paralytic and redemptive modalities of the rhetoric of failure. When we speak of US-Mexico relations, the "Colossus of the North" is typically represented as a looming ogre, ready to crush, usurp, and force its southern neighbor's will with the slightest provocation, and Mexico wears the garb of the victim. This Manichean division caricaturizes both parties to their detriment. Moreno and Zambrano allow the traumatic past to overcome them, to extinguish the positive lessons that Castro Leal hoped Mexican readers might pull from a correct understanding of the war. Their attitude toward the invasion might be best summarized by Dresser and Volpi's mocking suggestion that Mexican educators teach anti-American limericks punctuated with the occasional vulgarity to their students in order to create "un sentimiento positivo de rencor histórico que nos permita seguirnos lamentando, echándole la culpa de todos nuestros problemas a la mala suerte geográfica" [a positive sentiment of historical anger that allows us to continue lamenting our condition, blaming all of our problems on geographic bad luck] (69). By contrast, as with Del Paso's hope that Mexicans would accept Maximilian as one of their own, Solares expects Mexicans to evaluate the state of their political souls. They will ultimately be the judges. If things have not improved, it is up to them to do something about it. Abelardo confesses to posterity in the hope that it will redeem the past by correcting the present.

Conclusion: Bicentennial Reflections on Failure

Mexico celebrated the bicentennial of its independence and the centennial of its revolution amid fanfare and gunfire. While the federal government planned a massive celebration of the nation's history, an ongoing war against and among drug cartels has claimed the lives of more than forty thousand people since 2006. Celebratory banners hung in the capital city's downtown area eerily paralleled the mutilated corpses hanging from overpasses in the major cities of the northern states. Today, many small border towns in Chihuahua, Tamaulipas, and Nuevo León are hard-pressed to fill vacancies left by law enforcement officers who have been assassinated by narcos. Beyond drug violence, roughly half of the population lives in poverty, and stratification continues to widen the economic gap. Concerns about impunity still plague the judicial system as criminals escape maximum security prisons in laundry carts and climb over the walls using ladders.

The serendipitous coincidence of the bicentennial and a moment of significant crisis has underscored the disparity between these two competing visions of the nation. On the one hand, the federal government has promoted a monumental vision of the nation's progress and prosperity through massive public spectacles, military parades, historical reenactments, and artistic commissions for films and literature. The message expressed in "El futuro es milenario," the official anthem of the bicentennial composed by Jaime López and performed by pop star Aleks Syntek, neatly summarizes the image that the Calderón administration wanted to portray. Syntek croons about parties in the streets, differences being cast aside, and the entire nation standing together, united against whatever may come, and all this to the sound to the bicentennial beat. Aside from bubblegum pop conventions like the much derided "shalalá" and uninspired nationalist platitudes, the song was universally panned because it shellacs Mexico's social problems with a thin patina of meaningless, buoyant cheerfulness. On the other, intellectuals have openly denounced the violence, poverty, lawlessness, and criminal impunity that continue to plague the nation. Many seemed to share the sense of exasperation expressed by Mauricio Tenorio prior to the celebrations when, in *México y sus centenarios* (2009), he suggested that the central theme of the bicentennial celebration should include plans to resolve Mexico's most pressing problems and not simply rehash the mythical and revolutionary utopias (54). After the fireworks burned out and the streets were swept, editorialists and cultural critics moved on to evaluating what, if anything, the celebrations had produced. The near unanimous opinion was that little had been accomplished, that a singular moment had been wasted, and that the celebrations—like Syntek's lyrics—were ultimately empty.

Despite the dissatisfaction that intellectuals have felt regarding the outcomes of the national celebrations, I cannot help but find a proverbial silver lining because the bicentennial reflects both the opportunities and problems that Friedrich Nietzsche identified in his essay, "On the Utility and Liability of History for Life" (1874). History is only valuable to society inasmuch as it inspires us to improve upon our current state, he argues. "We only wish to serve history to the extent that it serves life," he continues, "but there is a way of practicing history and a valorization of history in which life atrophies and degenerates" (85). The bicentennial offered the nation an opportunity to reflect upon two hundred years of the failures that Monsiváis once called the stellar moments of Mexican history, those seemingly antithetical instances of defeat that have come to shape the way that the nation thinks about itself. While the government took the easy and ultimately barren route of triumphal nationalism, the very critics who expressed their frustration with the celebrations offered a constructive counternarrative akin to what we have seen in *Cult of Defeat*. What becomes evident, when we study the rhetoric of failure in Mexico's historical imagination, is that Mexican intellectuals are not naysaying pessimists who adopt resigned airs for the joy of somehow appearing more interesting for their angst. What the novels discussed in this book and others like them demonstrate is the potentially transformative effect that the rhetoric of failure has. Throughout this book I have argued that the rhetoric of failure in Mexico's historical imagination forges a story of resilience and perseverance from the debris of history. In the hands of a skilled writer, it can offer a means toward critically identifying contemporary problems, as we have seen in Ibargüengoitia's incisively keen evaluations of political theatricality and Serna's ability to slip pointed critiques about Mexican civil society into a novel that mercilessly slanders Santa Anna. But, for mediocre authors like Moreno and Zambrano or outstanding ones like Paz who get lost in the poetics, the rhetoric of failure is laden with pitfalls, the chief among them being the subtle shift from description to prescription.

The misfortune of these authors is that they become paralyzed by an excessive awareness of history's shortcomings. They paradoxically discuss the mistakes of the past in order to warn against them but, in doing so, they are overcome by these same failures.

Fueled by the recent anniversaries, historical fiction has enjoyed unprecedented success in Mexico. More than thirty novels retelling significant moments of national history have appeared in the last five years, and this does not account for all of the other ways that history has been offered up as a good for mass public consumption. The impetus behind this boom of historical fiction are the powerhouse publishers like Planeta Mexicana, Joaquín Mortiz, and Grijalbo Mondadori, which inundated the market with a deluge of historical novels in response to a growing public demand for new ways to engage with important national mythologies. So much so, in fact, that nearly every publisher in Mexico put all nonhistorical texts on hold until after the bicentennial celebrations ended. As is often the case with such floods, the quality of these works varies between novels of exceptional quality like Álvaro Uribe's *Expediente del atentado* (2008) and Eduardo Antonio Parra's *Juárez: El rostro de piedra* (2008) to ones that, by dint of their unimaginative and unremarkable engagement with the past, will quickly and quietly fade from the bookstands. In each of these novels, regardless of their aesthetic charm or ideological orientation, we find representations of the national past that confront failure and defeat. I hope that the analyses in *Cult of Defeat* point to new ways of engaging these portrayals of Mexico's, and Latin America's, stellar moments. What I read in these historical novels is not resignation, but a testimony to Mexico's long legacy of weathering historical maelstroms with self-critical and constructive humor. Under the surface of pessimism about the past and present, I find latent hope that the future will be better. At the heart of Mexico's cult of defeat is faith in its history of perseverance.

Works Cited

Note: The following are what the abbreviations in this section stand for:

FCE (Fondo de Cultura Económica), CONACULTA (Consejo Nacional para la Cultura y las Artes), and INBA (Instituto Nacional de Bellas Artes).

Abreu Gómez, Ermilo. *Juárez: su vida contada a los niños.* Mexico City: FCE, 1969. Print.

Adams, Hazard. *Critical Theory Since Plato.* Rev. ed. Fort Worth: Harcourt Brace Jovanovich, 1992. 38–48. Print.

Aínsa, Fernando. "La nueva novela histórica hispanoamericana." *Plural* 240 (1991): 82–85. Print.

Alamán, Lucas. *Historia de Méjico desde los primeros movimientos que prepararon su independencia en el ano de 1808, hasta la época presente.* 1852. Mexico City: Talleres Tipográficos de El Tiempo, 1989. Print.

Alonso, Carlos J. *The Burden of Modernity: The Rhetoric of Cultural Discourse in Spanish America.* New York: Oxford UP, 1998. Print.

Alter, Robert. *Partial Magic: The Novel as a Self-Conscious Genre.* Berkeley: U of California P, 1978. Print.

Anderson, Benedict R. *Imagined Communities: Reflections on the Origin and Spread of Nationalism.* Rev. ed. London and New York: Verso, 2006. Print.

Anna, Timothy E. *The Mexican Empire of Iturbide.* Lincoln: U of Nebraska P, 1990. Print.

Arias, Ángel. "Ibargüengoitia y la nueva novela histórica." *RILCE* 17.1 (2001): 17–32. Print.

Ariza, Eileen N. "Role Reversal: The Problems of a Spanish-Speaking Anglo Teaching Spanish to English-Dominant Puerto Rican Children." *Foreign Language Annals* 31.3 (1988): 431–36. Print.

Arroyo, Jossianna. *Travestismos culturales: literatura y etnografía en Cuba y Brasil.* Pittsburgh: Insituto Internacional de Literatura Iberoamericana and U of Pittsburgh, 2003. Print.

Ashcroft, Bill. "Constitutive Graphonomy." *The Postcolonial Studies Reader.* Ed. Bill Ashcroft, Gareth Griffiths, and Helen Tiffin. New York: Routledge, 1995. 298–302. Print.

Auerbach, Erich. *Mimesis; the Representation of Reality in Western Literature.* Princeton, NJ: Princeton UP, 1973. Print.

Avilés Fabila, René. *Borges y yo.* Mexico City: Grupo Editorial 7, 1991. Print.

Azuela, Mariano. *Los de abajo*. Mexico City: FCE, 1984. Print.

Badiou, Alain. *Handbook of Inaesthetics*. Trans. Alberto Toscano. Stanford, CA: Stanford UP, 2005. Print.

Barrientos, Juan José. *Ficción-historia: La nueva novela histórica hispanoamericana*. Mexico City: UNAM, 2001. Print.

Barrón, Luis. "Los relámpagos críticos: La revolución de Jorge Ibargüengoitia." *Istor: Revista de Historia Internacional* 35 (2008): 3–12. Print.

Beckett, Samuel. *Worstward Ho*. New York: Grove P, 1983. Print.

Benjamin, Walter. *Illuminations: Essays and Reflections*. Trans. Harry Zohn. Rev. ed. New York: Schocken Books, 2007. Print.

Bhabha, Homi. "DissemiNation: Time, Narrative, and the Margins of the Modern Nation." *Nation and Narration*. Ed. Homi K. Bhabha. London and New York: Routledge, 1990. 139–70. Print.

———. *The Location of Culture*. London and New York: Routledge, 1994. Print.

———. "Of Mimicry and Man: The Ambivalence of Colonial Discourse." *October* 28 (1984): 125–33. Print.

Biddiss, Michael D. *Father of Racist Ideology: The Social and Political Thought of Count Gobineau*. New York: Weybright and Talley, 1970. Print.

Biron, Rebecca. "Joking Around with Mexican History: Parody in Ibargüengoitia, Castellanos, and Sainz." *Revista de Estudios Hispanos* 34 (2000): 625–44. Print.

Blake, Linnie. *The Wounds of Nations: Horror Cinema, Historical Trauma and National Identity*. Manchester: Manchester UP, 2008. Print.

Blanchot, Maurice. *The Writing of the Disaster*. Trans. Ann Smock. Lincoln: U of Nebraska P, 1988. Print.

Bobadilla Encinas, Gerardo Francisco. "Apuntes sobre *El seductor de la patria* de Enrique Serna, o el epistolario no escrito de Antonio López de Santa Anna." *Revista de Literatura Mexicana Contemporánea* 9.21 (2003): 89–96. Print.

Borges, Jorge Luis. *La cifra*. Buenos Aires: Editorial Emecé, 1981. Print.

———. *Obras completas de Jorge Luis Borges (1923–1972)*. Buenos Aires: Emecé Editores, 1974. Print.

Boullosa, Carmen. "Guilt of Popularity." *The New York Times* 19 Apr. 2005: A21. Print.

Bourdieu, Pierre. "The Field of Cultural Production, or: The Economic World Reversed." *Poetics* 12 (1983): 311–56. Print.

Bradu, Fabienne. "*Noticias del imperio* de Fernando del Paso." *Vuelta* May 1988: 48–50. Print.

Bruce-Novoa, Juan and David Valentín. "Violating the Image of Violence: Ibargüengoitia's *El atentado*." *Latin American Theatre Review* 12.2 (1979): 13–21. Print.

Brushwood, John S. *México en su novela: Una novela en busca de su identidad*. Mexico City: FCE, 1973. Print.

———. *Narrative Innovation and Political Change in Mexico*. New York: Peter Lang Publishing, 1989.

———. *La novela mexicana, 1967–1982*. Mexico City: Grijalbo, 1985. Print.

Burke, Kenneth. *A Rhetoric of Motives*. Berkeley and Los Angeles: U of California P, 1969. Print.

Butler, Judith. "Performative Acts and Gender Constitution: An Essay in Phenomenology and Feminist Theory." *Theatre Journal* 40.4 (Dec. 1988): 519–31. Print.

Camp, Roderic Ai. *Intellectuals and the State in Twentieth-Century Mexico*. Austin: U of Texas P, 1985. Print.

———. "The Time of the Technocrats and Deconstruction of the Revolution." *The Oxford History of Mexico*. Ed. Michael C. Meyer and William H. Beezley. Oxford: Oxford UP, 2000. 609–36. Print.

Campesino, Juan. *La historia como ironía: Ibargüengoitia como historiador*. Guanajuato: Universidad de Guanajuato, 2005. Print.

Carballido, Emilio. "Drama y novela de Jorge Ibargüengoitia." *El atentado, Los relámpagos de agosto: edición crítica*. Ed. Juan Villoro and Víctor Díaz Arciniega. Nanterre: ALLCA XX, Universite Paris X, 2002. 263–65. Print.

Cárdenas, Noé. "A rizar rizos." *Letras Libres* Dec. 2006: 75–77. Print.

Caruth, Cathy. *Unclaimed Experience: Trauma, Narrative, and History*. Baltimore, MD: Johns Hopkins UP, 1996. Print.

Castañón, Adolfo. "*Noticias del imperio* de Fernando del Paso." *Vuelta* Sep. 1988: 32–33. Print.

Castellanos, Rosario. *El uso de la palabra*. Mexico: Ediciones de Excélsior, 1975. Print.

Castro Leal, Antonio. "Introduction." *Recuerdos de la invasión norteamericana*. Vol. 1. By José María Roa Bárcena, 1883. Mexico: Porrúa, 1947. vii–xiii. Print.

Chiang, Lan-Hung Nora and Chih-Hsiang Sean Yang. "Learning to be Australian: Adaptation and Identity Formation of Young Taiwanese-Chinese Immigrants in Melbourne, Australia." *Pacific Affairs* 81.2 (2008): 241–58. Print.

Christensen, Inger. *The Meaning of Metafiction: A Critical Study of Selected Novels by Sterne, Nabokov, Barth, and Beckett*. New York: Columbia UP, 1981. Print.

Clark, Stella T. and Alfonso González. "*Noticias del imperio*: La 'verdad histórica' y la novela finisecular en México." *Hispania* 77 (1994): 731–37. Print.

Cohn, Deborah. "The Mexican Intelligentsia, 1950–1968: Cosmopolitanism, National Identity, and the State." *Mexican Studies / Estudios Mexicanos* 21.1 (2005): 141–82. Print.

Corona, Ignacio. "La construcción de la subjetividad y lo aparente. El discurso periodístico de Jorge Ibargüengoitia." *El atentado, Los relámpagos de agosto: edición crítica*. Ed. Juan Villoro and Víctor Díaz Arciniega. Nanterre: ALLCA XX, Universite Paris X, 2002. 469–74. Print.

Corral Peña, Elizabeth. *Noticias del imperio y los nuevos caminos de la novela histórica*. Jalapa: Universidad Veracruzana, 1997. Print.

Crankshaw, Edward. *The Fall of the House of Habsburg*. New York: Penguin, 1983. Print.

De Groot, Jerome. *Consuming History: Historians and Heritage in Contemporary Popular Culture*. New York: Routledge, 2009. Print.

Delillo, Don. *Great Jones Street*. New York: Vintage Books, 1983. Print.

Derrida, Jacques. "Plato's Pharmacy." *Dissemination*. Trans. Barbara Johnson. Chicago: U of Chicago P, 1981. 61–171. Print.

———. *Specters of Marx: The State of the Debt, the Work of Mourning and the New International*. Trans. Peggy Kamuf. New York: Routledge, 1994. Print.

Díez Cobo, Rosa María. "La reescritura de la historia en la narrativa mexicana contemporánea." *Tendencias de la narrativa mexicana actual*. Ed. José Carlos González Boixo. Madrid and Frankfurt: Iberoamericana / Vervuert, 2009. 31–87. Print.

Dimock, Wai-Chee. *Through Other Continents: American Literature Across Deep Time*. Princeton, NJ: Princeton UP, 2009. Print.

Domínguez Ruvalcaba, Héctor. *Modernity and the Nation in Mexican Representations of Masculinity: From Sensuality to Bloodshed*. New York: Palgrave Macmillan, 2007. Print.

Dong, Jie Kathy. "Isn't It Enough to Be a Chinese Speaker: Language Ideology and Migrant Identity Construction in a Public Primary School in Beijing." *Language & Communication: An Interdisciplinary Journal* 29.2 (2009): 115–26. Print.

Dormeus, Anne T. *Culture, Politics, and National Identity in Mexican Literature and Film, 1929–1952*. New York: Peter Lang, 2000. Print.

Dresser, Denise and Jorge Volpi. *México: Lo que todo ciudadanos quisiera (no) saber de su patria*. Mexico City: Santillana Ediciones Generales, 2006. Print.

Dudley, Michael. "Melancholy or Depression, Sacred or Secular?" *International Journal for the Psychology of Religion* 2.2 (1992): 87–99. Print.

Duncan, Robert. "Embracing a Suitable Past: Independence Celebrations under Mexico's Second Empire, 1864–6." *Journal of Latin American Studies* 30.2 (1998): 249–77. Print.

———. "Political Legitimation and Maximilian's Second Empire in Mexico, 1864–1867." *Mexican Studies / Estudios Mexicanos* 12.1 (1996): 27–66. Print.

Earle, Peter G. "Underdogs and Top Dogs in the Mexican Novel." *Revista Hispánica Moderna* 49.2 (Dec. 1996): 299–307. Print.

Echegoyen, Maruja. "Nuevas conversaciones con Fernando del Paso." *Cuadernos de marcha* 24.23 (1983): 24–37. Print.

Eng, David and David Kazanjian. "Introduction: Mourning Remains." *Loss: The Politics of Mourning*. Ed. David Eng and David Kazanjian. Berkeley: U of California P, 2003. 1–25. Print.

Ehrman, Bart D. *Jesus: Apocalyptic Prophet of the New Millennium*. Oxford: Oxford UP, 1999. Print.

Escalante, Evodio. "La ironía de Jorge Ibargüengoitia." *El atentado, Los relámpagos de agosto: edición crítica*. Ed. Juan Villoro and Víctor Díaz Arciniega. Nanterre: ALLCA XX, Universite Paris X, 2002. 498–503. Print.

Fiddian, Robin W. *The Novels of Fernando del Paso*. Gainesville: UP of Florida, 2000. Print.

Flores Magón, Ricardo. "El apóstol." *Cuentos de la revolución mexicana*. Ed. Luis Leal. Mexico: Universidad Nacional Autónoma de México, 1993. 1–5. Print.

Foucault, Michel. *The Archaeology of Knowledge & The Discourse on Language*. 1972. Trans. A. M. Sheridan Smith. New York: Pantheon Books, 1982. Print.

Fowler, Will. "All the President's Women: The Wives of General Antonio López de Santa Anna in 19th Century Mexico." *Feminist Review* 79 (2005): 52–68. Print.

———. *Mexico in the Age of Proposals, 1821–1853.* Westport: Greenwood P, 1998. Print.

———. Rev. of *Para mexicanizar el segundo imperio: el imaginario político de los imperialistas,* by Erika Pani. *Journal of Latin American Studies* 35.3 (2003): 636–38. Print.

———. *Santa Anna of Mexico.* Lincoln: U of Nebraska P. 2007. Print.

Freud, Sigmund. "On Mourning and Melancholia." *The Standard Edition of the Complete Psychological Works of Sigmund Freud.* Trans. James Strachey. Vol. XIV. London, Hogarth and the Institute of Psycho-Analysis, 1986. 237–60. Print.

———. "Remembering, Repeating, and Working-Through: (Further Recommendations on the Technique of Psycho-Analysis II)." *The Standard Edition of the Complete Psychological Works of Sigmund Freud.* Trans. James Strachey. Vol. XII. London, Hogarth and the Institute of Psycho-Analysis, 1986. 147–56. Print.

Fuentes, Carlos. *La campaña.* Madrid: Mondadori, 1990. Print.

———. *La muerte de Artemio Cruz.* Mexico City: FCE, 1968. Print.

———. *Myself with Others: Selected Essays.* New York: Farrar, Straus, and Giroux, 1988. Print.

Garber, Marjorie. *Vested Interests: Cross-Dressing and Cultural Anxiety.* New York: Routledge, 1992. Print.

García, Gustavo. "Maten al negro." *Nexos* 10 Jan 1979. Web. 19 Oct. 2010.

García Canclini, Néstor. *Hybrid Cultures: Strategies for Entering and Leaving Modernity.* Minneapolis: U of Minnesota P, 1995. Print.

García Flores, Margarita. "¡No soy humorista!" Ibargüengoitia, Jorge. *El atentado, Los relámpagos de agosto: edición crítica.* Ed. Juan Villoro and Víctor Díaz Arciniega. Nanterre: ALLCA XX, Universite Paris X, 2002. 406–21. Print.

Garduño, Susana. "Ignacio Solares: La frontera con los Estados Unidos: Esa gran herida que no ha cerrado." *Club de Lectores.* Web. 5 July 2011.

Giménez, Manuel María. *El coronel D. Manuel María Giménez: su vida militar en 52 años, sus servicios en su patria en 7 años, sus servicios en 43 años en la que fue república mexicana y hoy es imperio, escrita por él mismo. Documentos inéditos ó muy raros para la historia de México.* Ed. Genaro García. Mexico: Porrúa, 1974. 280–408. Print.

González Echevarría, Roberto. *Myth and Archive: A Theory of Latin American Narrative.* Durham: Duke UP, 1998. Print.

———. *The Voice of the Masters.* Austin: U of Texas P, 1985. Print.

Gordon, Avery F. *Ghostly Matters: Haunting and the Sociological Imagination.* Minneapolis: U of Minnesota P, 2008. Print.

Grützmacher, Łukasz. "Las trampas del concepto 'la nueva novela histórica' y de la retórica de la historia postoficial." *Arte Poética* 27.1 (2006): 141–67. Print.

Guerrero, Elisabeth. *Confronting History and Modernity in Mexican Narrative.* New York: Palgrave Macmillan, 2008. Print.

———. "The Plotting Priest: Jorge Ibargüengoitia's *Los pasos de López*." *Hispanófila* 133 (2001): 103–21. Print.

Gutiérrez Estrada, Don J. M. *Méjico y el Archiduque Fernando Maximiliano.* Paris: Librería española de Garnier hermanos, 1862. Print.

Hale, Charles A. "Lucas Alamán, Mexican Conservative." *Mexico: From Indepedence to Revolution (1810-1910).* Ed. D. W. Ratt. Lincoln: U of Nebraska P. 128-34. Print.

———. *Mexican Liberalism in the Age of Mora.* New Haven, CT: Yale UP, 1968. Print.

———. Rev. of *Monuments of Progress: Modernization and Public Health in Mexico City, 1876–1910*, by Claudia Agostini. *Journal of Latin American Studies* 36.2 (2004): 390–92. Print.

———. "The War with the United States and the Crisis in Mexican Thought." *The Americas* 14.2 (1957): 153–73. Print.

Haw, Dora Luz. "Analizan *México mutilado*: Vende el libro 100 mil ejemplares en 90 días." *Reforma* 17 February 2005, Cultura: 4. Print.

Herman, Judith Lewis. *Trauma and Recovery.* New York: Basic Books, 1992. Print.

Herz, Theda. "Carnivalizing the Mexican Ethos: Comedic Gesture, Self-Deprecating Anecdote and the 'Pobre Diablo' in Jorge Ibargüengoitia's Prose." *Romance Quarterly* 43.1 (1996): 31–46. Print.

———. "Jorge Ibargüengoitia's Carnival Pageantry: The Mexican Theatre of Power and the Power of Theatre." *Latin American Theatre Review* 28.1 (1994): N. pag. *Academic Search Premier.* Web. June 24, 2011.

Herzog-Silva Márquez, Jesús. "Una defensa de la traición." *Nexos* April 2001: 16. Print.

Honig, Bonnie. *Democracy and the Foreigner.* Princeton, NJ: Princeton UP, 2001. Print.

Hoyle, Rafael Dent. "Writing Against the Grain: Ignacio Solares' Novels of the Mexican Revolution." Diss. U of Texas, 2003. Print.

Hutcheon, Linda. *Narcissistic Narrative: The Metafictional Paradox.* Waterloo: Wilfrid Laurier UP, 1980. Print.

———. *A Poetics of Postmodernism: History, Theory, Fiction.* New York: Routledge, 1988. Print.

Ibargüengoitia, Jorge. *Estas ruinas que ves.* Mexico City: Joaquín Mortiz, 1981. Print.

———. "La consumación: principio, no fin." *Instrucciones para vivir en México.* Mexico City: Joaquín Mortiz, 1990. 36–8. Print.

———. "El grito, irreconocible." *Instrucciones para vivir en México.* Mexico City: Joaquín Mortiz, 1990. 39–41. Print.

———. "El lado bueno de los próceres." *Instrucciones para vivir en México.* Mexico City: Joaquín Mortiz, 1990. 22–24. Print.

———. "La conspiración vendida." *Teatro III.* Mexico City: Joaquín Mortiz, 1987. 215–99. Print.

———. *Los pasos de López.* 1982. Mexico City: Joaquín Mortiz, 2004. Print.

———. *Los relámpagos de agosto.* 1964. Mexico City: Joaquín Mortiz, 2004. Print.

———. "Revitalización de los héroes." *Instrucciones para vivir en México.* Mexico City: Joaquín Mortiz, 1990. 34–35. Print.

Ibsen, Kristine. "Dissecting the Exquisite Cadaver: On Collections and Colonialism in Fernando del Paso's *Noticias del Imperio.*" *Bulletin of Spanish Studies* LXXX.6 (2003): 715–28. Print.

———. *Maximilian, Mexico, and the Invention of Empire.* Nashville, TN: Vanderbilt UP, 2010. Print.

———. "La poética del fragmento y el tercer espacio de la historia en *Noticias del imperio* de Fernando del Paso." *RILCE* 22.1 (2006): 91–103. Print.

Jameson, Fredric. "Marx's Purloined Letter." *Ghostly Demarcations: A Symposium on Jacques Derrida's* Specters of Marx. Ed. Michael Sprinkler. New York: Verso, 1999. 26–67. Print.

Jiménez Marce, Rogelio. "Historia y literatura en *Su Alteza Serenísima* de Victoriano Salado Álvarez." *Tawka* 11–12 (2007): 73–104. Print.

Jitrik, Noé. *Historia e imaginación literaria: Las posibilidades de un género.* Buenos Aires: Editorial Biblios, 1995. Print.

Johannsen, Robert W. "The Meaning of Manifest Destiny." *Manifest Destiny and Empire: American Antebellum Expansionism.* Ed. Sam W. Haynes and Christopher Morris. College Station: Texas A&M P, 1997. 7–20. Print.

Joseph, Rhawn. "The Limbic System and the Soul: Evolution and the Neuroanatomy of Religious Experience Source." *Zygon* 36.1 (2001): 105–36. Print.

Juan-Navarro, Santiago. *Archival Reflections: Postmodern Fiction of the Americas (Self-Reflexivity, Historical Revisionism, Utopia).* Lewisburg, PA: Bucknell UP, 1999. Print.

Kavanagh, James H. "Ideology." *Critical Terms for Literary Studies.* 2nd ed. Ed. Frank Lentricchia and Thomas McLaughlin. Chicago: U of Chicago P, 1995. 306–20. Print.

Kenner, Hugh. "The Arranger." *James Joyce's Ulysses: A Casebook.* Ed. Derek Attridge. Oxford: Oxford UP, 2004. 17–32. Print.

Kermode, Frank. *The Sense of an Ending: Studies in the Theory of Fiction: With a New Epilogue.* New ed. Oxford and New York: Oxford UP, 2000. Print.

Knight, Peter. *Conspiracy Culture: From the Kennedy Assassination to* The X-Files. New York: Routledge, 2000. Print.

Krauze, Enrique. *Siglo de caudillos: biografía política de México (1810–1910).* Mexico City: Tusquets, 2002. Print.

Kristeva, Julia. "The Strangers." *Partisan Review* 58.1 (1991): 88–100. Print.

Kurz, Andreas. "La literatura mexicana contemporánea entre regionalismo y cosmopolitismo." *Revista de literatura mexicana contemporánea* 9.21 (2003): 17–23. Print.

Labanyi, Jo. "History and Hauntology: or, What Does One Do with the Ghosts of the Past? Reflections on Spanish Film and Fiction of the Post-Franco Period." *Disremembering the Dictatorship: The Politics of Memory in the Spanish Transition to Democracy.* Ed. Joan Ramon Rasina. Amsterdam & Atlanta: Radopi, 2000. 65–82. Print.

LaCapra, Dominick. *Writing History, Writing Trauma.* Baltimore: Johns Hopkins UP, 2001. Print.

Layera, Ramón. "Mecanismos de fabulación y mitificación de la historia en las 'comedias impolíticas' y las *Coronas* de Rodolfo Usigli." *Latin American Theater Review* 18.2 (1985): 49–55. Print.

Leñero, Vicente. *El evangelio según Lucas Gavilán*. Barcelona: Seix Barral, 1979. Print.

———. *Los pasos de Jorge*. Mexico City: Joaquín Mortiz, 1989. Print.

Lomnitz, Claudio. *Deep Mexico, Silent Mexico: An Anthropology of Nationalism*. Minneapolis: U of Minnesota P, 2001. Print.

Long, Ryan F. *Fictions of Totality: The Mexican Novel, 1968, and the National-Popular State*. West Lafayette, IN: Purdue UP, 2008. Print.

Lukács, Georg. *The Historical Novel*. Trans. Hannah Mitchell and Stanley Mitchell. Rev. ed. Lincoln: U of Nebraska P, 1983. Print.

Lund, Joshua. *Impure Imagination: Toward a Critical Hybridity in Latin American Writing*. Minneapolis: U of Minnesota P, 2006. Print.

Lyotard, Jean-François. *The Postmodern Condition: A Report on Knowledge*. Trans. Bennington, Geoff and Brian Massumi. Minneapolis: U of Minnesota P, 1984. Print.

Mahin, Dean. *Olive Branch and the Sword: The United States and Mexico, 1845–1848*. Jefferson: McFarland & Co., 1997. Print.

Manickam, Samuel. "*El seductor de la patria*: A Dialogic Response to the Historic Santa Anna." *Chasqui* 39.2 (2010): 17–27. Print.

Marcus, Greil. *The Dustbin of History*. Cambridge, MA: Harvard UP, 1995. Print.

Martí, José. "Nuestra América." *Voces de Hispanoamérica: Antología literaria*. 3rd ed. Ed. Raquel Chang-Rodríguez and Malva E. Filer. Canada: Heinle Cengagle, 2004. 216–20. Print.

Martin, Gerald. *Journeys through the Labyrinth: Latin American Fiction in the Twentieth Century*. London: Verso, 1989. Print.

Martínez Assad, Carlos. "El revisionismo histórico por medio de la novela." Ibargüengoitia, Jorge. *El atentado, Los relámpagos de agosto: edición crítica*. Ed. Juan Villoro and Víctor Díaz Arciniega. Nanterre: ALLCA XX, Universite Paris X, 2002. 228–45. Print.

Maximilian of Austria. *Reglamento para el servicio y ceremonial de la Corte*. Mexico City: J. M. Lara, 1865. Print.

McKee Irwin, Robert. *Mexican Masculinities*. Minneapolis: U of Minnesota P, 2003. Print.

Menton, Seymour. *Latin America's New Historical Novel*. Austin: U of Texas P, 1993. Print.

Mercieca, Jennifer R. *Founding Fictions*. Tuscaloosa: U of Alabama P, 2010. Print.

Miller, Nicola. *In the Shadow of the State: Intellectuals and the Quest for National Identity in Twentieth-Century Spanish America*. New York: Verso, 1999. Print.

Mleczko, Agata. "Identity Formation as a Contemporary Adaptation Strategy: Chinese Immigrants in Italy." *European Education* 42.4 (2011): 25–48. Print.

Molloy, Silvia. *At Face Value: Autobiographical Writing Spanish America*. Cambridge: Cambridge UP, 1991. Print.

————. "The Politics of Posing." *Hispanisms and Homosexualities*. Ed. Sylvia Molloy and Robert McKee Irwin. Durham, NC: Duke UP, 1998. 141–60. Print.

Monsiváis, Carlos. "¿Cómo se dice 'México' en español, lenguas indígenas y espanglish?" *Proceso* 19 September 2004: 14–5. Print.

Mora, José María Luis. *México y sus revoluciones*. Vol 3. Mexico City: FCE, 1986. Print.

Moreno, Francisco Martín. *México mutilado*. Mexico City: Alfaguara, 2004. Print.

————. *México secreto*. Mexico City: Alfaguara, 2002. Print.

————. *México acribillado*. Mexico City: Alfaguara, 2008. Print.

————. *México negro*. Mexico City: Joaquín Mortiz, 1986. Print.

————. *México ante Dios*. Mexico City: Alfaguara, 2007. Print.

————. *México sediento*. Mexico City: Joaquín Mortiz, 1998. Print.

Morgan, Edmund Sears. *Inventing the People: The Rise of Popular Sovereignty in England and America*. New York: Norton, 1988. Print.

Morris, Stephen D. "States Exploring Mexican Images of the United States." *Mexican Studies / Estudios Mexicanos* 16.1 (2000): 105–39. Print.

Mosqueda, Raquel. "Los muchos modos del esperpento: la narrativa de Enrique Serna." *Literatura mexicana* 12.1 (2001): 115–39. Print.

Muñoz, Rafael F. *Santa Anna: El dictador resplandeciente*. 1945. Mexico City: Utopia, 1976. Print.

————. *Santa Anna: El que todo lo ganó y todo lo perdió*. Spain: Espasa-Calpe, 1936. Print.

New, W. H. "New Language, New World." *The Postcolonial Studies Reader*. Ed. Bill Ashcroft, Gareth Griffiths, and Helen Tiffin. New York: Routledge, 1995. 303–08. Print.

Nietzsche, Friedrich. "On the Utility and Libility of History for Life." 1874. *Unfashionable Observations*. Trans. Richard T. Grey. Stanford, CA: Stanford UP, 1995. 83–168.

Ochoa, John A. *The Uses of Failure in Mexican Literature and Identity*. Austin: U of Texas P, 2004. Print.

O'Connell, Joanna. *Prospero's Daughter: The Prose of Rosario Castellanos*. Austin: U of Texas P, 1995. Print.

Ortega y Gasset, José. *La deshumanización del arte. Ideas sobre la novela*. 2nd ed. Madrid: Revista de Occidente, 1928. Print.

O'Sullivan, John. "Annexation." *United States Magazine and Democratic Review* 17.1 (1845): 5–10. Print.

Osuna Osuna, Gabriel. *Literatura e historia en la novela mexicana de fin de siglo*. Madrid: Editorial Pliegos, 2008. Print.

Pani, Erika. *Para mexicanizar el segundo imperio: el imaginario político de los imperialistas*. Mexico City: Colegio de México and Centro de Estudios Históricos, 2001. Print.

Parkinson Zamora, Lois. *The Usable Past: The Imagination of History in Recent Fiction of the Americas*. Cambridge: Cambridge UP, 1997. Print.

Parra, Enrique Plascencia de la. "Conmemoración de la hazaña épica de los niños héroes: su origen, desarrollo y simbolismos." *Historia Mexicana* 45.2 (1995): 241–79. Print.

Paso, Fernando del. *News from the Empire*. Trans. Alfonso González and Stella T. Clark. Champaign & London: Dalkey Archive P, 2009. Print.

———. *Noticias del imperio*. Mexico City: Planeta, 1999. Print.

———. *Palinuro de México*. Mexico City: Alfaguara, 1977. Print.

———. *José Trigo*. Mexico City: Siglo XXI, 1966. Print.

———. *Obras III: Ensayo y obra periodística*. Mexico City: UNAM, Colegio Nacional, and FCE, 2000. Print.

Pastor Bodmer, Beatriz. *The Armature of Conqest: Spanish Accounts of the Discovery of America, 1492–1589*. Trans. Lydia Longstreth Hunt. Stanford, CA: Stanford UP, 1992. Print.

Paz, Ireneo. *Su Alteza Serenísima*. Mexico City: FCE, 1982. Print.

Paz, Octavio. *El laberinto de la soledad*. 1950. New York: Penguin, 1997. Print.

———. *El ogro filantrópico : historia y política, 1971–1978*. Mexico City: Joaquín Mortiz, 1979. Print.

Perkowska, Magdalena. *Historias híbridas. La nueva novela histórica latinoamericana (1985–2000) ante las teorías posmodernas de la historia*. Madrid and Frankfurt: Iberoamericana / Vervuert, 2008. Print.

Perry, Ruth. *Women, Letters, and the Novel*. New York: AMS P, 1980. Print.

Piérola, José de. "At the Edge of History: Notes for a Theory of the Historical Novel in Latin America." *Romance Studies* 26.2 (2008): 151–62. Print.

Piglia, Ricardo. *Artificial Respiration*. Trans. Daniel Balderston. Durham and London: Duke UP, 1994.

———. *Respiración artificial*. 1980. Barcelona: Editorial Anagrama, 2001. Print.

Pons, María Cristina. "*Noticias del imperio*: Entre la imaginación delirante y los desvaríos de la historia." *Hispamerica* 23.69 (1994): 97–108. Print.

Prescott, William H. *The Conquest of Mexico*. 1843. New York: Dutton, 1957. Print.

Price, Glenn W. *Origins of the War with Mexico: The Polk-Stockton Intrigue*. Austin: U of Texas P, 1970. Print.

Quackenbush, L. Howard. *El "López" de Jorge Ibargüengoitia: Historia, teatro y autorreflexibilidad*. Mexico City: CONACULTA, 1992. Print.

Quemain, Miguel Ángel. "Entrevista con Fernando del Paso: La exhuberante brevedad." Instituto Nacional de Bellas Artes. Web. 24 Jun. 2011.

Rama, Ángel. *The Lettered City*. 1984. Trans. John Charles Chasteen. Durham: Duke UP, 1996. Print.

Rancière, Jacques. *The Politics of Aesthetics*. Trans. Gabriel Rockhill. New York: Continuum, 2006. Print.

Rao, Raja. "Language and Spirit." *The Postcolonial Studies Reader*. Ed. Bill Ashcroft, Gareth Griffiths, and Helen Tiffin. New York: Routledge, 1995. 296–7. Print.

Renan, Ernst. "What Is a Nation?" Trans. Martin Thom. *Becoming National: A Reader*. Ed. Geoff Eley and Ronald Grigor Suny. Oxford and New York: Oxford UP, 1996. 41–55. Print.

Revueltas, José. *Los días terrenales*. Mexico City: Editorial Stylo, 1949. Print.

Reyes, Juan José. "Los berrinches del caudillo: *El seductor de la patria* de Enrique Serna." *Letras Libres* Nov. 1999: 90. Print.

Rodríguez Cadena, María de los Ángeles. "*Los pasos de López* y el 'relajo literario' de la Independencia de México de 1810." *Bulletin of Hispanic Studies* 85.5 (2008): 695–716. Print.

Rodríguez Marcos, Javier. "Entrevista: Ignacio Solares: El novelista llena los huecos que deja la historia." *El País*. 18 Mar. 2006. Web. 24 Jun. 2011.

Roeder, Ralph. *Juarez and His Mexico: A Biographical History*. New York: Viking P, 1947. Print.

Rulfo, Juan. *El llano en llamas*. 1953. Madrid: Cátedra, 2004. Print.

Runia, Eelco. "Spots of Time." *History & Theory* 45.3 (2006): 305–16. Print.

———. "Presence." *History & Theory* 45.1 (2006): 1–29. Print.

Salado Álvarez, Victoriano. *Episodios nacionales mexicanos*. Mexico City: INBA and FCE, 1984. Print.

Sánchez Prado, Ignacio M. "Dying Mirrors, Medieval Moralists, and Tristram Shandies: The Literary Traditions of Fernando del Paso's *Palinuro of Mexico*." *Comparative Literature* 60.2 (2008): 142–63. Print.

———. *Naciones intelectuales: Las fundaciones de la modernidad literaria mexicana, 1917–1959*. West Lafayette: Purdue UP, 2009. Print.

Santa Anna, Antonio López de. *Historia military y política (1810–1874)*. Mexico City: Porrúa, 1974. Print.

Santi, Enrico Mario. *Pablo Neruda: The Poetics of Prophecy*. Cornell: Cornell UP, 1982. Print.

Scholes, Robert. *Fabulation and Metafiction*. Urbana: U of Illinois P, 1979. Print.

Schmitt, Carl. *The Concept of the Political*. Expanded ed. Trans. George Schwab. Chicago: U of Chicago P, 2007. Print.

Sedwick, Frank. *A History of the Useless Precaution Plot in Spanish and French Literature*. Chapel Hill: U of North Carolina P, 1964. Print.

Serna, Enrique. *El miedo a los animales*. 1995. Mexico: Joaquín Mortiz, 2003. Print.

———. "La opulenta México." *Letras libres* Aug. 2002: 68. Print.

———. "La religión del fracaso." *Letras libres* Feb. 2000: 79. Print.

———. "Santa Anna en la historia y en la ficción". *Historia y novela histórica. Coincidencias, divergencias y perspectivas de análisis*. Ed. Conrado Hernández López. Mexico City: Colegio de Michoacán, 2004. Print.

———. *El seductor de la patria*. Mexico City: Joaquín Mortiz, 1999. Print.

———. *Señorita México*. Mexico City: Plaza y Janés, 1993. Print.

———. *Uno soñaba que era rey*. Mexico City: Plaza y Janés, 1989. Print.

———. "Vidas de Santa Anna." *Letras libres* Aug. 1999: 81. Print.

Sheridan, Guillermo. "La historia como farsa en Jorge Ibargüengoitia." *La memoria histórica en las letras hispánicas contemporáneas*. Ed. Patrick Collard, Ingeborg Jongbloet, and María Eugenia Ocampo y Vilas. Geneva: Drox, 1997. 249–59. Print.

Shumway, Nicolas. *The Invention of Argentina*. Berkeley and Los Angeles: U of California P, 1993. Print.

Sierra, Justo. *Evolución política del pueblo mexicano*. Mexico City: Casa de España, 1940. Print.

Sifuentes-Jáuregui, Ben. *Transvestism, Masculinity, and Latin American Literature.* New York: Palgrave, 2002. Print.

Silva-Herzog Márquez, Jesús. "Una defensa de la traición." *Nexos* Apr. 2001: 16. Print.

Simpson, Lesley Bird. *Many Mexicos.* Berkeley: U of California P, 1966. Print.

Solares, Ignacio. *La invasión.* Mexico City: Alfaguara, 2005. Print.

———. *Madero, el otro.* Mexico City: Joaquín Mortiz, 1989. Print.

———. *La noche de Ángeles.* Mexico City: Editorial Diana, 1991. Print.

———. "El jefe máximo." *Teatro histórico.* Mexico City: Coordinación de Difusión Cultural / UNAM, 1996. 9–62. Print.

———. "Los mochos." *Teatro histórico.* Mexico City: Coordinación de Difusión Cultural / UNAM, 1996. 179–204. Print.

———. *Yankee Invasion.* Trans. Timothy G. Compton. Minneapolis: Scarletta P, 2009. Print.

Soler Frost, Pablo. *1767. Una novela sobre el destierro de los jesuitas mexicanos.* Mexico City: Joaquín Mortiz, 2004. Print.

Sotelo Gutiérrez, César Antonio. "*El seductor de la patria* de Enrique Serna: la novela histórica como instrumento de análisis político." *Revista de literatura mexicana contemporánea* 5.12 (2000): 62–69. Print.

Spires, Robert. *Beyond the Metafictional Mode.* Lexington: U of Kentucky P, 1984. Print.

Su alteza serenísima. Dir. Felipe Cazals. Perf. Alejandro Parodi, Ana Berta Espín, Rodolfo Arías, and Pedro Armendáriz Jr. Serenísima Films, 2000. Print.

Syntek, Aleks. "El futuro es milenario." Mexico 2010. Web. 24 June 2011.

Tavira, Luis de. "Un atentado a la solemnidad de la historia." *El atentado, Los relámpagos de agosto: edición crítica.* Ed. Juan Villoro and Víctor Díaz Arciniega. Nanterre: ALLCA XX, Universite Paris X, 2002. 469–74. Print.

Tenorio Trillo, Mauricio. *Historia y celebración: México y sus Centenarios.* Mexico City: Tusquets, 2009. Print.

Torres, Vicente Francisco. "Los novelistas las prefieren gordas." *La palabra y el hombre* 113 (2000): 135–41. Print.

Troillot, Michel-Rolf. *Silencing the Past: Power and the Production of History.* Boston: Beacon, 1995. Print.

Tsu, Jing. *Failure, Nationalism, and Literature: The Making of Modern Chinese Identity, 1895–1937.* Stanford: Stanford UP, 2005. Print.

Usigli, Rodolfo. *Corona de sombra, Corona de fuego, Corona de luz.* 4th ed. Mexico: Porrúa. 1982. Print.

———. *Teatro completo.* Vol. 5. Mexico City: FCE, 1963. Print.

Vargas Llosa, Mario. *La fiesta del Chivo.* Spain: Grupo Santillana, 2000. Print.

Vasconcelos, Jose. *Breve historia de México.* Rev. ed. Mexico: Editorial Continental, 1956. Print.

Vásquez, Josefina Zoraida. "Verdades y mentiras de *México mutilado*." *Letras Libres* May 2005: 28–32. Print.

Vedder, Paul. "Language, Ethnic Identity, and the Adaptation of Turkish Immigrant Youth in the Netherlands and Sweden." *International Journal of Intercultural Relations* 29.3 (2005): 317–37. Print.

Villanueva Benavides, Idalia. "Identidad y máscaras en *Ángeles del abismo* de Enrique Serna." *Revista de literatura mexicana contemporánea* 12.30 (2006): vii–xv. Print.

Volpi, Jorge. "La desaparición de México." *Proceso* 11 (Jul. 2004): 21–22. Print.

Weatherford, Douglas J. "Reading and revolution in the novels of Ignacio Solares." *Studies in the Literary Imagination.* 33.1 (2000): 73–92. Print.

White, Hayden. *Metahistory: The Historical Imagination in Nineteenth-Century Europe.* Baltimore: Johns Hopkins UP, 1973. Print.

———. *Tropics of Discourse.* Baltimore: Johns Hopkins UP, 1985. Print.

Wittgenstein. Ludwig. *Tractatus-Logico Philosophicus.* Trans. D. F. Pears and B. F. McGuiness. New York: Routledge and Kegan Paul, 1963. Print.

Yáñez, Agustín. *Santa Anna, espectro de una sociedad.* Mexico City: Ed. Océano, 1982. Print.

Zambrano, Guillermo. *México por asalto.* Mexico City: Grijalbo, 2008. Print.

Zamora Plowes, Leopoldo. *Quince Uñas y Casanova aventureros.* Mexico City: Talleres Gráficos de la Nación, 1945. Print.

Žižek, Slavoj. *First as Tragedy, Then as Farce.* New York: Verso, 2009. Print.

———. *Living in the End Times.* New York: Verso, 2010. Print.

Index